The Editor Function

The Editor Function

Literary Publishing in Postwar America

ABRAM FOLEY

UNIVERSITY OF MINNESOTA PRESS
MINNEAPOLIS · LONDON

Works by Charles Olson published during his lifetime are held in copyright by the Estate of Charles Olson; previously unpublished works are copyright of the University of Connecticut; reprinted here with permission. Excerpts from Gilbert Sorrentino are copyright and courtesy of the Gilbert Sorrentino Estate. Excerpts from Paul Metcalf are reprinted courtesy of the Paul Metcalf Estate. Letters from Nathaniel Mackey are copyright and courtesy of Nathaniel Mackey. "Manchile" by Kamau Brathwaite, from BLACK + BLUES, copyright 1976, 1994, 1995 by Kamau Brathwaite; reprinted by permission of New Directions Publishing Corporation. Excerpts from Eliot Weinberger are copyright and courtesy of Eliot Weinberger. Excerpts from John Taggart are copyright and courtesy of John Taggart. Excerpts from Wilson Harris are reprinted courtesy of Michael Mitchell. Lines from Al Young's poem "What Is the Blues?" were originally published in *Hambone* 2, ed. Nathaniel Mackey (Santa Cruz, Calif.: Hambone, 1982), 57; reprinted here with permission. Excerpts from Will Alexander are copyright and courtesy of Will Alexander. Excerpts from Amiri Baraka reprinted with permission by Chris Calhoun Agency, copyright Estate of Amiri Baraka.

Every effort was made to obtain permission to reproduce material in this book. If any proper acknowledgment has not been included here, we encourage copyright holders to notify the publisher.

Copyright 2021 by the Regents of the University of Minnesota

All rights reserved. No part of this publication may be reproduced, stored in a retrieval system, or transmitted, in any form or by any means, electronic, mechanical, photocopying, recording, or otherwise, without the prior written permission of the publisher.

Published by the University of Minnesota Press
111 Third Avenue South, Suite 290
Minneapolis, MN 55401-2520
http://www.upress.umn.edu

ISBN 978-1-5179-1166-9 (hc)
ISBN 978-1-5179-1167-6 (pb)
A Cataloging-in-Publication record for this book is available from the Library of Congress.

The University of Minnesota is an equal-opportunity educator and employer.

UMP LSI

Contents

Introduction: The Editor Function	1
1. Editing and the Open Field: Charles Olson's Letters to Editors	29
2. Editing and the Institution: John O'Brien and Dalkey Archive Press	63
3. Editing and the Ensemble: Nathaniel Mackey's *Hambone*	93
4. Editing and Eros: Chris Kraus, Semiotext(e), and *I Love Dick*	127
Coda: Editing and *Entropy*	163
Acknowledgments	177
Notes	181
Index	217

INTRODUCTION

The Editor Function

The Editor Function shifts around two observations: that editing has often been taken up as an artistic and political practice in postwar American culture; and that editing generates its own modes of creative and critical thought. This study explores the complementary aspects of these observations by moving between them and gauging their tensions, for editing is always at odds with itself, both a practice and an art, realized and unrealizable. It is contextually situated and conceptually unbound, or at least it wants to be. If, as the editor and poet Peter Gizzi has written, "editing, like writing, is fundamentally about composing a world,"[1] then it is a process of composition that takes place in a world, this one, different from the one it seeks. At work in many editorial projects is a conceptual vision of community, of art, of new politics and different futures that at once drives an editor and flees before her, even as she builds the apparatus that might momentarily capture her vision. Editing feeds off of and adds to such productive tensions—between this world and a sought-after one, between a practice and those ideas deriving from it, between textual media and the riddling texts they bear into unknown places and futures—making editing a process that artfully encompasses practice and theory. *The Editor Function* studies this process.

Yet the idiom of encompassing is troublesome at the outset. The editors and editorial practices I study here are less interested in enclosure

2 Introduction

than in the ongoing open-endedness to which editing and publishing give rise. The incorporating mechanisms of literary practices and the creative economy have been well documented in recent years, showing how criticism and the literature it studies are often guided by the centripetal currents of the creative and capitalist economy.[2] Nearly everything swirls toward the vortex of discursive or capitalist incorporation. Such studies are valuable for delineating the structures of power that comprise the literary field, particularly in the postwar era when the American publishing industry underwent extensive corporate consolidation.[3] This study, however, seeks to move in a different direction by following the chaotic lead of literary editors, particularly those who set up small and independent journals and presses because or in spite of the conglomeration of the publishing industry in the postwar period. Editors are often characterized as "gatekeepers"[4] who regulate the flow of texts, deciding what passes into print and what remains outside the gates.[5] Many disappointed writers have no doubt experienced editors as such, including some who play key roles in this book. Yet many editors in the postwar United States responded to this characterization of editorship by taking up the task of editing as a means of opening up and disordering the literary field as they perceived it to exist, even as the corporate interests of publishing intensified.

The Editor Function thus examines publishing formations that took shape in response to and in protest of more dominant trends shaping postwar American literary culture. Take, for instance, *Assembling*, an anarchic experiment in both editorship and self-publishing founded by Richard Kostelanetz and Henry James Korn in 1970. Korn and Kostelanetz would invite contributors to submit one thousand printed copies of up to four pages of their work. They then assembled or collated the material in alphabetical order, sent three copies to each author, and sought to sell the rest via bookshops to cover additional costs.[6] In an essay titled "Why *Assembling?*" originally published in Bill Henderson's inaugural book for the Pushcart Press, *The Publish-It-Yourself Handbook: Literary Tradition and How-To* (1973), Kostelanetz explains that he and Korn "abrogated editorial authority not because we were lazy but because we wanted a structural contrast to the 'restrictive, self-serving

Introduction 3

nature of traditional editorial presses,'" with the phrase Kostelanetz quotes here coming from the form invitation letter he and Korn initially sent to invited contributors (221). In the same form letter to potential contributors, Korn and Kostelanetz emphasize that "the long-range goal of *Assembling* is opening the editorial/industrial complex to alternatives and possibilities" (222). With obvious reference to Eisenhower's military–industrial complex but also with more subtle echoes of Theodor Adorno and Max Horkheimer's study of "the culture industry,"[7] Korn and Kostelanetz, a self-identified anarchist,[8] attempt to imagine an editorship without editors, a conceptual maneuver that pushes them toward the language of the more mechanistic or instrumental tasks of "collating" and "assembling." Nicholas Thoburn has pointed out that their project did not escape editorship entirely, with a themed issue, for instance, chosen by the editors serving as an organizing principle at one point.[9] Asking authors to cover the costs of reproducing and even mailing one thousand copies of up to four pages of work also meant that contributors generally believed in the work they were submitting.[10] And even Kostelanetz acknowledges that their invite-only policy led to the kind of editorial oversight they sought to abandon. Their solution: refusing to invite a handful of contributors from one issue to contribute to the next, a Dada-like or surrealist-influenced attempt to reject the role of editorial taste-making and judgment, even if the gatekeeping function of the editor remains intact in the act of non-invitation. Nevertheless, Korn and Kostelanetz sensed the intensifying regulative function of "editorial presses" and their increasing "profit-hunger."[11] They countered with a publication whose "blatant chaos marked [it] as a counter-book or anti-book (though not a 'non-book') which nonetheless gains its cohering definition (which is approximately repeatable) from its unprecedented diversity."[12]

Offering anarchy in lieu of order, Kostelanetz obliquely addresses one of the landmark concepts of modern literary culture from which this book derives its name: the author function. When Michel Foucault theorized "the author function" in his essay "What Is an Author?" (1969), he proposed that the author served a limiting function that effectively regulates the proliferation of textual meaning. The author,

Cover of *Assembling Assembling* (1978), supplement to the eighth issue of *Assembling*, edited by Henry James Korn and Richard Kostelanetz. Courtesy of Richard Kostelanetz.

Introduction

Foucault writes in a well-known passage, "is a certain functional principle by which in our culture, one limits, excludes, and chooses . . . The author is therefore the ideological figure by which one marks the manner in which we fear the proliferation of meaning."[13] Foucault is theorizing and historicizing the characteristics of an entire discursive regime of modernity in this essay purportedly on "the author," with the aim to understand how limits are placed on textual practices of meaning-making. This book shows how editors and publishers undertook a related critical analysis of textuality and meaning-making in the period but proceeded through the work of editing and publishing itself rather than through formal theoretical statements such as Foucault's. The counter-editorial work of Korn and Kostelanetz, who were conceptualizing what *Assembling* was and how it would operate at nearly the same time that Foucault wrote his essay, shows one obvious point of conjunction between theory and editorial practice. Yet a wealth of critically engaged textual theorists became editors in the postwar period, to the point that author–editor Roxane Gay could observe in her 2011 essay aptly titled "Too Many of Us, Too Much Noise" that "everyone wants to be a writer, but increasingly, everyone wants to be an editor too."[14] The noise Gay identifies signals the postwar rise of the editor not as gatekeeper, nor as a limit function on the proliferation of meaning, but as a figure of excess and discord in the literary field.

Even as editors explore the manifold aspects of literary practice and production in order to test the author function and the "editorial/industrial complex" of postwar conglomeration, this book proposes that editing nevertheless advances its own legible theories of textuality and meaning-making. The editing studied here seeks radical alternatives to the world (of letters) as an editor perceives it to exist, but it seeks them through here-and-now practices—of correspondence, judgment, friendship and rivalry formation, proofreading—that remain historically situated and so available to critical analysis. Put differently, editing cannot achieve the escape velocity needed to abandon this world for an entirely new one. Its utopian drive always falters in practice, even if it often remains intact. Kostelanetz notes, for instance, that *Assembling* acquires coherence as the result of repeatable diversity. Patterns form, undercutting

6   Introduction

the magazine's desire for disorder. Peter Gizzi summarizes simply that editing is a balance of "consistency and openness."[15] Nathaniel Mackey, by comparison, characterizes his editorship of *Hambone*—the subject of chapter 3—as "a particularist undertaking—yet with a certain drive, which every magazine should have, toward ensemblist identity and definition."[16] Coherence through diversity. Consistency and openness. The particular and the ensemble. *The Editor Function* shows how editors derive theories of literature and textuality from the complementary dynamism active in the practice of editing itself.

In each of the above characterizations of editing, order and disorder strike a balance that recalls Maurice Blanchot's conclusion to *The Unavowable Community* (French 1983; English 1988). There, Blanchot reflects on "*the always uncertain end* inscribed in the destiny of community."[17] For Blanchot, this "uncertain end" keeps the political and ethical stakes of inscription open—and Blanchot is thinking by way of writing here—because it requires a certain disposition toward thinking in the present. In particular, Blanchot concludes that orienting ourselves toward the uncertain end inscribed in any formation of community "does not permit us to lose interest in the present time which, by opening unknown spaces of freedom, makes us responsible for new relationships, always threatened, always hoped for, between what we call work, *oeuvre,* and what we call unworking, *désoeuvrement*" (56). Editing advances a theory resonant with Blanchot's, giving shape to the substantive work (*oeuvre*) while also generating conceptual disorder—the unworking *désoeuvrement*—that inheres in the work and countersigns its legible form. The task of this book is to develop a critical method that can move between work and unworking while studying their complementarity. Editorial practices often leave recorded histories that remain legible to the critic. But they also generate conceptual theories that vex that historical record, probe the limits it has set, and seek to open pathways to new forms of knowledge by way of editorial assembly. This is how I think of work (*oeuvre*) and unworking (*désoeuvrement*) in relation to what I am calling the editor function.

My aim with *The Editor Function,* however, is not to romanticize the radical or theoretical potential of editing. Like any creative-critical task,

Introduction

editing is a historical-political practice that can readily reproduce intellectual formations that demand further critique. My first two chapters, on Charles Olson and Dalkey Archive Press, for instance, conclude by examining how their innovative conceptions of editing and publishing engage with and sometimes replicate colonial imaginaries and racialized histories of print culture. To resist romantic idealizing in favor of critical analysis, *The Editor Function* seeks to show how the unworking of the work, which forms the conceptual opening to new forms of knowledge and politics, comes about only through work itself, by which I refer to the intellectual labor and quotidian practices of editing. If editing appeals to a world (of letters) that's other than this one, then that world becomes available only as a result of the work that takes place here and now. Put differently, the "beyond" that editors so often seek—and that the editors and publishers I study configure and conceptualize in varied ways—is immanent in editorial work, not elsewhere.[18] When the poet, editor, and critic Nathaniel Mackey sought to relaunch his literary journal *Hambone* in the early 1980s, he wrote a letter to the poet Robert Kelly soliciting work. Instead of offering an elaborate sketch of the journal's conceptual vision, Mackey writes, "Can't offer much of an overture as far as the thrust I want to give the mag is concerned. 'Crossings' is a word which comes to mind, as does the much more widely worked expression 'New World poetics'— but I wouldn't want to push either one of them beyond what particular works give substance to."[19] This book likewise attends to intricate political and theoretical formations that particular editorial work gives substance to, and balances that against the conceptual, historical, and political claims that editors so often make to frame their projects. Sometimes these take form as a theory of editing and the open field, as I explore in chapter 1. Other times, as a meditation on the relationship between eros and editing, as my chapter on Chris Kraus and Semiotext(e) examines. Or, in the case of my coda on Janice Lee and *Entropy*, sometimes editing exhausts itself and is intended to reflect on the precarious conditions under which much editorial labor takes place. The editor function forms against the backdrop of a rapidly consolidating publishing industry, in the midst of "the program era," and, later on, in

8   Introduction

the context of a newly lauded creative economy that seeks to secure creative labor within the workings of capitalism.[20] These historical formations and processes provide contexts through which to understand the work of creative-critical editorship. Yet each editorial project evolves its own idiosyncratic theories of editing, assembled form, and historical context by way of the work of editing itself, a process that encompasses practice and theory and that demands the kinds of critical examination that this book begins to explore.

Media Histories of the Editor Function

Until very recently, the history of U.S. literature since World War II has been written largely in the absence of books. This is not to say that books disappeared. Nor is it to invoke recurrent claims about the death of the book in the digital age. I mean something much simpler: books, and the practices such as editing associated with publishing books and other textual objects, have until recently been largely overlooked as subjects for serious critical attention in postwar American criticism.[21] As the book historian Leah Price has noted, "literary critics only use books; they study texts."[22] Her statement speaks particularly well to postwar American literary studies. In a period when the author died, the work became a text, the American novel faced charges of both "greatness" and impending obsolescence, and poetry engaged new media and information theory, books remained nearly immaterial.[23] They have been hiding in plain sight, and one can extend this observation, as I do in this study, to include a range of printed formats and textual practices that both set and test the limits of what postwar American literature is and where it takes shape.[24]

Although numerous factors have no doubt contributed to the relative invisibility of print culture and its associated practices in critical studies of postwar American literature, several stand out for the active role they played in structuring dominant trends in the literary field. Rapidly corporatizing publishers, for instance, sought ever increasing returns on their investments in "literary" authors. One strategy for increasing returns in corporate publishing is to publicize and promote a

Introduction 9

small handful of authors who are eager or at least willing to take on roles as literary celebrities and popular intellectuals.[25] Consider that the two or three decades following World War II not only gave rise to "middle-brow" literary icons such as Norman Mailer and James Michener[26] but also produced the last profusion of what some critics have insisted on calling "the Great American Novel."[27] Directly related to the idea of the great American novel is the great American novelist: Bellow, DeLillo, Ellison, Mailer, Morrison, Pynchon, and Roth, all of whom have been included as exemplary in critical books about either literary celebrity or the great American novel, and all of whom were published primarily by corporate publishing houses.[28] The simultaneous emergence of these canonical figures and an increasingly profit-driven publishing industry is not coincidental. Foucault recognized in "What Is an Author?" that the author function results from diverse operations in the literary field; but the discursive establishment of the author function ultimately conceals the diversity of those operations.[29] The very structures and practices that allow for her existence make the author appear autonomous, thereby consolidating the author as a powerful function for the creation of both cultural and actual capital. Corporate publishers, in short, have a vested interest in promoting their authors in such a way that the guiding hands of editors, publishing houses, marketers, and the market remain invisible. In corporate publishing, the author's name, more than the publishing house's colophon, is the most valuable sign in a profit-driven literary economy.

Textual ideologies of the immediate postwar period also helped to hold up this power relation between the author and the literary field that made the author's seemingly autonomous existence possible. Oddly, we can look to a medievalist for clarification here. In a 1990 special issue of *Speculum* on the subject of "The New Philology," Stephen G. Nichols proposes that as books became the product of a more highly mechanized and refined mode of production, a critic could see a book's production and physicality as merely incidental to the text. Nichols, who is interested specifically in the "manuscript culture" of medieval texts, takes Erich Auerbach as his target, remarking that

10   Introduction

in Auerbach's view, philology represented a technological scholarship made possible by a print culture. It joined forces with the mechanical press in a movement away from the multiplicity and variance of a manuscript culture . . . Auerbach's generation installed a preoccupation with scholarly exactitude based on edited and printed texts. The high calling of philology sought a transfixed text as transparent as possible, one that would provide the vehicle for scholarly endeavor but, once the work of editing accomplished [sic], not the focus of inquiry. It required, in short, a printed text.[30]

While Nichols is in a philological turf war with one of the most well-known philologists of the twentieth century, his point is worth reflecting on, especially if we consider the New Critics among "Auerbach's generation." Auerbach published *Mimesis* in 1946; Cleanth Brooks published *The Well Wrought Urn* in 1947. To summarize Nichols's charge, and to extend it to Brooks: the literary text, in the absence of its media, stands transparently alone as a well-wrought urn; literary textuality is set free from history and contingency precisely because the production of texts has become so highly mechanical, the codes of the codex mastered.[31] Even if literary scholars have been reacting against New Criticism for decades, with René Wellek noting that it was "considered not only superseded, obsolete, and dead, but somehow mistaken and wrong" already by 1978,[32] the backlash against the New Critics in the United States did not necessarily redirect itself toward textual studies. A New Critical approach to literary textuality lives on in the study of postwar and contemporary American literature today, even while politically grounded historicism is now the basis for critical inquiry in most respects.

Although a highly formalized conception of textuality directed academic literary study in the immediate postwar period, writers and editors at that time began to examine literary textuality by way of the practices and channels that set the text on its course into the world. Charles Olson opens his influential essay on "Projective Verse" (1950) by opposing "projective or OPEN verse" to "the NON-Projective (or what a French critic calls 'closed' verse, that verse which print bred."[33] Olson's

Introduction

characterization of closed verse as "that verse which print bred" turns out to be an opening shot in a war against the unmediated version of literary textuality the New Critics had been promoting. Indeed, in an early draft of projective verse that took form as a letter to Frances Boldereff, Olson pits projective verse against "the non-projective (the 'closed' as some french guy puts it, the lyric, poysonal, OMeliot,"[34] with "OM" apparently playing on the Order of Merit T. S. Eliot had received in 1948 in order to make Eliot into an omelet. In the published version of "Projective Verse," Olson simply declares in his conclusion that "O. M. Eliot is *not* projective."[35] Olson offers several reasons for identifying Eliot's verse as non-projective, some of which I will address in the first chapter. I am more interested here, however, in the shift that happens from the early draft of "Projective Verse" to the final draft. In Olson's early letter–draft, "OMeliot" occupies the exact place that "that verse which print bred" takes up in the published essay several months later. The revision hints at the correspondence in Olson's thinking between New Criticism's conception of textuality, here represented by T. S. Eliot, and an ideology of textuality dependent on inconspicuous modes of textual production and transmission such as print.[36] Just three years after the publication of Cleanth Brooks's *The Well Wrought Urn*, Olson identifies what Nichols outlines more explicitly forty years later: a highly mechanized print culture made possible an ideology of literary textuality that omits a range of situated medial practices associated with textual expression. According to Olson, print allowed verse to "close" itself to the material processes of poetic making, and as I show in chapter 1, these processes include editing and publishing.[37]

The well-wrought text began to show cracks in the postwar period due in part to some writers and editors shifting their focus from the thing made (the urn, the poem, the literary text) to the process of its making (practice, process, modes of transmission). Olson was an important figure in instigating this shift for poetry—a change made possible in part through his engagement with artists working in sound, visual, and performance arts[38]—and his influence reverberates in a later essay on artistic practice by LeRoi Jones (later Amiri Baraka), who called "Projective Verse" "the manifesto of a new poetry."[39] In a 1964

12   Introduction

essay titled "Hunting Is Not Those Heads on a Wall," Jones subordinates the art "artifact" to the active process of making art, what he calls "art-ing."[40] He writes, "The academic Western mind is the best example of the substitution of artifact worship for the lightning awareness of the art process. . . . The process itself is the most important quality because it can transform and create, and its only form is possibility. The artifact, because it assumes one form, is only that particular quality or idea. It is, in this sense, after the fact, and it is only important because it remarks on its true source" (174). Jones tips the scales toward the active processes of art-ing rather clumsily here. His notion that the artifact can express only one particular quality or idea becomes a convenient straw man version of how a literary text means and what a reader or critic, situated in history, brings to the encounter of reading. More generously, however, his is a description of the art object, or the poem, as conceived of by New Criticism: a thing unto itself, complexly unified in its mode of expression.

Jones's desire to emphasize art-ing as an active process signals the changes taking place in the postwar period with regard to the relationship between texts and textual practices, and as this book shows, these changes continue to influence our understanding of literature and literary practice at present. Jones's theory of "art-ing" as an act of *poiesis* takes on different valences, for instance, when we consider his influential role as an editor of several little magazines and literary journals in the 1950s and 1960s. With his wife, Hettie Jones, he cofounded and coedited Totem Press and the magazine *Yūgen* in the late 1950s. Totem Press in fact brought out a pamphlet edition of Olson's "Projective Verse" in 1959, which the Joneses published alongside work by Diane di Prima, Paul Blackburn, and Jack Kerouac, among others, with Baraka priding himself on the way his editing brought various schools of poetry together, from the New York School to Black Mountain to the San Francisco Renaissance. Jones later played a variety of editorial roles for the influential magazine *Kulchur* from 1960 to 1965, headed at the time by Lita Hornick. In the early 1960s Jones also coedited the early issues of the poetry pamphlet *The Floating Bear* with Diane di Prima, though she eventually took over sole editorship.[41] I propose that when Jones

Introduction   13

develops his theory of art-ing as an act of *poiesis*, he sees this broad creative practice as including practices of editing and publishing, where the active dynamics of art-ing take material and social form. When Len Fulton wrote a 1971 overview of the "little magazine" scene of the 1960s, in which he includes a discussion of the Joneses' *Yūgen*, he remarks that in the 1960s "the little magazine began to acquire a new definition for itself, to become an ever-changing, moving process, a string of continuous events more than a series of contained and individual issuances."[42] Even more than *Yūgen*, *The Floating Bear* exemplifies Fulton's observation. Indeed, when Jones pitched the idea of coediting a new publication to di Prima, he described it as a "literary newsletter."[43] It was designed to thrive on process, taking advantage of the Gestetner mimeograph machine in the back of Robert A. Wilson's Phoenix Book Shop in Greenwich Village for rapid and affordable reproduction and distribution. Di Prima—and not Jones/Baraka—speaks to Fulton's observation best in reference to editing and producing *The Floating Bear*. In her memoir *Recollections of My Life as a Woman* (2001), after giving a detailed account of their editorial processes, di Prima moves her reflections in a more conceptual direction:

> Not only the publishing but the networking too felt familiar. The linking of all of us through the magazine: Olson, Duncan, Dorn, myself, John Wieners. A kind of sixth sense of who was actually speaking to whom in a poem, a review, or article. Where it might be heading.
>
> Years later, Charles Olson told me how important it was to him to know in those early days of the *Bear*, that he could send us a new piece of, say, *The Maximus Poems*, and within two weeks a hundred and fifty artists, many of them his friends, would read it. Would not only read it, but answer in their work—incorporate some innovation of line or syntax, and build on that. Like we were all in one big jam session, blowing. The changes happened that fast. (254)

Di Prima's reflection on the processes of assembling poetic coteries— "the linking of all of us through the magazine"—corresponds to Jones's interest in the process of "art-ing" as an act of poetic making. Di Prima,

14   Introduction

however, talks about the arts of making specifically in relation to editorial practice, noting how it gives rise to its own modes of thought—"a kind of sixth sense"—by way of the collective work of its editors and contributors. In this, di Prima extends Fulton's observation that little magazines became a "string of continuous events rather than a series of contained and individual issuances" to propose that the process of editing in fact creates collective ways of thinking where the individual utterance can be understood only in the context of a broader social milieu. For di Prima, editing becomes a means for conceptualizing and thinking through the social and medial conditions of postwar writing.

The emphasis that editors like di Prima place on the poetics of literary practices—by which I mean the self-reflective recognition that editing, publishing, and distribution themselves have a poetics and play an active part in shaping how we can think about the literary field—corresponds to conceptual engagements with the mediated nature of "literature" that were also taking place in postwar U.S. literary culture. Consider, for instance, that Jones's plea to take the process of artistic creation into account was collected in *Home: Social Essays* in 1966, the year Brian McHale has argued marks the beginning of postmodernism. Among McHale's pieces of evidence supporting his polemical claim: John Barth's *Giles Goat-Boy*, which McHale says "consolidates the encyclopedic 'meganovel' genre that came to dominate American fiction in the postmodernist era."[44] In *The Program Era* (2009), Mark McGurl dedicates several pages of his introduction to *Giles Goat-Boy*, describing the book as "technomodernist," a descriptor that marks the continuity of postwar American fiction with "the modernist project of systematic experimentation with narrative form, even as it registers a growing acknowledgment of the scandalous continuity of the literary *techne* (craft) with technology in the grosser sense—including, most importantly, media technology."[45] McGurl identifies the continuity between *techne* and technology in one of the novel's conceits: "Formally divided not into parts but into magnetic computer tape 'Reels,' it may have been written by the all-powerful WESCAC [computing system] itself" (43). In other words, Barth crafts his novel in light of his technological milieu, including the advancements in computing taking place in

Introduction 15

the Cold War American university, where Barth's novel is set. In the context of *The Program Era,* which is a history of postwar American fiction in light of the rise of creative writing programs, it makes sense that McGurl homes in on the computer to illustrate the relationship between technomodernism and the Cold War university, where Barth "[associates] creative writing in the university not with the dusty workshop but with the modern Cold War laborator[ies]" on American campuses (42).

The supercomputer, however, is not Barth's only overt acknowledgment of medialogical intervention into narrative structure. Barth begins his "meganovel" with twenty-odd pages of prefatory materials related to publishing: a "Publisher's Disclaimer"; four discrete reader's reports by infighting associate editors concerning the manuscript's suitability for publication; a summary of the logic for choosing to publish the manuscript by the editor in chief; and a "Cover-Letter to the Editors and Publisher" signed by "J.B."[46] These prefatory materials, unaddressed in both McHale's and McGurl's studies, locate the work in a long-established and therefore more easily overlooked operating media system: the field of publishing. The prefatory texts are fictional satires, but they nevertheless confirm and redirect the continuities between experimentalism and technomodernism that McGurl identifies, turning them in this case toward a more archaic and often invisible form of mediated textuality—literary publishing—that was undergoing significant changes at the time. In *Giles Goat-Boy,* the publisher's disclaimer explains that the author named on publisher's title page, that is, John Barth (there is a second, fictional title page), has been adamant that the manuscript came to him by way of "one Stoker Giles or Giles Stoker—whereabouts unknown, existence questionable—who appears to have claimed in turn 1) that he too was but a dedicated editor, the text proper having been written by a certain automatic computer, and 2) that excepting a few 'necessary basic artifices' the book is neither fable nor fictionalized history, but literal truth" (ix). Barth adapts the framed story conceit of the found or edited manuscript, a narrative technique used to great effect over the history of narrative experimentation, often for making claims to the veracity of the story as Barth does here. Looking back to eighteenth-century novels such as Daniel Defoe's *Roxana* (1724) and Jonathan Swift's *Gulliver's Travels* (1726), both of which include fictionalized statements from editors and publishers, Barth's playful prefatory texts point explicitly to the people and processes that guide his book into print.[47] Instead of adding these materials solely to make a truth claim for the text, however, Barth includes them to add another layer to the position he advances with his claim that WESCAC wrote the text: that acknowledging more quotidian practices of mediation—including editing, publishing, distribution, and marketing—exposes traditional "authorship" as but one limited function in a set of practices that affect how we think about literary textuality. Saying that a Cold War supercomputer composed the manuscript is indeed one technomodernist way to challenge modern conceptions of authorship. But Barth's insistence on including four readers' reports and a letter to the editor provides another, more subtle glimpse at how procedures of textual production and transmission become means for theorizing literary textuality and authorship in a postwar media environment.

The task of making the text's mediated nature apparent in the prefatory materials of *Giles Goat-Boy* has a correlated consequence: it transforms Barth, like Stoker Giles or Giles Stoker, into "a dedicated editor." Barth's change of position in the literary field is a fictional sleight of hand in the novel, and unlike many of his contemporaries Barth himself never took on any major editorial projects. Yet the fictional conflation of author and editor addresses the collapsing distinction between the two that was taking place at the time. Eight years later, for instance, Ronald Sukenick announced the emergence of the "Author as Editor and Publisher" in a full-page "Guest Word" editorial published in the *New York Times Book Review.* He begins by declaring that "the publishing industry can no longer support quality fiction. For novelists this situation may be an opportunity in the guise of a disaster."[48] To seize the opportunity, Sukenick argues, authors need to take on the roles of editors and publishers themselves. To this end, he and some other writers have founded the cooperative Fiction Collective "to select, edit, produce and distribute the books of its peers on the basis of literary

Introduction 17

merit, free of the implicit commercial standards of the book business" (55). This novel move for fiction writers in the United States—at least in terms of publishing books rather than literary journals—would allow authors to add parity to publishing by freeing themselves and their peers from the commercial interests that increasingly drove corporate houses, even if this new attempt at parity relied on the contentious criterion of merit. In his 1978 overview of the Fiction Collective, which had published around twenty-six books of fiction in its first four years, Larry McCaffery notes that the quality of the books was very good, and that the editorial strategy had generally worked to plan. But the press foundered in its early coterie emphasis on East Coast and mostly male writers.[49]

Nevertheless, McCaffery sees the Fiction Collective's model of a writer-run cooperative publishing house as an important addition to the American publishing scene, made necessary by the divergent interests of formally demanding writers and the commercial presses that no longer supported more than a small handful of them at a given time. The major houses were still putting out works by authors who were contemporary literary stars and would achieve canonical status—Ishmael Reed's *Mumbo Jumbo* came out with Doubleday in 1972, Thomas Pynchon's *Gravity's Rainbow* appeared with Viking in 1973, E. L. Doctorow's *Ragtime* was published by Random House in 1975, the same year Bantam published Samuel R. Delany's *Dhalgren*, and Alfred A. Knopf published William Gaddis's *JR*, and Knopf published two of Toni Morrison's early novels, *Sula* and *Song of Solomon*, in the mid-1970s as well. But these houses were not openly theorizing the "editorial/industrial complex" and its effect on American literature. Those discussions were being held instead by newfound editors and publishers who turned their hands to the work of assembling contemporary literature. So, while Sukenick the author has been identified "among the founders and standard-bearers of American postmodernist fiction,"[50] his longer-lasting legacy might in fact be his work, collectively undertaken, as an editor and publisher.

The tremendous surge in the number of literary journals and independent presses operating today is a remarkable development in the

18   Introduction

postwar United States.[51] Many of these ventures operate under editors like Sukenick who make editorial practice into a means of testing and conceptualizing the contexts of postwar literary production and its attendant ideologies of literary textuality. *The Editor Function* studies a small handful of such editors and editor-adjacent figures, and I choose them for the stories they allow me to tell about editing as a conceptually dynamic literary practice. Still, a wealth of significant and critically nuanced editorial projects could have guided this book: whether Danielle Dutton and Martin Riker's influential and women-focused Dorothy, a publishing project; or the more sci-fi, surreal, and fantasy focused work of Small Beer Press, run by Kelly Link and her husband and fellow writer Gavin J. Grant; or Diane Williams's editorship of *Noon* and its attention to and promotion of a new literary minimalism. Or what about Make Now Books, who write on their "About" page that "small presses, like independent record labels, are instrumental to the living everyday of a literary community. Hundreds of small editing practices keep new works circulating. They make discovery more interesting. The history of 20th century literature is half done if the role of the editor is explored less stringently"?[52] This admittedly whimsical shadow list poses a problem I have faced throughout my work on this project: when the editorial projects doing critical and creative work are so abundant, questions about exemplarity come to the fore. Indeed, as Make Now Books acknowledges, the subject this book studies forms in countless "small editing practices," many of which will only be reflected on in the process of editing itself. And yet, as Make Now's statement also makes clear, the critical history of literature is only half written if critics do not extend their attention to practices of editing and publishing. *The Editor Function* is thus best read as a critical opening into a vast set of practices that it can only begin to address, but that must be addressed, if not here, then in the ongoing work of the editor function itself.

The Editor Function in Theory

The Editor Function explores the work of writers and editors who conceived of editorial and publishing projects as artistic and theoretical undertakings. As the title of this subsection suggests, this book is not

Introduction 19

interested in material histories of publishing alone. Its focus is rather on the complementary aspects of material and theoretical work, between the workaday tasks of editing and the textual theories that both inform it and stem from it. Indeed, the editors whose work I examine recognize the text's modes of production and distribution as active components of the literary imagination.[53] Such a recognition derives from a tension always propelling the editor function onward: historical and medial limitation is the condition of artwork, by which I refer to the process of making art and to the resultant work itself. Although we saw Olson rail against the "closed verse" that print bred earlier in this introduction, his aim was not a poetics conceived in the absence of poetry's media. It was rather to give more medial and historical nuance to poetic expression, allowing the conditions of the poem's composition and transmission to enter into conceptions of what and how a poem expresses.[54] In "Letter 5" of his *Maximus Poems* sequence (1950–70), Olson calmly notes that "Limits / are what any of us / are inside of."[55] This is not an expression of futility. On the contrary, Olson's purpose is to make medial limitation into an active element of a new postwar poetics. Nathaniel Mackey similarly conceptualizes a Black centrifugal poetics by proclaiming that "centrifugal work begins with good-bye . . . begins with what words will not do, paint will not do, whatever medium we find ourselves working in will not do."[56] Here again, limits specific to certain media incite a theory of art in which centrifugal practice "begins with" the condition of limitation. As I show in chapters 1 and 3, each of these poetic theories is tested, extended, and redirected by way of the editor function, where the "limits any of us are inside of" take material form as little magazines, literary journals, and contemporary configurations of the literary field.

In their proposals that medial limitation becomes conceptually productive for postwar poetics, Olson and Mackey put themselves in conversation with Theodor Adorno's theory of "second reflection" developed in the 1960s. In *Aesthetic Theory* (1970), Adorno proposes that certain kinds of postwar art operate in a mode of "second reflection" that takes the modernist project of questioning mimetic "reflection"—where an artwork mirrors the world—in more radical directions. Adorno builds

20 Introduction

his theory of second reflection with some observations on the contemporary work of art, remarking for instance that "in sharp contrast to traditional art, new art accents the once hidden element of being something made, something produced."[57] He adds to this the observation that "all efforts to secret away the process of production in the work could not but fail" in postwar art (26). However, this apparent self-knowledge of art and artmakers—that is, acknowledging that their processes of composition, production, and even distribution may be openly on display—does not result in an entirely apparent or legible work of art. Quite the opposite actually. By making the media and procedures of art's production and transmission apparent in art's expression, artists and artworks in fact signal how the mediated aspect of art produces opacity. In other words, sly nods toward the behind-the-scenes operations of art do not lay bare art's artifice but rather acknowledge art's operations and media as generative limits imposed on the working artist.

Working off this counterintuitive observation that in making art's procedures apparent one acknowledges art's opacity, Adorno advances his theory of second reflection:

> The truth of the new, as the truth of what is not already used up, is situated in the intentionless. This sets truth in opposition to reflection, which is the motor of the new, and raises reflection to a second order, to second reflection. It is the opposite of its usual philosophical concept, as it is used, for instance, in Schiller's doctrine of sentimental poetry, where reflection means burdening artworks down with intentions. Second reflection lays hold of the technical procedures, the language of the artwork in the broadest sense, but it aims at blindness. (26–27)

It helps to emphasize a key point that Adorno is working through here. For him, following from Schiller, first reflection expresses the *intention* of the artist for his artwork to mimetically reflect the world. "The truth of the new" now, however, "is situated in the intentionless." This is to say, the reflective work of art that was thought to be the product of an

Introduction 21

artist's intention is no longer the locus of art's novel truths, to adopt Adorno's language.

Adorno appears to bear an odd resemblance to the New Critics here. William Wimsatt and Monroe Beardsley's essay on "The Intentional Fallacy" (1946) in particular encouraged critics to abandon the "fallacy" that understanding an author's intention offers a key into a text. Poems and their language of expression are more independent of intention than such a fallacy lets on. In the place of authorial intention Wimsatt and Beardsley offer the poem whose expressive means inhere in the specific configuration of words on the page. But while both Adorno and Wimsatt and Beardsley take aim at artistic intention, Adorno's "intentionless" art is something different than what Wimsatt and Beardsley propose. Adorno's aim is rather to develop a theory of new art that points to itself as something made and as existing within the limits of art's media. In this, second reflection aligns more closely with Olson's understanding of projective verse or Mackey's theory of centrifugal poetics. That is, Adorno develops his theory of second reflection by acknowledging the medial limitations imposed on the working artist: "Second reflection lays hold of the *technical procedures,* the language of the artwork in the broadest sense, but aims at blindness."[58]

For Adorno, the unsettled conjunction between "laying hold of" and "aiming at blindness" exposes the limits of intention when channeled through the "technical procedures" of art. And I take these "technical procedures" to include the active processes of editing and publishing in the context of this book. The initial "laying hold of" is active, to be sure, and yet "aiming at blindness" suggests that the desired outcome of that action is for opacity or non-intention to introduce itself into intentionality. In Adorno's thinking, a medial apparatus for the unforeseen redirection of intention intervenes in the process of artmaking. Avant-gardists have made the desire for such unforeseen intervention operative for much of the twentieth century, with John Cage's prepared pianos, for instance, inviting the apparatus to become a constitutive element of any piece played on a prepared piano. This seems to me a good example of laying hold of in order to arrive at the unintentional.

Adorno's broader point with second reflection, then, is that artists in the postwar period increasingly understand the diverse procedures of art—including its material procedures—as constituting medial limits that: are nonidentical to the reflective intention of the artist and thus challenge artistic idealism; and are at the same time active and constitutive components of artmaking, where the nonidentity between artist and artwork becomes a critical and dynamic element of the postwar work of art.

The conjunction Adorno theorizes with second reflection aptly describes the editor function and forms a crux that this book returns to from different angles over the course of its chapters: between the material and conceptual components of postwar editing. *The Editor Function,* that is, examines how practices of editing can themselves be generative of new practice-based theories of writing and its attendant media. This book thus advances a theory of postwar editing and writing by insisting that editing is itself a theoretical practice rather than a purely instrumental one. As such, this book takes part in a reassessment of theory's legacy in literary studies today, a reassessment that has sought in some instances to join theory with the material practices of literary work. In his 2006 essay on "Ideas of the Book and Histories of Literature: After Theory?" Peter D. McDonald takes the publication of Terry Eagleton's *After Theory* (2003)—along with a handful of other pronouncements on the death of theory—as the impetus for considering what might be done with theory after its decline. McDonald, who has a background in book history, develops his reassessment between two poles: on the one hand, staunchly historicist book history, which Leah Price notes critics saw as a space of retreat and refuge during critical theory's heyday in the 1970s and 1980s;[59] and high theory itself, which according to McDonald often operated as an intensified expression of New Criticism's understanding of literary textuality, where meaning (or its deconstruction) were thought to be immanent to the literary text.

McDonald's path between these polarized positions rests on perhaps the most famous phrase of poststructuralist theory: "*Il n'y a pas de hors-texte.*" Gayatri Chakravorty Spivak translated Derrida's phrase from *Of*

Introduction   23

Grammatology (French 1967; English 1976) as "There is nothing outside the text"; Derek Attridge as "There is no outside-the-text."[60] With
his knowledge of book history, its technical apparatuses, and the jargon specific to the process of making books, McDonald points out that
both Spivak and Attridge miss the pun in Derrida's phrase. "Hors-
texte" in fact sets "*hors-texte,* a technical bookmaking term roughly
translated as 'plate' (as in 'This book contains five color plates'), alongside *hors texte,* which Attridge's translation comes closest to capturing"
(222–23). McDonald acknowledges that the play on words, relying on
a single hyphen, might not force an immediate rewriting of the history of theory. But "it does indicate . . . that '*Il n'y a pas de hors-text*'
announced neither a triumphant nor a culpable break with history.
The play on words inventively underscored Derrida's sustained commitment to putting in question received assumptions about what is
outside and what is thought to be inside writing" (223). Particularly
relevant here: "plate" (*hors-texte*) refers both to the physical plate that
is part of the bookmaking process and the portion of the book made
by such an apparatus. This dual denotation of plate—where the feature of the book adopts the name of the apparatus of its making—
signals the complementary aspects of literature itself, where literary
text and textual practice conjoin. Operating in tandem with Derrida's
theory of textuality: the apparatuses of textual impression and production, the technical procedures of the work of art.

Like McDonald's reframing of Derrida, *The Editor Function* asks us to
think further about the practices from which our theories of writing and
literature emerge. This appeal is indebted to book history, which continually works between books and texts. "One is a tangible object," Leah
Price summarizes, "the other a verbal structure."[61] Together these form
what McDonald calls the "testing doubleness" of literature, whereby
material histories of the book converge with and contest intellectual
histories and textual ideologies.[62] At the same time, however, this
appeal arises directly from the editorial and publishing practices that
this book studies. It is here that the working and unworking of writing
and literature takes place. And it is here, in practice, that theories of
postwar writing take form, coalescing in published books and literary

24 Introduction

journals that themselves rest on excessive records of correspondence, proofs, solicitations, and the often difficult-to-trace contours of friendship, rivalry, careers, and communities. *The Editor Function* follows editors into this impossible object of study, whose richness in provocations and contradictions is not only the basis for this book but also the locus of postwar theories of literature.

Conclusion: The Editor Function in Practice

Each editorial venture I examine was born out of necessity and borne on particularity. As such, the chapters that follow seek to balance histories of specific editing–publishing formations with commentary on the literary practices that inform them and close readings of texts that speak to the conceptual interests of the editor–publisher. Indeed, each of the chapters that follows seeks to demonstrate how the specific interests, practices, and contexts of working editors and publishers lead to their novel theorizations about literary practice and mediated textuality. So while every chapter adds to a broader history and theory of the editor function, the specific editorial theory each advances stems from the idiosyncratic work of editing and publishing. One of my hopes for this book is to show that an abundance of work remains to be done on the relationships among literary practices and the texts and textual objects they create, particularly for critics of postwar writing where this relation has been less studied until recently. If scholars and critics investigate the practical and theoretical work already undertaken by editors and publishers during this ongoing period, we might yet develop new methods for reflecting on the works and workings of postwar American writing today. This book seeks to develop some of those methods.

In chapter 1, "Editing and the Open Field," I explore the relationship between Charles Olson's poetic epic, *The Maximus Poems,* and his letters and letter–poems to editors of little magazines regarding the conceptual aspects of editorial work. Although Olson is the only figure in this book who was not extensively involved in editing himself—at least not editing that led to the production of books or literary journals—his meticulous interest in editing and publishing was directed toward a

Introduction 25

retheorization of literary textuality in the immediate postwar period. His critical turn toward thinking about postwar writing through the practices of editing and publishing has two primary sources: the corporatization of print culture in postwar America that he addresses in *The Maximus Poems*; and his idea that a radically "open" poetics, which must include poetic processes of making, will undermine the New Critics' interest in what Olson identified in 1950 as "'closed verse,' that verse which print bred."[63] For Olson, the well-wrought poem might acquire new dynamism by introducing the historically situated work of literary practice into conceptions of what poetry is and how it works. This introductory chapter offers an account of Olson's success in opening "closed" verse to historical contingency by way of a highly theoretical understanding of literary practice. However, I conclude by exploring a line of argument less discussed in criticism on Olson: that his theory of textuality was based in part on ideologies of writing and inscription made available through earlier colonial imaginaries, particularly with regard to Olson's study of Mayan glyphs, which he undertook at the same time that he outlined his theory of editing and publishing in his letters to poet–editors Cid Corman and Robert Creeley.

The second chapter, "Editing and the Institution," changes focus from the open field poetics of Olson and his editor–correspondent Cid Corman to the institutionally entangled publishing house Dalkey Archive Press. Whereas Olson and Corman were writing and editing in a period when the study of contemporary literature within academic institutions was still a relatively novel practice—and one Olson explored extensively in his several years directing Black Mountain College— Dalkey Archive Press formed in part as a result of the newly sanctioned status of contemporary literature within universities.[64] Founded in 1984 by a disgruntled early-career scholar of contemporary writing, Dalkey Archive Press began by bringing out-of-print works of contemporary and modernist writing back into print, thereby serving a critical function in the field of contemporary literary studies. In this chapter, I argue that Dalkey Archive Press draws on the legacy of Irish literary modernism to show how literary institutions—from the academy to corporate publishers—effectively limit what comes to be known as "contemporary literature" in the decades following World War II. Because John O'Brien, the founder of the press, floundered in his attempts at writing criticism on contemporary literature, editing and publishing allowed him to expose the institutionally built field of "contemporary literature" to the abandoned and forgotten writers and literary works on which it rests. Yet even a publishing house designed to lay bare the inequities of field formation can reproduce some of the logics of the field it criticizes. I therefore conclude my chapter on Dalkey Archive Press by reflecting on the place of Black writers in the formation of Dalkey Archive Press. Although John O'Brien earned his PhD in the early 1970s by producing a dissertation (and then book) called *Interviews with Black Writers* (1973) in which he interviews some of the leading African American fiction writers of the twentieth century—including Ralph Ellison, Ernest J. Gaines, Clarence Major, Ann Petry, Ishmael Reed, and John Edgar Wideman, among others—Dalkey Archive Press subsequently published very few African American writers aside from Ishmael Reed. Rather than trying to account for the disparity in O'Brien's focus on African American writing in his two major critical projects (his sole book and his publishing house), I instead take the disparity as an opportunity to address the present absences in Dalkey Archive Press, partly by recalling my time working at Dalkey Archive Press and my mostly failed attempt to reissue a series of works by Black writers.

My third chapter, "Editing and the Ensemble," focuses on Nathaniel Mackey's editorship of the literary journal *Hambone*. Since its inception in 1982, *Hambone* has offered an open call to writers looking to experiment with poetic form. Its "bassline," however, has been formed by an ensemble of African American, Caribbean, and Euro-American writers who establish the cross-cultural terrain that Mackey seeks to examine with his journal.[65] This chapter argues that *Hambone*'s purposefully eccentric ensemble of American and international authors derives from and coalesces around theories of intellectual labor and creative hospitality that can be traced through the vernacular of Hambone's history. Hambone is the figure of a call-and-response rhyme—"Hambone, Hambone, where you been?"—arising from a tradition that understands creative labor to be a process of collective experiment, expression, and

Introduction   27

organization. My goal in this chapter is to show how Mackey draws on *Hambone* and the figure's history to develop a theory of the ensemble and ensemblist form that dislocates the locus of creative conception while also historicizing it through the cross-cultural practice of editing.

Chapter 4, "Editing and Eros," takes the title of Chris Kraus's first novel—*I Love Dick* (1997)—as a point of departure for studying the erotics of editing, but where the erotic extends beyond the sexual to include love for friends and fellow artists. Like my chapter on Mackey, this one examines editing as a practice of community formation, evident especially in Kraus's written and editorial interest in art scenes. However, I begin my investigation into arts scenes and editing from a perhaps unexpected angle: by establishing Kraus's epistolary *I Love Dick* as an elaborate response to Henry James's *The Turn of the Screw* (1898), where an economy of letters—including editing and making public—frames a story about love and desire. *The Turn of the Screw* is in some sense a tale of love and desire that "*won't* tell . . . in any literal vulgar way."[66] *I Love Dick,* by comparison, tells all and so literalizes its protagonist Chris's desire through publication. And yet, as the chapter goes on to show, Chris's love letters to Dick have multiple addressees, many of whom enter the narrative as ghosts of Chris's dead friends who lived as marginalized artists and writers in postwar America. In the first book of his *Spheres* trilogy, Peter Sloterdijk proposes that "love stories are stories of form, and that every act of solidarity is an act of sphere formation."[67] In the second part of this chapter, I show how Kraus draws on eros in order to make editing an act of erotic solidarity with lovers and lost friends.

The coda, "Editing and *Entropy,*" explores the proposition that editing ultimately exhausts itself and that this exhaustion is related to the conditions of labor under which most noncorporate literary editing now takes place. I end the book with this brief coda on Janice Lee and *Entropy,* an eclectic online magazine and community space for the arts, because *Entropy's* organizational structure is shaped by and responds to the working conditions of many early career writers, critics, editors, and publishers at work—and out of it—today. *Entropy* began publishing in 2014, six years after the onset of the recession and relately six

28 Introduction

years into the continued contraction of the academic job market in the United States that the recession intensified. The coda examines how an editorial response to such large-scale social and structural changes takes shape, with *Entropy* effectively asking: To what end should a journal seek to make order out of the chaos that our economic and academic systems generate? To answer this question, Lee conceptualizes editing as what I call an "editorial long take"—a concept I develop by reading Lee's editorship alongside her written engagements with the Hungarian filmmaker Béla Tarr—where the open dynamic of the long take allows intimacy and empathy to emerge in response to increasing precarity. For Lee and the dozens of editors that now make up *Entropy's* editorial board, dwelling in chaos and disorder becomes a means for attending to solidarity with others in this precarious present.

Yet *Entropy's* disorder—its unruly drive—equally tests this book's aim to develop critical methodologies for studying the work of editing. I end with *Entropy* quite deliberately, then, as a means of reflecting on the broader aims of this project. This book proposes that the editor function looks beyond the limiting function of the author to show how editors, author–editors, and publishing formations make editorial work into a dynamic mode of textual and extra-textual meaning-making.[68] But as one moves beyond the limiting function of authors and into the disruptive and often disordered world of the editor, one's subject of study becomes increasingly manifold. It emerges through the work of specific editors and the numerous material histories feeding into and deriving from editorial work. It emerges through intellectual histories and histories of intellectual labor. And it emerges through the texts and textual theories that transform and are themselves transformed by what this book designates broadly as the editor function. These varied formations do not always so much cohere as conjoin. And it is through studying their points of conjunction that *The Editor Function* takes shape.

1

Editing and the Open Field

Charles Olson's Letters to Editors

Of the many letter–poems that comprise Charles Olson's *Maximus Poems,* a poetic epic written from the late 1940s until Olson's death in 1970, few set the tone and the stakes as well as a three-poem sequence addressed to a beleaguered literary editor. "Letters" 5, 6, and 7 of *The Maximus Poems* find Olson, by way of Maximus, responding to a recent issue of Vincent Ferrini's literary journal *4 Winds* in which Olson had just published "Letter 3" of his fledgling epic.[1] Because *4 Winds* was published in Gloucester, Massachusetts, the small city that Olson's epic seeks to bring to life, it was an especially fitting venue for an early Maximus poem. In "Letter 3," the hero addresses the citizens of this "root city" in an attempt to outline his vision for a new "polis" in the postwar era. His vision has a limited purview, however, with Maximus conceding that "Polis now/is a few," a line speaking less to the small population of Gloucester than to Olson's sense that he and a select few needed to build a postwar poetics from the ground up.[2] These few would form "a coherence not even yet new (the island of this city" (I.11).[3] At once a diagnosis of postwar American literary culture in decline because of those who "use words cheap" (I.9) and a remedy in the form of a poetics "not even yet new," the poem establishes its epic vision by linking return with rejuvenation. Gloucester is the restorative source

29

30   Editing and the Open Field

that will help Maximus to find his "few" in order to establish a new yet historically grounded poetic polis.

While Maximus dreams of making Gloucester his model polis through a sequence of poems, Olson's expectations for *4 Winds* were hardly less grand. Ferrini and his little magazine were to be among the "few" that would establish Gloucester as a new literary center. The magazine would allow the letters of Maximus to find their recipients, thereby shaping the "evanescent, idealized political possibility" that polis represents in Olson's thought.[4] *4 Winds* would also situate that possibility squarely and materially within Gloucester. Olson's high expectations for Ferrini's magazine explain his eventual disappointment at the double issue, numbers 2–3, to which Maximus letters 5, 6, and 7—which I call the Ferrini Letters—respond. Far from being pleased with seeing "Letter 3" published in Gloucester, Olson scolds and patronizes Ferrini for "this sheet you've had the nerve / to put upon the public street" (I.18). In a moment of pride disguised as vulnerability, Olson merges his own voice with that of Maximus to wonder if Ferrini feels "(as vulnerable as I am / brought home to Main St / in such negligible company)" (I.20), the last line of which captures Olson's opinion of the other poems published in the issue.[5] Maximus's triumphant arrival home eludes him. Yet his printed appearance in *4 Winds* compels Olson to consider how editorial work and literary journals shape the conceptual and political formations of postwar writing. In the Ferrini Letters, the conditional processes of editing and publishing recast the utopian vision of polis that Olson had outlined in "Letter 3." The Ferrini Letters thereby open an investigation into—and so acknowledge—the limits that editorial practices place on the more metaphysical and idealist poetics that Olson had in fact been advancing.

Olson's transition from the utopian polis of "Letter 3" to the more personal and pedantic Ferrini Letters introduces the close and complementary relation between process (Ferrini Letters) and metaphysics ("Letter 3") in Olson's larger body of work. This chapter explores that relation through an examination of editing, publishing, and print culture. It shows how Olson often anchors his poetics in the process-based

Editing and the Open Field 31

economy of literary editing and publishing; and it argues that his poetry nevertheless withdraws from the practical and procedural aspects of editing and publishing as it moves toward the metaphysical, symbolic, and theoretical.[6] Olson addresses the association between process and metaphysics in a 1952 essay on "The Materials and Weights of Herman Melville." According to Olson, Melville understood the "given physicality" of things and moved literature from a concern with "essence" to a concern with "kinetics," a statement that at first opposes the "essential" forms of metaphysics to the "given physicality" of things. Olson shores up this position by declaring that modern writing must approach its objects not through metaphysical "essence alone" but also through "*dimension,* that part of a thing which ideality—by its Ideal, its World Forms or its Perfections—tended to diminish."[7] Yet while Olson seeks to abandon essences, particularly those he associates with "Ideal" forms, he nevertheless retains metaphysics. "For the metaphysic now to be known," Olson announces, "*does* lie inside function, methodology is form" (117). Thinking by way of Melville, Olson stresses that metaphysics inhabits function and methodology. This conception of a functional or process-oriented metaphysics, which numerous scholars have rightly traced back to the influence of Alfred North Whitehead's process philosophy, manifests itself in a variety of ways in Olson's body of work.[8] I focus here on its manifestation in his relationship to editing and print culture, where active methods of writing, editing, and publishing at once ground Olson's poetry and give it metaphysical dimension.

The Ferrini Letters aptly illustrate Olson's complementary shifts between material process and metaphysics. On the one hand, the letters see Olson acknowledge the editorial and medial limitation that *4 Winds* places on the utopian vision that "Letter 3" set forth. On the other hand, Olson goes on in the letters to envision the poetry journal as both a material and conceptual print–poetic dwelling. *4 Winds,* that is, both limits and generates poetic possibility. Olson arrives at his theory of the literary journal through broader reflections on print media and what he calls the "limits of literacy." In "Letter 5," Maximus asserts that

32   Editing and the Open Field

> The habit of newsprint
> (plus possibly the National Geographic)
> are the limits of
> literacy[9]

In this criticism of the print cultural industries—with "newsprint" the epitome of "those who use words cheap, who use us cheap" (I.9)—publishers who decide what is fit to print ultimately also form the horizon of legible public knowledge. Yet following his criticism of the "limits of literacy," Maximus concedes that

> I am not at all aware
> that anything more than that
> is called for. Limits
> are what any of us
> are inside of (I.17)

In a change of stance, Maximus grants the limits prescribed by newsprint without much complaint, for he understands that thought is a situated practice. Proposing any easy transcendence of limits would lead Olson into a direct contradiction with the argument he developed in "The Materials and Weights of Herman Melville" just a year earlier. At the outset of the Ferrini Letters, then, we find Olson, via Maximus, acknowledging "limits" as a condition of possibility. Such position-taking is characteristic of Olson's poetics, with David Herd observing that Olson's poetic project was to develop a "conception of the poem grounded in relation; an aesthetic that made relatedness (of people, objects, and ideas) axiomatic to the poem's form and creative practice."[10] In "Letter 5," that relatedness begins to take shape by way of editing and publishing. Ferrini's *4 Winds* becomes a ground of relation that Olson's projective verse initially set out to examine.

This examination, however, is guided as much by poetic figuration as it is by medial limitation. Olson establishes the link between the two most clearly in "Letter 5," where he develops the conceit of the little magazine as a neighborhood where Maximus and Ferrini can meet. Still upset by the negligible company he is forced to keep within the pages of *4 Winds*, Maximus suggests to Ferrini that they meet "anywhere you

Editing and the Open Field 33

say" (I.22). He then proposes several places in Gloucester, embellishing them with local lore and populating his polis and his poem with houses, inns, sailors, and early colonial settlers. After several attempts to locate a meeting place, Maximus abandons his efforts:

> I begin to be damned to figure out where we can meet. I liked your own
> house,
> that first day I sought you out (you will recall that I came to your door
> just because I had read a poem by you in just such a little magazine
> as you now purport to edit (I.23)

Irritated, Maximus convinces himself that the meeting place he seeks cannot be found and finds solace in recollection. He remembers Ferrini's home, which he sought out after reading Ferrini's poetry "in such a little magazine / as you now purport to edit." The little magazine was in fact their meeting place, an at once real and figural space whose coordinates were laid out in print. As Maximus explains:

> A magazine does have this "life" to it (proper to it), does have streets,
> can show lights, movie houses, bars, and, occasionally,
>
> > for those of us who do live our life quite properly in print
> > as properly, say, as Gloucester people live in Gloucester
> you do meet someone
> as I met you
> on a printed page (I.24)

The magazine is not simply a place to meet. It has streets and bars; it shows movies. It is, for Olson, a print–poetic polis with a life of its own. The "island city" manifests itself through the typography "on a printed page" and through the process-derived metaphysics of literary work. The close associations among poetics, polis, and print culture— by which I refer to the active processes of editing and publishing as well as to the media with which those processes engage—signal here the dynamic relation between *medial configuration* and *poetic figuration* in Olson's work.

I begin *The Editor Function* with Olson, then, because he saw the manifold nature of editorial and publishing work: it has a limiting

34   Editing and the Open Field

function—to draw once again on the Foucauldian author function discussed in the introduction—that situates Olson's own poetry in the active processes of editorial labor and literary production; and it has a figural function that allows Olson to conceptualize the workings of the literary field in more abstract ways. Ferrini is not the only editor who makes his way into *The Maximus Poems* after all. The sequence in book form, in fact, begins with Olson's 1960 dedication "for ROBERT CREELEY / —the Figure of Outward" (3). According to George F. Butterick, who edited and published ten volumes of correspondence between Olson and Creeley, the dedication responds to "the possibilities Creeley offered as publisher and editor."[11] The dedication is particularly sharp, since "edit" stems from the Latin "to put forth" or "to put out," an etymology perhaps not lost on Olson. In Olson's own words from a late-in-life note found among his papers,

> the Figure of Outward means way out way out
> *there:* the
> 'World'[12]

In his role as correspondent, editor, and publisher, Creeley offered Olson ways out into the "World." Olson's placement of the "World" in quotation marks gives reason for pause, however, because it makes it impossible to distinguish the world to which he refers. Is it the world we live in? The world of letters? Or an imagined, poetic, fictional world, like the Gloucester he imagines in the pages of *4 Winds*? There is no singular answer to these questions. Olson's work shifts between worlds and their dimensions, from physical, to literary historical, to metaphysical, and back again. He makes these shifts by way of processes of editing and publishing, and via the editors and publishers—those "figures of outward"—who make such shifts possible. Together Olson and his editors figure the outward and thereby introduce one of the threads that runs through *The Editor Function*: situated literary practices guide writers, editors, and publishers alike toward theories of textuality in which historical and material specificity meet with the conceptually unbound.

"On a Printed Page"

Olson's commitment to print in the Ferrini Letters—"occasionally / [. . .] you do meet someone / as I met you / on a printed page"—gives reason for pause, not least because Olson opens his most famous essay on poetics, "Projective Verse" (1950), by denouncing what he calls "'closed' verse, that verse which print bred."[13] Later in that essay he levels the charge that "what we have suffered from, is manuscript, press, the removal of verse from its producer and its reproducer, the voice" (245). In his early attempts to establish a "projective or OPEN verse" (239), one attuned to its limits and conditions of possibility while not giving itself over to totalizing limitation, Olson tips the scales momentarily in favor of the orality of voice and the breath. Yet he quickly balances his stress on the voice by singling out the typewriter as the machine with which the poet can "indicate exactly the breath . . . which he intends" (245), thereby transferring the poetic breath to the typed page. The introduction of the typewriter into Olson's projective poetics invites us to consider that his assertive denunciations of print work less to rid us of print altogether than they do to reconfigure our conception of print and type as media of poetic expression. Olson implicitly asks how to conceptualize printed poetry in such a way that verse remains open to and aware of its conditions of production.

Before assessing Olson's process-oriented conception of print in greater detail, however, I want to contextualize his apparently dogged anti-print position. Olson has taken various stances against print, most often linking it to limits of literacy, closure, and commercialism. His suspicion of print stems from his conviction that the written word has enforced logocentrism since the times of Socrates, Plato, and Aristotle. Rather than *logos* meaning simply "word" as it once did, for Olson it has become a unit of ratio and measurement that leads to the abstraction of thought. Consider the position Olson takes against *logos* in "Human Universe":

> We have lived long in a generalizing time, at least since 450 B.C. And it has had its effects on the best of men, and the best of things. Logos, or discourse, for example, in that time, so worked its abstractions into our

36   Editing and the Open Field

concept and use of language that language's other function, speech, seems so in need of restoration that several of us go back to hieroglyphs or to ideograms to right the balance. (The distinction here is between language as the act of the instant and language as the act of thought about the instant.)[14]

Olson pits the abstractions of *logos* against the seeming immediacy of speech, or "language as the act of the instant." Although Olson does not name print or writing here specifically, his lament that "language's other function, speech," has been abandoned implies that language's primary mode has become written expression. He associates this mode with an unwanted sense of mediated removal—"language as the act of thought about the instant"—thereby tethering thought's abstraction to written and printed language.

Olson solidifies the link he sees between *logos* and alphabetic writing by offering nonalphabetic writing systems—the ideogram and the hieroglyph—as alternatives for inscribed communication. In Olson's thinking, hieroglyphs and ideograms, like speech, access language's other function: its nonrational, processual potential. Joseph Riddel has argued that, for Olson, a glyph "is a metonym for a poem, a means of communication and not a closed work reflecting (upon) itself."[15] The glyph, like the poem, shows language in action. Building on Riddel's argument, William Spanos explains that by invoking ideograms and hieroglyphs Olson aligns himself with Ernest Fenollosa's *The Chinese Written Character as a Medium for Poetry* (1920). Like Fenollosa, Spanos writes, Olson destroys "the hardened logocentric metaphysical tradition beginning with Plato and Aristotle" by stressing "the verbal or active element evoked by the occasion, the speech 'motion' the ideogram enacts."[16] It is not so much that Olson abandons graphic expression outright. Rather, Olson seeks to discover a balance between speech and its graphic manifestation in the forms of ideograms and hieroglyphs. He retains his suspicion of the alphabetically written and printed word in his attempt to counter the power of *logos* in Western thought. But he also insists that some forms of graphic expression—and as this chapter

Editing and the Open Field 37

argues, the practices associated with these forms such as editing and publishing—provide means for language's active use.

Olson's evident wariness of print and logocentrism in "Projective Verse" and "Human Universe" extends to literacy as well. In his 1959 "Letter to Elaine Feinstein," Olson restates his claim from "Projective Verse" that "form is never any more than an extension of content," but adds the clarification "—a non-literary sense, certainly."[17] The non-literary holds Olson's interest in this letter because it helps him to reflect again on the relationship between speech, alphabetic literacy, and poetic language. "The only advantage of speech rhythms," he explains to Feinstein, "is illiteracy: the non-literary, exactly in Dante's sense of the value of the vernacular over grammar—that speech as a communicator is prior to the individual and is picked up as soon as and with ma's milk."[18] In going back to Dante, Olson accesses two monumental figures of the vernacular at once: Dante himself, who composed *The Divine Comedy* in Italian rather than Latin; and the figure of the mother, once conceived of as the source of a "primary orality."[19] For Olson, speech is illiterate and nonliterary because it finds its source in the figure of the mother before the onset of literacy. Yet even while Olson idealizes primary orality with the figure of the mother, he grounds his idealization in Dante, who brought the vernacular voice to the written page. Dante's vernacular triumph was not that he spoke Italian, but that he wrote in it. For all of Olson's championing of illiteracy and the nonliterary, illiteracy often refines Olson's thinking about what literacy entails rather than working as a starry-eyed dismissal of literacy altogether.[20]

Olson aims his rethinking of literacy and logocentrism at thought's abstraction, particularly as this abstraction intensifies the association Olson sees between print culture and commercialism. In his letter to Elaine Feinstein, Olson clarifies his position on speech rhythms: "I couldn't stress enough on this speech rhythm question," he says, for the results exhibit "a non-literate, non-commercial and non-historical constant daily experience" (250). Olson had made similar observations on the relation between commercialism and literacy several years earlier in "The Songs of Maximus" (1953):

38   Editing and the Open Field

>   colored pictures
> of all things to eat: dirty
> postcards
>   And words, words, words
> all over everything
>   No eyes or ears left
> to do their own doings (all
> invaded, appropriated, outraged, all senses
> including the mind, that worker on what is (I.13)

This song makes graphic media, written and visual in this case, objects for consumption. Olson and his contemporaries gorge on "colored pictures," "dirty / postcards," and "words, words, words," but in doing so are themselves "appropriated" by the machinations of commerce and the culture industry. The result is that postwar cultural consumers lose their senses: eyes and ears are passively appropriated and become the property of graphic commercialism.

Olson's entrenched suspicion of the relation between print and logocentrism displays itself most forcefully in "Projective Verse." As we have seen, Olson condemns "'closed' verse, that verse which print bred," and laments that "What we have suffered from, is manuscript, press, the removal of verse from its producer and its reproducer, the voice" (245). The voice, which stands in for the poetic and therefore noncommercial use of language in Olson's thought, has been evacuated by and to the page, making Olson's purpose in "Projective Verse" recuperative. The breath and ear become poetry's recuperative apparatuses. William Spanos sees Olson's turn to the ear and voice as an attempt to "dis-cover the primordial meaning of the *logos* covered over and finally forgotten by the hardening of the recollective emphasis of the ontotheological tradition."[21] Olson's turn away from print and toward the breath, in other words, discloses a relationality that scrapes away the hardened crust of the "ontotheological tradition." According to Spanos, Olson "dis-covers" the primordial meaning of *logos,* and thereby reenters a sense of relationality in time made impossible by logocentrism, by turning to the "temporal sense *par excellence,* the ear, that is to say, speech as oral/aural activity as agency of knowledge" (46). In this reading of

Editing and the Open Field 39

Olson's projective poetics, only the oral/aural enacts poetic activity as the agency of knowledge.

A problem arises here, however, which has tended to distort the reception of Olson's work: the too-ready embrace of the oral/aural at the expense of graphic expression. Thomas Ford has argued that the apparent pressure to choose either the oral/aural or the graphic underwrites many of the tensions of twentieth-century poetry. "The main currents of Anglophone modernism were neither phonocentric nor graphocentric," he writes,

> but no poetry could afford to ignore the agonistic struggle between these rival poles. The purities of script and the absolutism of voice acted as historical limit cases for twentieth-century poetry. Between them they defined the media space available to poets. In fact, much of the history of twentieth-century poetics can be understood as a story of strategic positioning within this technical space.[22]

Olson's body of work indeed presents itself as a series of strategic positionings between the poles of phonocentric and graphocentric poetics. Yet the "laws and possibilities of the breath" that drive Olson's argument in "Projective Verse" have often led critics to neglect the role of print in Olson's projective project (239). Spanos makes the ear the temporal sense "*par excellence*" for registering the agency of knowledge in time. He warns that critics should be wary of the oral/aural presence that underwrites logocentrism, but makes little mention of writing's place in the discovery of the "primordial meaning of *logos*."

Although "Projective Verse" is best known for its breathing poet, the essay also makes a strong case for writing and print as media for projective engagement. Any careful reading of "Projective Verse" has to account for the fact that the poet's breath, which produces the syllable, forms only half of Olson's poetic equation. The other half is the poetic line. "Together, these two," he writes, "the syllable and the line, they make a poem, they make that thing" (242). The breath and the line complement one another in the creation of the poem: "And the line comes (I swear it) from the breath, from the breathing of the man

40   Editing and the Open Field

who writes, at the moment that he writes, and thus is, it is here that, the daily work, the WORK, gets in" (242). In the act of writing, the poet registers the breath because the breath "gets in" to verse by way of its graphic manifestation. Olson and the Black Mountain poets "are usually remembered for endorsing a speech-based poetics," as Brian Reed has remarked.[23] Yet writing and print often balance the aural/oral claims for which Olson's essay is renowned.[24] Indeed, the meeting of voice and page is nearly mythologized in Olson's awe of the typewriter. Immediately after Olson laments how poetry suffers from "manuscript, press," he goes on to say that

> the irony is, from the machine has come one gain not yet sufficiently observed or used . . . It is the advantage of the typewriter that, due to its rigidity and its space precisions, it can, for a poet, indicate exactly the breath, the pauses, the suspensions of syllables, the juxtaposition even of parts of phrases, which he intends.[25]

By means of the typewriter, the poet can "indicate how he would want any reader, silently or otherwise, to voice his work" (245). The illiterate ear and the literate eye work in concert, making the split between orality and literacy in Olson's work a red herring at best, or, at worst, an exacerbation of the very logocentrism that this critical tradition sets out to challenge.

Origin, Editing, and the Poetics of Print

Olson's extension of the poetic breath to the poetic line in "Projective Verse" extends still further to printed journals and little magazines. The early 1950s correspondence between Olson and Cid Corman, a poet and editor of the literary journal *Origin*, sees Olson elaborating his conception of projective verse by way of the little magazines that publish his work. These expansions of Olson's projective poetics are prompted by Olson's attempt to posit just what a little magazine is and how it works in relation to "composition by field" (239). Olson's initial letter to Corman in *Letters for Origin* replies to Corman's invitation to be a

Editing and the Open Field

contributing editor for his little magazine. The letter begins cautiously before Olson explains, "I am an older animal. And smell thrice, as I go around a new baby, just, to make sure . . . to be mighty sure, there's breath BREATH in it" (1). Olson's emphasis on breath here certainly plays into his metaphor that presents *Origin* as a newborn baby. The emphatic repetition of "breath BREATH," however, also links this letter—and by association *Origin*—to the "laws of breath" that govern projective verse.

Once Olson and Corman's relationship developed, Olson began to see even stronger connections between "composition by field" and the actual composition of *Origin* as a material and metaphorical field of practice for projective poetics. In a 1951 letter written in Campeche, Mexico—at the same time that Olson was writing his influential *Mayan Letters* to Robert Creeley—Olson responds to *Origin*'s first issue. Declaring his pleasure that the issue works, like a book, as a single unit of expression, he adds the qualification that a book articulates the thought of a single author. The little magazine, by comparison, emerges via thoughtful collaboration between the editors and the authors. For an editor of a little magazine, "the pieces, he is composing, are, someone else's (chiefly), in other words . . . he is the agent of a, collective" (48). If "Projective Verse" forms "a conception of a poem grounded in relations" as David Herd has pointed out,[26] then Olson's engagement with *Origin* advances a projective verse that includes editing, publishing, and print as active variables within this field of relations.[27] *Origin* acts on Olson's thought, pushing it in directions he had neither intended nor foreseen. He is no longer concerned solely with "the breathing of the man who writes," but also with the editing of the person who publishes.

Olson's increasing interest in editing, assembling, and publishing was not without false starts. When Olson began theorizing about the process of editing and publishing in his letters to Corman, he at first lit on "taste" as a defining element of editorial work. Because an editor selects "the pieces, he is composing," according to Olson, the editor's "taste" shapes the ambiguous collective he presents. Unlike with a single-author book, the editor's work revises the "taste" of authors—

Cover of *Origin* 1 (1951), edited by Cid Corman. This issue led to an extended exchange between Corman and Olson regarding the function of the little magazine for postwar American writing. Courtesy of Granary Books / From a Secret Location with permission from the Cid Corman Estate.

the stylistic idiosyncrasies and thematic signs under which they are to be consumed—by placing them side by side. On the one hand, thinking via taste appeals to Olson, because it enables him to consider how the assembled form of a little magazine works against any singular taste of the author or editor. Assembled form, in short, becomes yet another way for Olson to think about how limits might generate their own openings. In this case, the taste of the editor jostles writers by putting them side by side in a methodical but never completely controlled fashion. Always moving among viewpoints, however, Olson soon runs against the limits of taste as his overarching metaphor, for a little magazine also has the potential to turn into "a fearful compounding" of "taste" that could hinder poetic expression. That is, taste runs the danger of becoming an "inherited mold" that might simply reproduce and compound cultural and poetic norms.[28] The question then becomes: how does one edit without simply becoming a functionary of social reproduction, a process that would further shape poetry into a closed aesthetic form? (48–49). This question has no definitive answer, of course, and the critics I cite above have shown convincingly that Olson relied heavily on a network of mostly like-minded White men to advance his poetics and his position in the field of postwar American poetry, with Olson's epistolary exchange with Frances Boldereff a terrific exception. Yet the impossibility of answering this question drives Olson's thinking about the poetics of editing and publishing, even if, in hindsight, he reproduced some of the oppressive social formations of midcentury America that made it more difficult for women and writers of color to attain recognition in the world of poetry.

Seeing that his line of approach with taste has begun to hit limits of encroaching social reproduction, Olson tries to open editorial and publishing work back up by changing its governing principle from "taste" to "force," a term that anchors his newfound editorial poetics in "Projective Verse." After he explains to Corman that each issue of *Origin* should be conceived of as a field of force, he remarks, "Which brings us to the mat: in what way can a magazine for the 'creative' be at once the inevitable act of the taste of the editor and at the same time be, wholly, inside itself, a, field of force[?]."[29] Given the vitality of Olson's

44   Editing and the Open Field

writing throughout this letter, one expects a potent answer to the question he poses to himself and Corman. Instead, Olson concedes that the answer is undecidable:

> THAT ORIGIN PRESENTS THE SAME PROBLEM AS—I take it—A POEM OR A STORY DOES, now:
>
>> that, because it is OPEN, & it already implies that ENERGY is the source of, taste [. . .]
>
>> > that THE DEMAND
> ON YOU, CID CORMAN, is, to accomplish each issue—to see it, always clearly, exhaustively, as—A
>
>> FIELD OF FORCE
>
> that is, that, as agent of this collective (which ORIGIN is going to be) the question is larger than, yr taste, alone: it has the same sort of confrontation as—in any given poem—a man faces: how much energy has he got in, to make the thing stand on its own feet as, a force, in, the fields of force which surround everyone of us, of which we, too, are forces: to stand FORTH
>
> This is getting to sound altogether too much like a P[rojective] V[erse] thing! (50)

Here, the magazine acts as a force in the field of forces in which Olson situates his poetic theory. Whereas a critic such as Spanos associates this kind of active force with Heideggerian Being and oral/aural situated action, Olson proposes that editing and publishing also participate in the active processes of *poiesis*: the editor function is an engaged form of making. Indeed, instead of distancing this poetics of publishing from his foundational statements about projective verse, Olson makes the connection explicit. "This is getting to sound altogether too much like a PV thing!," he concludes, acknowledging how the tenets set forth in "Projective Verse" take new shape via the operations of editing a little magazine.

Editing and the Open Field

Still, Olson has not yet answered the question he has set for himself: how can a magazine be both an expression of taste and an expression of force? The answer, finally, emerges in graphic expression, particularly as graphic expression is the manifestation of quotidian literary practices. Toward the end of his letter to Corman, Olson offers a numbered summary of the points he has covered:

> (I), Keep clear of the insides of, any assumptions which are part of, or colored by "Western", or "Christian", history
>
> (2) which means most of our assumptions abt taste and "the aesthetics of" any art (as proceeding fr, the Greeks, & first formulated significantly by Aristotle, and Longinus, etc.
>
> (3) offset to I & 2, kinetics of contemporary physics, say, as more healthful than, either of above, and of the *graphic* as a better runner for the sleigh or cart than, humanism (51)

Olson distances himself from Western aesthetics yet again and offsets aesthetics with kinetics and "the *graphic.*"[30] Kinetics traces the transfer of force from one place to another, from the breath to the line, as we have seen, or from the line to the little magazine. Instead of situating the graphic as the final expressive means in a series of kinetic transfers, however, Olson characterizes the graphic as the horse before the cart. This position differs significantly from the one Olson takes in "Projective Verse." His targets remain the same: Western and Christian history; and aesthetic assumptions as markers of closed cultural systems, extending to and including "closed verse." His operative media and practices, however, have changed: the kinetics of the graphic and the practices of editing and publishing.

Islands Hidden in the Blood: Print to Polis

Islands hold a unique place in Olson's literary topography. In "Cole's Island" (1964), written after the death of Olson's wife and one of the most haunting *Maximus* poems, Olson uses insular topography to present an ethereal experience.[31] The poem opens, "I met Death—he

46 Editing and the Open Field

was a sportsman—on Cole's / Island," suggesting that islands are spaces for otherworldly experience dressed in quotidian garb. "Cole's Island," writes Olson,

> is a queer isolated and gated place, and I was only there by will
> to know more of the topography of it lying as it does out
> over the Essex River. And as it now is, with no tenants that one can
>   speak of,
> it's more private than almost any place one might imagine. (III.69)

This is not a place one stumbles upon. Maximus is "only there by will," for this remote island rests beyond the perhaps stygian river Essex. Yet despite the many eerie markers that set Cole's Island apart from the world, Olson remarks that "it's more private than almost any place one might imagine," suggesting in passing that Cole's Island is not an entirely imagined place. And it is not: Cole's Island rests under ten miles from Gloucester, though not beyond the Essex River, at least not as one would get there from Gloucester. Characteristic of the movement between quotidian, historical, metaphorical, and mythical modes that propel the Maximus sequence, Maximus's Cole's Island is at once imagined and not, otherworldly and worldly. Its insular location, floating between that which is here and that which is elsewhere, provides a strangely removed point of entry to the insular topography of *The Maximus Poems*.

Like Cole's Island, the poetic polis of Gloucester is a queerly isolated place. Although Olson plumbs Gloucester's history over the course of the sequence, seeking to bring Gloucester to life, Olson's "root city" nevertheless emerges as an otherworldly and insular space of poetic retreat where diverse forces gather and unlikely figures meet. By the end of the sequence, for instance, Olson likens Gloucester to Atlantis, their close relationship signaled by the syntax and absent punctuation of the phrase: "just south of Atlantis Gloucester" (III.205). Olson's conceptualization of Gloucester as an island city—an example of the idealized polis we saw outlined earlier in "Letter 3"—shows how Olson draws on insular topography as a trope for poetic retreat, imagination, and mythmaking. He draws on this insular trope throughout the sequence,

Editing and the Open Field 47

from the late placement of Gloucester in close proximity with Atlantis (January 1, 1969)[32] to the very opening lines of Olson's poetic epic, likely composed in May of 1950.[33] Introducing the sequence, Maximus speaks among islands:

> Off-shore, by islands hidden in the blood
> jewels & miracles, I, Maximus
> a metal hot from boiling water, tell you
> what is a lance, who obeys the figures of
> the present dance (I.1)

These forceful opening lines address both the citizens of Gloucester and the reader of the poem. For all the force of his address, however, Maximus speaks from a distance, from "Off-shore, by islands hidden in the blood." In the opening lines, the epic space once committed to invoking the muses, Maximus favors an address withdrawn in poetic retreat. From this space, he mines jewels and miracles and emerges as the decorated epic hero he remains throughout the Maximus sequence.

Maximus's opening retreat invites us to reconsider Olson's poetics, which has often been understood to eschew poetic detachment and artifice.[34] William Spanos, we have seen, focuses on the active agency of speech in order to short-circuit poetry's abstractions into "logocentric metaphysics." Paul Bové has turned to Olson's work precisely because he understands it to flout the poetics of detachment associated with New Criticism and its solipsistic vision of modernist poetry, a version of modernist poetry that has admittedly been challenged since the publication of Bové's book in 1980.[35] In *Destructive Poetics: Heidegger and Modern American Poetry*, Bové sets out to expose the "metaphysical critical tradition" that the New Criticism had underwritten.[36] For Bové, modernist habits of reading "are based on critical theories of aesthetic distance" that insist on "a continuous, unchanging tradition maintained by the exclusive definition of poetry as ironic, closed form" (x, xii). Bové's own critical position and vocabulary hew closely to those that Olson developed in the early 1950s, with Bové nearly replicating Olson's argument in his letters to Cid Corman about taste being a closed form of cultural reproduction. It should be no surprise, then, that Bové sees Olson as

48   Editing and the Open Field

subvert[ing] the traditional language of abstract concepts and ironic
symbols to displace not only the continuous linearity of the Western
onto-theological tradition, but to discover that the very notion both of
"tradition" as a centered canon and of "history" are Western *myths* used
to defend the aesthetic, distanced, disinterested privilege of antihistorical metaphysics. (xiv–xv)

Here again, Olson's writing is deemed exemplary for working against
the abstractions associated with "antihistorical metaphysics." Spanos
and Bové are often perceptive in their thinking about Olson's poetic
positioning against Eliotic modernism and the New Critics. Yet if their
readings of Olson are not without their own blind spots, then *The
Maximus Poems* ought to eschew modes of aesthetic and poetic retreat
associated with closed verse and modernist solipsism.

Queer, then, that Maximus opens his epic by retreating offshore to
islands hidden in the blood. The maneuver performs the very poetic
distancing that Bové and Spanos so eagerly jettison. Olson similarly
concludes the first book of *The Maximus Poems*—comprising the first
165 pages in the collected *Maximus Poems*—by invoking the insularity and detachment he establishes at the outset. Seeking a subdued
conclusion, Olson closes the first volume by connecting his island of
Gloucester to the mainland United States. The final six lines read:

to this hour sitting
as the mainland hinge

of the 128 bridge
now brings in

what,
to Main Street? (I.160)

Public infrastructure connects Gloucester to the continent, bringing
the unknown to its Main Street and an end to the first book of *The
Maximus Poems*. The correspondence between the mainland hinge (the
bridge on Route 128) and the sequence's terminus speaks to just how
generative Gloucester's figurative insularity is for Olson.[37] Olson brack-
ets the entire first book with insular address, lending it an undefined

Editing and the Open Field 49

connection to other places, including the very city it seeks to bring into being. Despite critical claims to the contrary, the figurations of insularity that Olson develops in *The Maximus Poems* show how modes of poetic artifice and detachment remain fundamental to Olson's developing poetics.

As we saw in Olson's transition from "Letter 3" to the Ferrini Letters, Olson understands the little magazine as another poetic hinge that connects the figural and the physical, where Olson's utopian polis is recast in light of Maximus's materialization in the printed pages of *4 Winds*. Such hinges return us once again to the relation between process and metaphysics in Olson's writing and eventually guide us back to the relation between Olson's poetry and the editor function. Consider Maximus's opening address once again. Maximus speaks from islands hidden in the blood, a place rich with "jewels and miracles." At the same time, however, he commands the "figures of / the present dance." These are not figures of poetic artifice alone. They are also medial figures: printed words related directly to the poetic line Olson writes about in "Projective Verse." It is not mere coincidence, then, that Olson first saw "Letter 1" as an invocation of the muses when he was preparing *Maximus Poems / 1–10* for publication with Jonathan Williams's Jargon Society. In a letter dated April 11, 1953, Olson writes to Williams:

> Am all fired out, just becoz, that you were going to do this, has revealed to me what I am abt in these / maxis / /
>
> Am in the process of gathering the thing together into a book mss to ship off to you, (air mail, through PM, N.Y., right?) / and ([Letter] I) suddenly reveals itself as INVOCATION, classic beginning. / Very damned pleased. [. . .] In any case, what we are embarked on is more than I'd guessed—and am very damned grateful already.[38]

We see here how the material dimensions of editing, publishing, and print lead Olson to unforeseen ideas about poetic figuration as it operates in his own sequence of poems. The opening address of *The Maximus Poems,* like Olson's preparation of "these maxis" for print, combines graphic and medial configurations with poetic figuration, thereby offering a glimpse into process-oriented metaphysics in his

50   Editing and the Open Field

poetry. Figuration is "the action or process of forming into figure,"[39] and Olson's poetics takes a keen interest in how highly mediated and material actions and processes interact with and even produce poetic figures.

The convergence of poetic figuration and graphic configuration found in Maximus's opening lines manifests ideas Olson first developed in "Projective Verse." As I noted above, Olson conceives of two primary media of poetic expression for projective verse: the breath and the line. Although Olson emphasizes the poetic breath early in his essay, he changes his focus to the line after several pages, writing that "it is the LINE that's the baby that gets, as the poem is getting made, the attention, the control, that it is right here, in the line, that the shaping takes place, each moment of the going" (242). The active "shaping" of poetry—its figuration—takes place here in the composition of the line as its fundamental graphic component. "The dance of the intellect is there," Olson remarks, where "the PLAY of the mind" is (242). Importantly, Olson grounds the intellect's playful dance in his turn to the poetic line: "And the threshing floor for the dance? Is it anything but the LINE?" (243). The dance of the intellect takes place on the floor of the line; material grounding (medial configuration) enables the play of figuration. When Olson opens *The Maximus Poems*, combining "islands hidden in the blood" with the "figures of the present dance," the sequence moves between poetic figuration and those words figured on a printed page.

The printed page referenced in the Ferrini Letters shows how the play of the intellect engages with its medial and historical limitations. As we saw earlier, Maximus tells Ferrini that a little magazine has a veritable life to it, and proposes that occasionally you meet someone, "as I met you / on a printed page" (I.24). Olson then continues to develop this belief:

You get my drift: 4 Winds

> (or let me call it "Island",
> or something more exact—
> "Gloucester", just that flat
> making my polis yours (I.24)

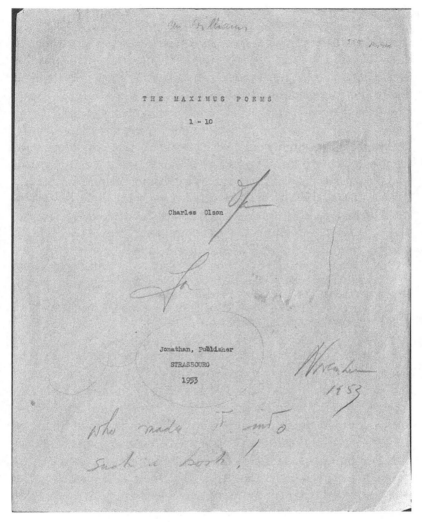

First typescript page of *The Maximus Poems / 1–10* (1953) submitted to Jonathan Williams, editor and publisher of the Jargon Society. The inscription reads: "for Jonathan, Publisher, Strasbourg, 1953, who made it into such a book!" Courtesy of the Poetry Collection of the University Libraries, University at Buffalo, the State University of New York. Works by Charles Olson published during his lifetime are held in copyright by the Estate of Charles Olson; previously unpublished works are copyright of the University of Connecticut; reprinted here with permission.

Olson discards Ferrini's chosen title, *4 Winds*, to suggest two alternatives: "Island" and "Gloucester." These alternatives hint at the way that the little magazine forms an Olsonian "Island," a space of both poetic retreat and emergence. And just as Olson dubs Gloucester his "island city" (I.11), we see the magazine here becoming an island city, for we can recall that a magazine "does have streets, / can show lights, movie houses, bars." In other words, Olson's construction of a poetic polis requires a medial foundation for figural building, and literary journals such as *4 Winds* and *Origin* ultimately set that foundation for him.

After Olson offers "Island" and "Gloucester" as alternative titles for *4 Winds*, he makes a third suggestion which is intended as a slight to Ferrini but which also displays the various literary and historical registers of Olson's work. He carries on with his suggestions:

> or if you have to be romantic
> why not call it "The Three Turks Heads"
> and have something at least which belongs to the truth of the place
> as John Smith so strikingly did? (I.24)

Olson seeks to chasten Ferrini by calling him "romantic," with "The Three Turks Heads" seeming to derive straight from the kinds of racist and romantic writing Edward Said associates with orientalism. This is correct in part, for the Three Turks Heads is the name John Smith—the American historical romance figure himself—gave to three islands off the eastern and southeastern point of Cape Ann, apparently "commemorating an incident from his earlier adventures in which he claims to have beheaded three Turkish warriors in successive single combats."[40] Although Olson implies his rejection of the romantic by using it to chastise Ferrini, he also recognizes that the romantic "belongs to the truth of the place / as John Smith so strikingly did." Both the name and John Smith are historical figures. The three islands exist as John Smith did. But they are figurations, too, bound as much to (imperial) romance as to factual history.[41] This reference to the Three Turks Heads is yet one more marker of the entanglements between romance and history in Olson's epic poem. The written record brings myth with it.

Editing and the Open Field

Romance, poetry, and graphic expression present themselves in new formations in Olson's bibliography to the *Mayan Letters*. Published in 1953 and initially written as letters to his friend and collaborator Robert Creeley from February to July 1951, the *Mayan Letters* record Olson's brief time researching a Mayan language near Campeche on the Yucatan Peninsula. Here, I want to focus less on the letters themselves and more on the bibliography that concludes the *Mayan Letters*. The bibliography, a word that refers to both the description of books and the writing of books ("biblio-graphy"), shows how Olson employs the bibliographic form to consider once again the associations between poetic figuration and medial configuration in the context of his postwar poetics.

The bibliography to the *Mayan Letters* is strangely literary in its formatting, by which I mean it combines description and annotation with irregular spacing, line breaks, and other typographic markers associated with experimental and poetic literary form. Olson introduces his bibliography with an epigraph from the early twentieth-century agricultural theorist Edward Hyams: "'The scientific bias taken by our civilization has . . . given to History and Archaeology a role, valuable and respectable, of course, but not inspired.'"[42] Olson chooses his epigraph wisely, because it connects several of his interests. First, Hyams's assertion that scientific bias has deadened our historical and archaeological methodologies dovetails with Olson's ambivalence about logocentrism and its rational biases. Second, Hyams touches on historical method, one of Olson's primary interests in the *Mayan Letters*. Early in the letters Olson clarifies to Creeley that his project entails "getting rid of nomination, so that historical material is free for forms now" (81). Like modernist poets before him, Olson seeks a methodology to perplex the inherited names of things so that he might derive new forms of expression from them, thereby grounding a new historicist methodology. Finally, Hyams moves from scientific form to "inspired" form. The word choice is significant, for it connects Olson's methodology with "inspiration." In "Projective Verse," Olson remarks that "the breath has a double meaning which the latin [*sic*] had not yet lost" (245). *Spiritus*, in Latin, means breath and spirit and joins physical method with poetic inspiration. This epigraph emblematizes the search for a methodology

54   Editing and the Open Field

linked to inspiration, a connection Olson develops throughout the bibliography for the *Mayan Letters*.

Olson concludes his bibliography for the *Mayan Letters* just as he begins *The Maximus Poems*: by retreating to an insular, secreted place. Olson has worked through most of his bibliography, having recorded and recommended works by authors as diverse as Brooks Adams's *The New Empire* (1902), Leo Frobenius on the topics of African rock paintings and Paideuma (1890s–1930s), Jane Harrison on Greek writing and religion in *Prolegomena to the Study of Greek Religion* (1903), Carl Sauer's *Environment and Culture in the Deglaciation* (1948), D. H. Lawrence's *Fantasia of the Unconscious* (1922), Herman Melville in general, and Ezra Pound's *Guide to Kulchur* (1938). These authors share Olson's interests in writing, ecology, ethnography, cultural analysis, and imperial history. Strange, then, that Olson concludes his bibliography with a retreat into the realm of eccentric and romantic literature. Fond of creating categories for organization in his bibliography, Olson labels the final section of his bibliography "(Addendum, Attic, Annex, Any hidden place" (129). Each of Olson's multiple designations indicates yet another hidden place in his writing and calls to mind Maximus's "islands hidden in the blood," or the queer isolation of "Cole's Island." Two of Olson's designations here are also bibliographic terms. An addendum is an addition to a text meant to clarify some earlier portion of the text. And an annex can be "an addition to a document; an appendix."[43] By combining bibliographic terminology with places that are hidden, subordinated, or supplemental, Olson draws a connection between bibliography and figural or metaphysical space. The "hidden place" of poetic figuration converges here with bibliographic codes. True to the trajectory of process-oriented metaphysics, what begins as a largely didactic exercise in bibliography ends as a statement about the emergence of the metaphysical within the confines of bibliography and literary methodology.

Literary Metaphysics, Colonial Imaginaries

The authors Olson mentions in his "addendum" support the proposition he develops elsewhere: that literary figuration binds itself to graphic expression. Yet they also form a bond between Olson's process-oriented

Editing and the Open Field   55

metaphysics and practices of philological investigation that developed under the conditions of expanding colonialism in the nineteenth century.[44] After labeling his final section "(Addendum, Attic, Annex, Any hidden place," the bibliography carries on: "for those who have the wit to tell the Unconscious when they see one, or for the likes of me, who was raised on the American Weekly, there are at least two men I want to mention (not to speak of Ignatius Donnelly on Atlantis, Churchward on Mu—or, for that matter, Rider Haggard!):".[45] Olson ultimately names the two men he mentions in passing here: Victor Bérard, "who wrote several books to show that the Odyssey was a rewrite from a Semitic original" (129), and L. A. Waddell, "who was sure that the Sumerians or the Hittites or the Trojans founded the British Hempire" (130). I will say more about these two presently. However, it is well worth pausing first to consider the three writers Olson refrains from elaborating on, but whom he nevertheless calls forth: Ignatius Donnelly, James Churchward, and H. Rider Haggard. Each of these men garnered renown for writing about those hidden places Olson refers to in the section heading, particularly lost worlds; each wrote work that drew on literary methodologies associated with philology, in which attentiveness to documents and writing systems plays a key role; and each wrote during a period of rampant colonialism. Together these writers offer clues for piecing together various aspects of Olson's thinking about poetry, poetics, and medial configuration. They show how the relations between medium-specific inquiry, literary methodology, and metaphysical figurations inform one another. They also suggest that Olson's hidden places—the metaphysical spaces made possible by literary practice—cannot entirely escape the histories and ideologies of textuality they seek to reconfigure. Limits, as Olson himself pointed out, are what any of us are inside of.

Closer examination of Olson's turn toward the metaphysical dimensions of textual practices makes apparent one further strand of intellectual history that feeds into projective poetics. Take Ignatius Donnelly. He is a fascinating figure of nineteenth-century American culture, having had a lively and active literary and political career. He is most famous now, and was quite famous then, for his books that offer unusual and

56   Editing and the Open Field

occult accounts of human history. One of his most well-known works, *Atlantis: The Antediluvian World* (1882), argues for the historical existence of Atlantis as the source of human civilization.[46] Olson's fascination with Donnelly stems from this work on Atlantis, with Ralph Maud noting that "Olson's interest in Atlantis goes back a long way to an early reading of H. Rider Haggard's *She,* though he did not keep the book; to Ignatius Donnelly's *Atlantis: The Antediluvian World* . . . though again he did not hang on to the book. He owned James Churchward, *The Lost Continent of Mu* . . . notes on it are found in a journal of 1939."[47] Following Olson, Maud links the three authors in his notes on Olson's reading, likely having noted their close association in the bibliography to the *Mayan Letters.*

The three figures are linked in their methods and their orientation toward textuality and literary metaphysics in more profound ways as well. Donnelly, for instance, wrote several other books that situate him as a significant occultist, fantasist, and pseudo-philologist in nineteenth-century America.[48] In his book *The Great Cryptogram: Francis Bacon's Cipher in the So-Called Shakespeare Plays* (1888), Donnelly claims to have discovered a cipher that decodes Shakespeare's plays and reveals them to be the work of Francis Bacon. In *The Codebreakers,* David Kahn characterizes Donnelly's decipherments as "deliriums, the hallucinations of a sick cryptology."[49] Brian Lennon observes that in fact "Donnelly's 'system' had its place in a nineteenth-century cultural polysystem organized by the imaginaries of so-called Oriental knowledge, whose reflection in the hermeticism of the American Renaissance and whose maturity in modernist U.S. poetry carry implications that have yet to be sorted out even today."[50] Lennon sees Donnelly's work as situated in a cultural system greatly influenced by orientalist imaginaries, wherein cryptographic work such as deciphering, code-breaking, and finding skeleton keys to a text are not far removed from more practical philological methods—translation and description of material documents— that were put into the service of empire building in the eighteenth, nineteenth, and twentieth centuries.[51]

In the work of Donnelly and Churchward in particular, the association between philological methods that pay close attention to media, language, and translation, and orientalist imaginaries is clear. Both

Donnelly and Churchward take an interest in mythical and lost worlds and civilizations, Donnelly in Atlantis and Churchward in its Pacific equivalent Lemuria or Mu. For both men, these lost worlds became accessible by way of philological comparison and translation. Donnelly, specifically, drew on the discourse and methods of philology and cryptology in order to claim the authenticity of his decipherments of Shakespearean texts. His work on the rediscovery of Atlantis was equally indebted to philology, or at least to the modicum of respectability that philology, as a discipline, lent to Donnelly's propositions. In order to prove that "the description of this island given by Plato is not, as has been long supposed, fable, but veritable history,"[52] Donnelly proposes that "the Phoenician alphabet, parent of all the European alphabets, was derived from an Atlantis alphabet, which was also conveyed from Atlantis to the Mayas of Central America" (2). Donnelly then devotes a chapter to "The Origin of Our Alphabet," where he places a variety of writing systems side by side in order to leap to fanciful conclusions about the existence of Atlantis (and by association the rooting of European civilization back in the West). Dotted throughout this section are quotations from orientalists working as scholars and philologists.[53]

James Churchward, who published seven books on Mu between 1926 and 1935, also sought to prove its existence through the translation of secret scripts to which he had gained access. "All matters of science in this work," he begins in *The Lost Continent of Mu*, "are based on the translations of two sets of ancient tablets. Naacal tablets which I discovered in India many years ago, and a large collection of stone tablets, over 2500, recently discovered by William Niven in Mexico."[54] Eager to establish the provenance of his specialist knowledge, Churchward then narrates how he learned to decipher these ancient texts. Nearly fifty years prior, there had been a famine in India and the young Churchward assisted the relief work undertaken by "the high priest of a college temple" (9). When the high priest sees Churchward "trying to decipher a peculiar bas-relief" (10), the men discover their mutual interest in archaeology. Churchward then studies under the still unnamed high priest for two years before, "in a talkative mood, he told me there were a number of ancient tablets in the secret archives of the temple. . . . Now he amazed me by the admission that the precious

58   Editing and the Open Field

tablets were believed by many to have been written by the Naacals" (10). Although the tablets are sacred and the high priest refuses to take them from the archive, Churchward eventually convinces the high priest to let him to have a look for the sake of assuring their longevity. "They may not be packed properly," he warns. "We should at least look at them to see if they are safe" (11). Churchward finally "obtain[s] access to the hidden treasures," after which he and the priest, two of the four people in the entire world with the knowledge to read the tablets, set about their philological work of discovering a lost world.

Olson concludes his bibliography with a brief reference to Victor Bérard, a "Mediterranean explorer, who wrote several books to show that the Odyssey was a rewrite from a Semitic original," and L. A. Waddell, a crypto-philologist who was eager to prove the Aryan origins of European culture and "who was sure that the Sumerians or the Hittites or the Trojans founded the British Hempire, and that Menes the Egyptian was Minos the Cretan and ended up dead, from the bite of a wasp, in Ireland, at the Knock-Many, the 'Hill of Many,' in County Tyrone."[55] Olson distances himself from these figures to a degree, noting in the bibliography that "no one but an herodotean may fool around with such fraudulence and fantasy practiced on document" (130). This is to say, only a historian working with a Herodotean method—where "'istorin . . . makes any one's acts a finding out for him or her self"[56]—should fool with the fraudulence and fantasy written by Donnelly, Churchward, Haggard, Bérard, and Waddell. Yet Olson considers himself "an herodotean" and actively engages with these crypto-philologists and orientalists in his writing and poetics, including in poems such as "All My Life I've Heard about Many." The poem traces the travels of Maximus:

> He went to Spain,
> the handsome sailor,
> he went to Ireland
> and died of a bee:
> he's buried, at the hill
> of KnockMany

Editing and the Open Field 59

He sailed to Cashes
and wrecked on that ledge,
his ship vaulted
the shoal, he landed
in Gloucester: he built a castle
at Norman's Woe (II.7)

Maximus here becomes the poetic figuration of Olson's fascination with alternate and orientalist literary histories. Waddell's literary history positing that Menes died of a bee sting in County Tyrone, Ireland, transforms into Maximus dying of a bee sting at Knock Many. But Olson revives him so that he may sail on to Gloucester, where he builds a new retreat, "a castle / at Norman's Woe," subtly introducing pseudo-philological Aryan literary history into Olson's poetic polis.

Olson's recourse to nineteenth- and twentieth-century crypto-philologists helps to establish the relation between process and metaphysics in his poetics. Churchward, Donnelly, and Waddell all relied on the medial practices of crypto-philology to imagine worlds into being, even if they were lost worlds. And Olson reservedly admired their "fraudulence and fantasy practiced on document." As Joseph Riddel remarks, Olson "would ultimately define poetry as 'document,' meaning that poetry is an assimilation and articulation of the fragments or records, the signs, by which any culture realizes its structural coherence, particularly its systems of communication and exchange, and thus becomes culture."[57] Riddel's comment is astute, but he does not point out that by documenting how fragments and signs of history morph into culture one might also capture, and be captured in, textual ideologies one sought to escape. The links between Olson and figures such as Churchward, Donnelly, and Waddell show that there is a history to Olson's process-oriented metaphysics that scholars cannot trace back to Whitehead alone, or even Heidegger as Spanos and Bové have done. Olson's process-oriented metaphysics also emerges from romantic and orientalist crypto-philology, and these in turn underwrite how Olson thinks about textuality and textual artifacts up to and including the little magazine.

Editing and the Open Field

I conclude, then, by turning back toward the earlier focus of this chapter, for crypto-philology provides a context for understanding Olson's significant turn toward editorial practice, print culture, and graphic expression in the early 1950s, after the publication of "Projective Verse." Olson wrote his most extensive theorization of the little magazine—his elaborate letter to Cid Corman—from Lerma, Campeche, on the Yucatan Peninsula on May 3, 1951. Olson was there to undertake amateur archaeological and philological investigations into Mayan culture and writing systems.[58] In a letter to Robert Creeley from April 1, 1951, also sent from Lerma, Olson writes that a "Mayan glyph is more pertinent to our purposes than anything else, because each of these people & their workers had forms which unfolded directly from content (sd content itself a disposition toward reality which understood man as only force in field of force containing multiple expressions."[59] The glyph, that is, provides a graphic model for reconsidering projective poetics.

Olson's turn toward the little magazines as a graphic manifestation of his field poetics is thus grounded in part in the philological fieldwork he undertook in 1951. His most significant letter on the function of editing a little magazine—quoted at length earlier in this chapter and requoted in part here for the new context—was written to Cid Corman just one month after his letter to Creeley and echoes his description of the glyphs found in that earlier letter:

> that THE DEMAND
>
> ON YOU, CID CORMAN, is, to accomplish each issue—to see it, always clearly, exhaustively, as—A
>
> FIELD OF FORCE
>
> that is, that, as agent of this collective (which ORIGIN is going to be) the question is larger than, yr taste, alone: it has the same sort of confrontation as—in any given poem—a man faces: how much energy has he got in, to make the thing stand on its own feet as, a force, in, the fields of force which surround everyone of us, of which we, too, are forces: to stand FORTH
>
> This is getting to sound altogether too much like a P[rojective] V[erse] thing![60]

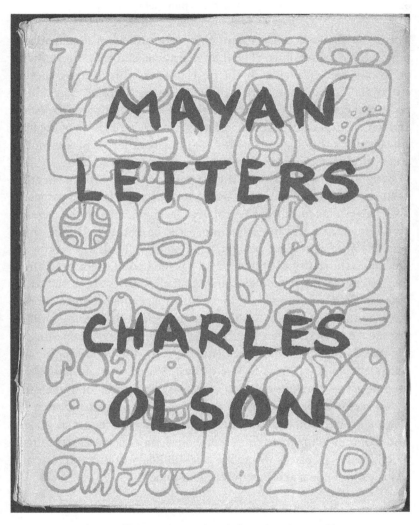

Divers Press edition of *Mayan Letters* (1953), based on letters Olson wrote to editor, publisher, and poet Robert Creeley during Olson's brief time undertaking amateur fieldwork in Lerma, Campeche, Mexico, in 1951. Courtesy of the Poetry Collection of the University Libraries, University at Buffalo, the State University of New York. Works by Charles Olson published during his lifetime are held in copyright by the Estate of Charles Olson; previously unpublished works are copyright of the University of Connecticut; reprinted here with permission.

The glyph shows humans to be "only force in field of force containing multiple expressions." The little magazine, similarly, must "stand on its own feet as, a force, in, the fields of force which surround every one of us." Olson's conception of *Origin* as an editorial extension of projective verse has its own antecedents in his amateur archaeological and philological investigations in Campeche. Olson's vision of the little "magazine," etymologically a storehouse, stores forms of knowledge and critical methodologies for which we still need to account.

Early in his poetic career, Olson transitions from a print-skeptical position in "Projective Verse" (1950) to a print-embracing stance in his letter–poems to Vincent Ferrini (1953). There, the printed pages of a little magazine and the active processes of editing and publishing help Olson to conceptualize his poetic polis while also extending its medial reach. *Letters for Origin* marks a pivotal point in this transition. Inspired by Olson's keen interest in Mayan glyphs, the letters that Olson wrote to Cid Corman propose that a little magazine becomes another force in a field of forces and that "the *graphic*"—that is, the written, printed, and inscribed—might become another means for opening up the closed forms of Western aestheticism and even for building a postwar poetic polis (51). It is in this context that editing and publishing become active elements of Olson's postwar poetics. Yet the *graphic* that Olson seeks to recover bears with it ideologies of textuality that his process-oriented metaphysics never entirely acknowledges or grasps. Those figures in the magazine's storehouse, the Olsonian attic, remain there, hidden in places where we can still discover them: in our and Olson's own textual and metaphysical methods.

2

Editing and the Institution

John O'Brien and Dalkey Archive Press

When James Joyce's Stephen Dedalus famously proclaims, "History is a nightmare from which I am trying to awake," he does so in the midst of a literary work (*Ulysses*) whose historical and geographic specificity is designed to bring Dublin to life.[1] However, Stephen does not denounce history in Dublin proper. He speaks the line while sitting uneasily in an educational institution in Dalkey, a town just south of Dublin. That space is the eponymous one of Flann O'Brien's *The Dalkey Archive* (1964).[2] More than mere coincidence, O'Brien responds to Stephen's nightmare-inducing Dalkey by making the same town a setting for fictional awakening. In *The Dalkey Archive,* James Joyce has survived World War II and renounced nearly all of his literary works, and in his last appearance in the novel he is offered a job washing the underpants of Jesuits, a joke fitting what O'Brien describes as his fictional "class of fooling" (35). Whereas *Ulysses* finds Stephen wishing to awaken from the nightmare of history, *The Dalkey Archive* awakens Joyce himself in the unlikely place of literary history. The novel's description of Dalkey as an "unlikely town . . . pretending to be asleep," where streets are "not quite self-evident as streets and with meetings which seem accidental" (7), works as a reflection on the curious diegetic space—and fictional pathways—developed in the novel, and on the inconspicuous modes of literary–historical succession that take place there.

63

64   Editing and the Institution

Extending the focus of the novel from which it takes its name, Dalkey Archive Press took shape around a constellation of literary–historical claims ranging from the intertextual to the institutional. The press formed in the suburbs of Chicago in 1984 primarily as a response to what the scholar-turned-publisher John O'Brien saw as the troubled status of contemporary fiction. Even when publishers took risks on publishing formally complex fiction, they too readily let those works go out of print, creating an archive of abandoned books within American letters. These out-of-print books, in O'Brien's eyes, were symptomatic of institutionally situated academics' failure to write about and teach works of fiction by lesser-known writers. Academic criticism perpetuated work by established authors—most often published by major houses with large marketing budgets—while neglecting small press and print run authors with little celebrity status.[3]

In 1980, O'Brien addressed these problems by founding the *Review of Contemporary Fiction*, which published brief critical essays on understudied authors and sought to "define contemporary fiction in terms of its aesthetics, its traditions, and its internal relationships."[4] Following the *Review*'s success, O'Brien broadened his literary–historical task by publishing out-of-print books with the newly established Dalkey Archive Press. The young literary historian turned away from a traditional academic path in order to found alternative outlets for contemporary fiction. The *Review of Contemporary Fiction* and Dalkey Archive Press continue to make contemporary fiction readily available to readers. They also present readers with contemporary fiction's alternative histories: books that have often fallen outside the purview of corporate publishing models and academic rubrics.

Dalkey Archive Press compels us to consider what institutional literary histories leave behind. While studies by Mark McGurl and Margaret Doherty, for example, provide institutional optics that bring obscure aspects of the literary field into focus, such histories often begin with the example of institutional success. McGurl's study of the effect creative writing programs have had on contemporary American fiction is a prominent example of scholarship that reads contemporary fiction

Editing and the Institution 65

through such an optic.[5] In Margaret Doherty's account of the relationship between the National Endowment for the Arts and literary minimalism in the 1980s, the NEA operates as an "overdetermined" influence on pervasive minimalist form.[6] In both accounts, the narrative forms and literary categories that have lodged themselves most firmly in institutions become the starting points for institutional accounting. I tread lightly here, for neither McGurl nor Doherty claims an entirely determining relationship between institutions and literary texts. McGurl addresses this point obliquely in the introduction to his book, where he writes, "This book will take up residence in the gap between freedom and necessity—or rather, in the higher educational institutions that have been built in that gap, with gates opening to either side."[7] McGurl's nod toward "freedom" here refers to Vladimir Nabokov's "assertion of artistic freedom" in writing *Lolita* while teaching at Cornell (2). Yet McGurl's position as an institution-bound critic might rely more on the necessities of institutional history and on the conditions of possibility set in place by current institutional configurations than his "residence in the gap" acknowledges.

Like the institution McGurl inhabits, Dalkey Archive Press occupies a gap between freedom and necessity: between "artistic freedom" and the necessity of the market. It levies into this gap the enigma of literary history. Robert Caserio has argued that literary history "might be all the more involved than history proper with the problematics . . . of unintelligible specificity. By suspending their immediate relation to contexts, the fictions that constitute literature simultaneously explain and do not explain themselves. They intrude a riddling specificity or singularity upon the historicizing enterprise."[8] The Dalkey Archive Press operates at the crux of history and literary history that Caserio identifies. One can write a history of Dalkey Archive as a literary institution. And to that end, the first section of this chapter offers an historical account of the foundation of the press. Yet the press remains open to—precisely because it is kept open by—the "riddling specificity or singularity" of the fictions it publishes. And to this end, this chapter proceeds from an institutional history of the press to a discussion of

66   Editing and the Institution

several key works by James Joyce, Flann O'Brien, and Gilbert Sorrentino that were foundational to the press's early self-conception. The literary history of Dalkey Archive reminds us that institutions derive from commitments to literary particularity as well as to institutional identity. Turning toward the riddling specificities of literature, as John O'Brien has done with Dalkey Archive Press, might offer us alternative starting points for arriving yet again—with our various institutions—in our literary present.

"'Contemporary literature' is only certain people . . ."

John O'Brien's career has long focused on the methodologies by which literary history emerges in critical and institutional discourse. A decade before he founded Dalkey Archive Press, the fledgling academic published a book titled simply *Interviews with Black Writers*.[9] Based on his doctoral dissertation, the book draws out a genealogy of literary experimentation by African American writers in an attempt to demonstrate two things: that these writers are fundamental to understanding experiments in fiction in the twentieth century; and that nearly all the writers, with the exception of Ralph Ellison, had been—up to that point—shamefully overlooked in critical accounts of American writing. O'Brien's experience interviewing writers ranging from Arna Bontemps and Ralph Ellison to Michael Harper and Ishmael Reed—who was just on the verge of publishing *Mumbo Jumbo*—led him to conceive of a second book of interviews with an array of overlooked writers. Although the second book never took shape, O'Brien's early inquiries for the collection put him into contact with author and editor Gilbert Sorrentino, without whose guidance O'Brien almost certainly would not have founded the *Review of Contemporary Fiction* or Dalkey Archive Press.[10] From his initial contact with Sorrentino in July or August of 1971, to the founding of the *Review* in 1980, to the founding of Dalkey Archive Press in 1984, and then to the end of Sorrentino's life in 2006, John O'Brien looked to Sorrentino as a friend and mentor who offered direction, editorial knowledge, and authors to O'Brien's quixotic project.

Sorrentino was forty-two years old when John O'Brien wrote to him, and he had a more stable position in American letters than the young

Editing and the Institution 67

academic did. Sorrentino had edited the little magazines *Neon* in the late 1950s and *Kulchur* in the early 1960s. By the late 1960s, Sorrentino had become an assistant editor at Grove Press, which was then at the height of its influence in American countercultural publishing.[11] Sorrentino had also written and published three books of poetry and two books of fiction by the time O'Brien contacted him in 1971. His first novel, *The Sky Changes,* was published by Hill and Wang in 1966 (later republished by Dalkey Archive), and his second novel, *Steelwork,* was published by Pantheon in 1970 (also republished by Dalkey Archive). In Sorrentino's first letter to O'Brien, dated August 20, 1971, he adds "P.S. My third novel, *Imaginative Qualities of Actual Things,* will be available from Pantheon next month. You might want to read it before talking to me."[12]

Although Sorrentino was already on the path of a well-established literary career, having gathered many literary contacts and experiences in publishing that would become essential to John O'Brien, his finances were less assured. He moved among jobs proofreading, editing, and teaching in order to fund his writing. His letters to O'Brien show that during the 1970s he was continually scrambling for financial security, some of which he sought through O'Brien's academic backing. On July 26, 1972, he wrote to O'Brien, "I'm going to apply for a Guggenheim this year and I wondered if I might use your name as a reference. Please let me know."[13] The friendship between O'Brien and Sorrentino was mutually beneficial. Sorrentino offered O'Brien access to the world of contemporary American letters and O'Brien in turn filled the role of academic advocate. When O'Brien solicited an editor of the *Chicago Review* to review *Imaginative Qualities of Actual Things,* Sorrentino responded gratefully: "Thank you for your conversation with the editor of the *Chicago Review.* I have a feeling that it is too late for reviews of *I Q* [*Imaginative Qualities*] to appear, but perhaps someone will be moved enough by the book to consider a critical essay."[14] Sorrentino's comment demonstrates the multiple time frames in the life of a novel that would later form the philosophy of Dalkey Archive: if it is not reviewed immediately in the press and taken up by a wide public, the next best opportunity for the book's longevity might be a belated academic essay

68   Editing and the Institution

about the book. Although he could not have known it at the time, an even better second life might be found in a new publishing house that would situate *Imaginative Qualities of Actual Things* within a complex institutional narrative about the history of modernist and contemporary fiction.

John O'Brien was early in his academic career when he and Sorrentino developed their friendship, and aside from *Interviews with Black Writers* his work met with repeated setbacks due in part to his interest in relatively obscure authors. His early letters to Sorrentino have three general themes: excitement at discovering new authors through Sorrentino's recommendations, including many O'Brien ultimately republished with his press, such as Brigid Brophy, Henry Green, and Nicholas Mosley; anger at the publishing industry for letting most books by such authors go out of print; and resentment about his stalled academic career. O'Brien shared his reservations about contemporary academia with Sorrentino, who in response to a particularly bleak letter from O'Brien outlined the reality of contemporary literary studies for his younger friend:

> It is permissible to be "interested in" contemporary letters, so long as you are interested in the right kind. The "line" runs from Henry Miller through Lawrence Durrell and thence to [John] Barth, [Donald] Barthelme, [Robert] Coover, [Thomas] Pynchon, down to our "peers"—[Ronald] Sukenick, [Richard] Brautigan, [Jerzy] Kozinski [*sic*], et al. You are still safe with O.K. black folks like Ish[mael] Reed and LeRoi [Jones], but outside those two, you're not too cool. What I'm saying, of course, is heresy, i.e., "contemporary literature" is only certain people.[15]

Sorrentino's heresy acknowledges the limited purview of the academy with regard to contemporary writing. O'Brien knew the limitation well. He likely even saw the purpose of anointing only a handful of contemporary writers out of the dozens or hundreds whose work literary critics could usefully address. After all, how can academics be attentive to the vast field of contemporary literature in a critical and evaluative manner? They cannot be. The academic map never matches its territory

Editing and the Institution

where contemporary literature is concerned.[16] Rather than succumb to despair in the face of this fact, O'Brien responded to the wealth of fiction and the limits of criticism by founding Dalkey Archive Press. The press attempted to offset the "line" of "contemporary literature" to which Sorrentino refers by constituting new and alternative models for literary history. Answering Sorrentino's quip that "'contemporary literature' is only certain people," the press made the validity of "contemporary literature" uncertain by reprinting work that apparently failed to be contemporary in its time.

In establishing the press to counter then-current academic versions of what contemporary literature was in terms of style, voice, and genre, O'Brien followed advice Sorrentino gave him in the aforementioned letter from late September 1974:

> I think that you should forget such shabby journals as *American Scholar* and their aberrant editors. Why don't you start contributing to "little little" magazines? God knows, they are spotty and half of the stuff they print is shit on toast, but they will print you, you'll get some kind of audience, and they are weak in the criticism department anyhow, by and large. They could use you . . . The great problem nowadays is that there is really not a first-rate magazine out of the muddy academic stream, viz., *Kulchur, Black M[ountain] Review, Origin*. What I'm really saying is that I think you should take a shot now at seeing what you can do out of academe. I don't want to sound fashionable, etc., but the university is a truly stultifying and depressing place, meant to be moved through rapidly, and then out of.[17]

Sorrentino's references to exemplary "little little" magazines such as *Black Mountain Review* and *Origin* show the lasting effect that Charles Olson and his editorial interlocutors had on a segment of immediate postwar publishing, with Sorrentino old enough to bridge the little magazine publishing culture of the 1950s and 1960s and the editorial projects John O'Brien set up in the 1980s. Sorrentino's nostalgic glance backward in 1974, however, suggests that the turbulent and exciting days of little magazine and small press publishing had died down.

27 September 1974

Dear Jack:

I am beginning to get the feeling that you are not welcome in the Middle West. I also suspect that your relationship to me and my work, however peripheral, is doing your career damage. (I am only half in jest when I say this.) It is permissible to be "interested in" contemporary letters, so long as you are interested in the right kind. The "line" runs from Henry Miller through Lawrence Durrell and thence to Barth, Barthelme, Coover, Pynchon, down to our "peers" -- SukenickBrautigan, Kozinski, et al. You are still safe with O.K. black folks like Ish Reed and LeRoi, but outside those two, you're not too cool. What I'm saying, of course, is heresy, i.e., "contemporary literature" is only certain people. And those certain people are absolute descendants of the old-time novel. The figure is the same in poetry. I flatter myself that my work comes out of Joyce, Ford, Lewis, and Beckett, and Williams. Sukenick has changed the "look" of novels by such folks as Dos Passos, Miller, Lawrence, etc. There is a difference of intent, asxwell as a difference of execution. He has more to do with Joyce Carol Oates than with Selby, even though the latter seems more "traditional." How can I say this except by insisting that there are two fictions, at least. I feel closre to Jean Rhys than to Diane Wakoski. Closer to Lewis than to Kozinski. All this has made me the stubborn son of a bitch that I am. And you, unfortunately, have seen that not all the residents of a hotel are members of the same lodge, even though the pretense is insisted upon by the world at large. In about 15 years, Imaginative Qualities will be "discovered." I know this almost as a certainty. And it has little to do with the fact that the assaults on certain specific figures will then be blunted by time. Somehow, someone will see that the book has an inner structure that is absolutely trim and tight...it will be recognized as a book that is not a sister to Up, or The Painted Bird, or Barth or Barthelme. Maybe 20 years, then. One thing is for sure. It will not be "seen" in time to prevent the yawns and shallowness that will greet the book I'm now in the process of completing -- that will be painted with the one word -- "Joyce" -- and that will about settle its hash. That is, if anyone will publish it, what with the papers full of the moans of publishers who are down to their last 10 million dollars, and fading fast.

I think that you should forget such shabby journals as American Scholar and their aberrant editors. Why don't you start contributing to "little little" magazines? God knows, they are spotty and half of the stuff they print is shit on toast, but they will print you, you'll get some kind of audience, and they are weak in the criticism department anyhow, by and large. They could use you. You mentioned Oyez, that's the kind of thing I mean. Forget PR and Chicago, etc. I also wasn't kidding about MD and your Henry Green stuff -- if you want, I'll write Laughlin.

I don't know. Maybe you should give the writing business a serious shot xxxi and try for a job out of the academic mill. It seems to me that you are being punished for writing anyway, or at least for what you are writing. The great problem nowadays is that there is really not a first-rate magazine out of the muddy academic stream, viz., Kulchur, Black Mt Review, Origin. What I'm really saying is that I think you should take a shot now at seeing what you can do out of academe. I don't want to sound fashioanble, etc., but the university is a truly stultifying and depressing place, meant to be moved through rapidly, and then got out. I cannot think that any serious work can be done therein, unless one is more or less free, like a big-shot "chair" professor, etc. The trouble there, of course, is that professors like that are usually Ihab Hassans, and their "freedom" is just freedom to further befoul the public prints with their trash -- or Federman on Sukenick -- ah, now there is a hip professor! I can just haer him, "My friend, Sam Beckett..."

I speak of course as your bitter correspondent. Sukenick, Federman, Barth, Coover, Gass, Gardner, and on and on are "modren" writers because they live onx campus; out in the real world, they are ho and hum. But they don't even know that.

Letter from Gilbert Sorrentino to John O'Brien dated September 27, 1974. Sorrentino tells O'Brien that "'contemporary literature' is only certain people," a problem that has driven the publishing strategies of John O'Brien and Dalkey Archive Press. Copyright and courtesy of the Gilbert Sorrentino Estate. Courtesy of the Department of Special Collections, Stanford University Libraries with permission from the Gilbert Sorrentino Estate.

Editing and the Institution 71

Loren Glass affirms Sorrentino's sentiment in his study of Grove Press, noting that "by the end of the 1960s, the avant-garde had in essence become a component of the mainstream, and Grove Press," for whom Sorrentino worked as an editor, was largely "responsible for this fundamental transformation, the consequences of which are still with us" (12). One consequence of the transformation Glass describes is that formally complex works of fiction became "components of the mainstream," at least to a degree, and were sometimes even published by mainstream publishers. Yet this does not mean that those books, once published, stayed in print. Dalkey Archive thus forms a response to the nostalgic mood Sorrentino describes, attempting to reinvigorate the once dynamic small press publishing scene—while also revealing some of the consequences of the mainstream (market) incorporation to which Glass alludes.

Within several years of Sorrentino's advisory letter, John O'Brien conceived of a little magazine that he planned to run with his colleague, John Byrne. The *Review of Contemporary Fiction* published its first issue—dedicated to the works of Gilbert Sorrentino—early in 1981 and operated on the following guidelines, which O'Brien wrote up in a prospectus for possible subscribers and sent to Sorrentino for suggestions:

PROSPECTUS: AIMS/PLANS

*** Will promote an on-going discussion of contemporary fiction, primarily through a consideration of one or two writers per issue.
*** Will consider the moderns in terms of their continuing presence in contemporary fiction.
*** Will regularly consider various schools and movements within the contemporary: the Beats, the Black Mountain school, the Kulchur group, etc.
*** Will treat the other arts in so far as their activities touch upon or parallel those in fiction.
*** Will publish essays on the work of younger contemporaries beginning in issue three.

72   Editing and the Institution

*** Will feature book reviews, forthcoming books, recommended books, and out-of-print books that should be reissued.

*** Will define contemporary fiction in terms of its aesthetics, its traditions, and its internal relationships.

*** Will treat expansively the work of Gilbert Sorrentino, Hubert Selby, Paul Metcalf, Wallace Markfield, Nicholas Mosley, William Gaddis, Douglas Woolf, Aidan Higgins, Paul Bowles, John Hawkes, Juan Goytisolo, Julio Cortázar, Robert Pinget, Paul Goodman, Coleman Dowell, Ishmael Reed, LeRoi Jones, William Eastlake, Jack Kerouac, Camilo José Cela, and José Lezama Lima.[18]

The absence of women in O'Brien's early conception of the *Review* deserves immediate mention, for it replicates in many ways the homosocial literary sphere formation we saw at work in Olson's circle in the first chapter. Dalkey Archive, however, has subsequently addressed this conspicuous absence to a degree by publishing works of Djuna Barnes, Christine Brooke-Rose, Brigid Brophy, Micheline Aharonian Marcom, Ann Quin, and Gertrude Stein, among others. Its first book of translated fiction, moreover, was not one of the major Spanish-language writers listed above but rather the Argentinian Luisa Valenzuela's *He Who Searches,* which Dalkey Archive reissued in 1987.[19]

Several points in O'Brien's prospectus for the *Review* anticipate the formation of the Dalkey Archive Press. First, O'Brien writes that the *Review* "will consider the moderns in terms of their continuing presence in contemporary fiction." This presence has long anchored the self-conception of the press, and Dalkey Archive continues to publish works within the tradition of literary modernism. O'Brien also notes that the *Review* would feature out-of-print books "that should be reissued," a task he eventually undertook himself. These two goals led to the literary–historical crux of the prospectus: the *Review* would "define contemporary fiction in terms of its aesthetics, its traditions, and its internal relationships." This set of interrelated points structures the literary–historical project that the press ultimately advanced. Dalkey Archive promoted contemporary fiction by republishing the work of those who, as Sorrentino remarked, failed to be "contemporary literature" in their

Editing and the Institution 73

time. In this sense, the texts Dalkey Archive published (and continues to publish) remind us that the critical category of "contemporary literature" is often itself a useful contemporary fiction for literary historians, and one that often obscures the contradictions and elisions that comprise literary history. Yet by publishing these books in a carefully edited list whose traditions and internal relationships become apparent through their inclusions in Dalkey Archive, O'Brien puts the category of contemporary fiction under pressure in other ways—for instance, by showing its always contended and contentious position in the ongoing narratives of literary history. These narratives develop in different kinds of institutions. O'Brien did not take Sorrentino's advice to retreat from the deadening academy, and he and the press have nearly always kept ties to academic institutions.[20] But O'Brien did turn away from his own formal academic writing. He instead founded alternative institutions—publishing projects—dedicated not only to studying but also advancing alternative histories of contemporary literature.

Literary History Founded upon a Void

The hundreds of letters O'Brien and Sorrentino sent to one another during the 1970s and 1980s abound with book recommendations from Sorrentino to O'Brien. Many of the authors cataloged in O'Brien's prospectus had been the topic of exchanges between him and his author–mentor. In a letter from February 8, 1974, for example, Sorrentino wrote to O'Brien, "If you can, get a book (Coward-McCann) called *Impossible Object* by Nicholas Mosley. It is extraordinary and brilliant. You see how everything conspires to keep these remarkable writers under wraps. He's British and has been publishing novels for apparently 20 years or so. But read it yourself. What a pleasure to see a conscious artist at work."[21] Seven years later, Mosley contributed a brief piece on Sorrentino's fiction for the first issue of the *Review of Contemporary Fiction*. Eight years later, *RCF* dedicated half an issue to Mosley's work. And at present, Dalkey Archive has seventeen of Mosley's books in print, including the remarkable five-novel Catastrophe Practice series. In the same letter in which Sorrentino recommends Mosley, he commands O'Brien to "write about Douglas Woolf. The stomach turns when one

74   Editing and the Institution

sees year after year go by with no one mentioning his name even in relation to the American novel." Ten years later, Douglas Woolf's *Wall to Wall* was one of the first three books published by Dalkey Archive. The other two were *Splendide-Hôtel* by Gilbert Sorrentino and *Cadenza* by the little-known Irish writer Ralph Cusack. In an introduction Sorrentino wrote for this last volume, he compared *Cadenza* favorably with the fiction of James Joyce and Flann O'Brien.[22]

The most significant point of correspondence between the writer and the future publisher was their mutual adoration of Irish fiction. Allusions to Flann O'Brien dot their epistolary exchange, with Sorrentino recommending that John O'Brien name his press "Flann Books, or, even better, The Dalkey Archive Press."[23] In an earlier letter from 1980, Sorrentino writes to John O'Brien about the affinity between Irish and American fiction: "if I were a scholar, I would write a book about Irish and American fiction, that is, how it is not only removed from, but at odds with, English fiction, that it is, operating at its best, 'blood brothers.'"[24] Sorrentino's claim has an illocutionary force that turns into an institutional formation; John O'Brien's early publishing strategies often followed the tactics of fictional mythmaking in three figures important to the press: James Joyce, Flann O'Brien, and Gilbert Sorrentino.

Among the many hypotheses Stephen Dedalus advances over the course of *Ulysses,* one from the "Scylla and Charybdis" episode bears particular significance for this chapter: that succession, including literary–historical succession, takes place upon a void. Well into the episode, Stephen spars with his intellectual rival, Buck Mulligan, who pokes fun at Stephen's scholastic lecture on spirit, matter, and genealogy in *Hamlet.* Provoked by Mulligan's skepticism, Stephen turns from literary genealogy in *Hamlet* to other forms of succession, asserting that "fatherhood, in the sense of conscious begetting, is unknown to man. It is a mystical estate, an apostolic succession, from only begetter to only begotten. On that mystery . . . the church is founded and founded irremovably because founded, like the world, macro and microcosm, upon the void. Upon incertitude, upon unlikelihood."[25] In conflating fatherhood and apostolic succession here, Stephen proposes that the

Editing and the Institution

truth of begetting undermines the stable foundations often claimed by genealogical institutions. He likens biological fathers to the church fathers, both of whom derive and maintain their powers from an unbroken, successive patriarchal line. Stephen draws two conclusions. First, he reasons that institutions can be founded on processes that remain obscure or even mystical. And second, he concludes that lineage just as often derives from elective processes of succession—where one chooses the line one will follow—as it does from more ontologically or biologically stable points of origin. Like literary history, the process is constitutive, drawing unlikely lines of descent and founding institutions upon uncertainty and unstable ground.

To the extent that "Scylla and Charybdis" takes literary genealogy as its theme, it equates literary history with churchly succession. Both are fictions built upon a void but that nevertheless have material antecedents and effects. Indeed, Joyce merges the clerical and the literary in "Scylla and Charybdis" through the Catholic conception of *limbus patrum*. Early in his lecture on *Hamlet*, Stephen asks his small audience, "Who is the ghost from *limbo patrum*, returning to the world that has forgotten him? Who is King Hamlet?" (9.147–51). In Catholic theology, *limbus patrum* denotes the limbo in which the saints from the Old Testament awaited the resurrection of Christ and consequently their own ascension to Heaven. Here, Stephen figures *limbus patrum* as the hazy locus from which the ghost of Hamlet's father returns to the world. Stephen's excursus on Hamlet's lineage, moreover, draws out Shakespeare from the strange *limbus partum* of literary history. Both Stephen and Joyce call on Shakespeare to situate themselves in a literary genealogy, Stephen as the precocious student and analogue to Hamlet, Joyce as Shakespeare's descendent and peer. As Joyce suggests, however, such claims not only call upon *limbus partum* but also rest upon a void. For Dalkey Archive, these claims draw out a tension in the construction of contemporary literature: it rests on stacks of unpublished and out-of-print writing. Its succession is based on a void not only conceptual but also material.

Flann O'Brien follows Stephen Dedalus's arguments in "Scylla and Charybdis" by making the novel a limbo-like space for constructing

76   Editing and the Institution

literary–historical and genealogical succession. In a passage from O'Brien's first novel, *At Swim-Two-Birds* (1939), the unnamed student narrator of the primary narrative frame (there are several narrative frames in the novel) proclaims that literary "characters should be interchangeable as between one book and another. The entire corpus of existing literature should be regarded as a limbo from which discerning authors could draw their characters as required, creating only when they failed to find a suitable puppet."[26] In a metacritical manner characteristic of O'Brien's fiction, this passage partly applies the process it describes. The student narrator's literary assertions "are intended to be a mockery of the overstatements, conscious posturings and squalid habits of James Joyce's Stephen Dedalus."[27] Yet even a mocking rejection of Dedalus's pretensions ultimately draws on, refigures, and continues the Joycean legacy. Even if the corpus of existing literature is a limbo, adding to that corpus might constitute lines of literary history in it but not necessarily lines of flight from it. The novel, for O'Brien, cannot extricate itself from the limbo of literary history upon which it rests.

O'Brien develops this point in the novel he wrote last, *The Dalkey Archive*, where the "unlikely town" of Dalkey corresponds to the "unlikelihood" and "uncertainty" of succession that Joyce attributes to institutions based upon voids. In O'Brien's novel, the "archive" of the title takes shape as a figural void, a limbo in which figures from the past return to the present. After the novel's opening description of the town, the protagonist Mick and his friend Hackett encounter the "theologist and physicist" De Selby, who tells them he has developed a substance, DMP, that removes oxygen from the surrounding environment.[28] Forming an analogue to O'Brien's conception of fiction, De Selby claims that if DMP is ignited in a hermetically sealed space it will create a vacuum where time ceases to exist and historical figures emerge from the past to present themselves in the present. Mick and Hackett doubt his claims, so De Selby invites them to a cave along Dalkey's shore. The cave has been sealed off by high tide and De Selby outfits the two young men with oxygen masks to swim into the sealed-off space. In the cave De Selby detonates a small charge of DMP, suspending time's apparent course.

Editing and the Institution

77

If the novel's opening passage hints at the "unlikely" spaces created by fiction, then here we find the rarified version of fiction's unlikely figurations: "Then Mick saw a figure, a spectre, far away from him. It looked seated and slightly luminescent. Gradually it got rather clearer in definition but remained unutterably distant, and what he had taken for a very long chin in profile was almost certainly a beard. A gown of some dark material clothed the apparition" (33). Just as Hamlet reacted with alarm to his father's ghost, Mick is startled by this vision. Before he can conceptualize his experience, however, De Selby addresses the apparition, who responds with a voice "from far away but perfectly clear" (34). Oddly, the specter has a Dublin accent but speaks about perhaps being African. Only when the ghost brings up his second book of confessions do we realize that the specter is Saint Augustine brought back to fictional life in the Dalkey archive, a figuration of the limbo-like space of the novel as a fiction as well as of the "corpus of existing literature" from which O'Brien draws his characters.

Following the specter's appearance in the cave, a lively discussion ensues, with De Selby asking questions about Saint Augustine's still murky life. O'Brien uses the scene as an opportunity for a range of jokes, mostly at Augustine's expense. The treatment Augustine receives in the novel even led O'Brien to include an epigraph to Saint Augustine: "I dedicate these pages to my Guardian Angel, impressing upon him that I'm only fooling and warning him to see to it that there is no misunderstanding when I go home" (5). O'Brien's use of the word "fooling" here is particularly important, because a brief interaction concerning "fooling" early in De Selby and Augustine's conversation returns us to Gilbert Sorrentino and the Dalkey Archive Press. Referring to Saint Augustine's renowned days of debauchery before turning to God, De Selby asks, "Were all your rutting ceremonials heterosexual?" Augustine responds passionately: "Heterononsense! There is no evidence against me beyond what I wrote myself. Too vague. Be on your guard against that class of fooling. Nothing in black and white" (34–35). The saint's pithy response to De Selby—there's nothing in black and white—hints at the passage's complexity. In particular, the "black and white" can be glossed in several ways. Most simply, the expression

78   Editing and the Institution

suggests that nothing exists in an either–or opposition; nothing is that simple. Yet Augustine, in his early years, was greatly influenced by Manichaeism, which sets spiritual light against the darkness of the material world. Manichean duality therefore lodges itself in Augustine's response as well.

Most importantly, Augustine's assertion that there is "nothing in black and white" refers to O'Brien's media: writing and print. Augustine emerges from a limbo in *The Dalkey Archive* and proceeds to empty writing of its significance. Yet his assertion about the vacuity of writing takes place in a novel whose response to literary tradition and whose own internal consistencies make it a singularly rich work of fictional meaning. In this light, Augustine's assertion fails to transform writing into a pure negation or a total void. What O'Brien attempts here is to empty writing of its content—of its historically factual content especially—in order to make it available as a "class of fooling," an especially fitting definition of fiction as Flann O'Brien understands it. In *The Dalkey Archive,* the Manichean dualism between the ideal and the secular—which would describe separate worlds of absolute aesthetic autonomy (total void) and positive factual history (all is present)—collapses into the limbo expressed in black and white: in this case, fiction. Fiction is neither factual history, nor total void. It is an uncertain form, a limbo. Calling to mind Auden's epigram that poetry makes nothing happen, *The Dalkey Archive* makes "nothing" happen in the printed language of the novel. It continues to make nothing happen in the formation of Dalkey Archive Press, in which O'Brien's theory of fiction and literary–historical mythmaking is strategically set into print.

Gilbert Sorrentino and Dalkey Archive Press, Redux

It is a coincidence of history that Flann O'Brien published *The Dalkey Archive* in 1964, the same year that Gilbert Sorrentino published a book of poetry titled *Black and White.* The close publication dates make it doubtful that Sorrentino had read *The Dalkey Archive* and had had time to make his book's title a reference to a brief passage in the novel.[29] Undoubtedly, however, Sorrentino's later novel, *Mulligan Stew* (1979), works as an elaborate extension of Flann O'Brien's oeuvre. Like

Editing and the Institution 79

O'Brien's *At Swim-Two-Birds,* Sorrentino's *Mulligan Stew* plays with the relationship between fictional authors and the fictional characters they adopt and create. Antony Lamont, the fictional author in *Mulligan Stew,* is a character created by the fictional author, Dermot Trellis, in Flann O'Brien's *At Swim-Two-Birds.* And as in *At Swim,* Sorrentino makes Dermot Trellis into Lamont's literary rival. The fiction that Lamont ultimately writes employs Ned Beaumont (a character from Dashiell Hammett's fiction), a "created" character named Martin Halpin, and Daisy Buchanan (moonlighting from *The Great Gatsby*) as its protagonists. Beaumont and Halpin are publishers in New York and the bane of Lamont's ever-worsening writing career. The novel does not have a plot as such and, as its title suggests, works more as a mix of narrative elements deployed to intensify increasingly absurd scenarios. Even so, as Antony Lamont becomes progressively frustrated with his stalled literary career, the chapters of his novel become more and more unruly. Making his central figure into a comically stymied author, Sorrentino fools with literary history just as Flann O'Brien does before him. But he also turns his novel into a reflection on and send-up of the extraneous pressures—primarily the publishing industry—exerted on the intra- and intertextual working of literary history.

The relationship between formal experimentation and authorial frustration in *Mulligan Stew* stems in part from Sorrentino's own experience as a working author. It is bitterly ironic, for instance, that Sorrentino himself failed to find a publisher for *Mulligan Stew* for several years, a demoralizing experience discussed at numerous points in his correspondence with O'Brien. When Grove accepted the book and published it in 1979, Sorrentino prefaced the novel—before the title page and copyright even—with eleven unnumbered pages of comically fictionalized rejection letters that dramatize the work's trials. Some letters lampoon the commercialism of for-profit publishing: "To be frank with you, I must show a profit to the parent company before I can even consider getting behind a project like yours."[30] This particular editor offers hope for future experimental works, however, which will be funded by the popular books he has recently published: "One already on the shelves, is, it seems to me, a necessary addition to 'Beatle lore'—

The Compleat Beatle Wardrobe Book."[31] The next letter mocks the contradictory logic at work within publishing houses: "the conclusion, I'm afraid, is that the narrative doesn't rise above its own irony—although one of our readers, a Sorrentino 'fan,' felt that the irony hasn't the precision to cope with the strong narrative."[32] Another letter ridicules publishing's association with corporations: "I am about to leave to join my senior colleague Dack Verlain in starting our own publishing house, a subsidiary, wholly owned, of Cynosure Oil."[33] Eventually, "Gil" sends a letter to Barney (Rosset of Grove Press), joking about the many suspicious characters who have rejected his work: "Can 'Dr. Mullion Blasto' exist? He sounds like one of my characters."[34] At Grove Press, *Mulligan Stew* finally receives an excellent review and recommendation to publish. The saga continues, however, because the larger publishing house that distributes Grove's books refuses to distribute *Mulligan Stew*. When Grove demands an explanation from "Hasard House," its legal counsel replies that "Hasard House did not elect to distribute Mr. Sorrentino's novel because it was not considered by our legal staff to be of sufficient merit to warrant the additional investment of inventory. 'Merit' in this context is to be spelled 'bottom line,' if you follow me."[35] Even with a good publisher behind it, *Mulligan Stew,* or some fictional version of it, is left in a legal limbo as tortuous as the lines of literary history developed in the novel's narrative.

Hasard House's final letter to Sorrentino and Grove Press—fictionalized as it may be—outlines the limbo between publication and distribution that Dalkey Archive Press sought to address. Arthur Gride, Hasard House's general counsel and also an old miser in Charles Dickens's *Nicholas Nickleby,* explains, "Our decision [not to distribute *Mulligan Stew*] is not a *rejection* of Mr. Sorrentino's manuscript, which presumably has been *accepted* by Grove Press, heaven knows why! Be that, however, as it may, we here at Hasard House simply have exercised our option under our contract with Grove not to distribute that work for Grove, nor to have anything to *do* with that work. Grove is now free to arrange for its distribution by others and, if I may say so, lots of luck!"[36] Whether they are drawn from actual letters Sorrentino received, or whether they are pure invention, these last sentences dramatize the

Editing and the Institution　　81

material and historical distributive limbo into which many lines of literary history lead. Hasard House is not *rejecting* Sorrentino's book; they simply refuse to make it available to readers.

Couched in Hasard House's refusal to distribute *Mulligan Stew* is the literary–historical problem that Dalkey Archive Press sought to make apparent: even a published novel can fall into a material–historical void. In *Mulligan Stew*, fiction enacts and shows the contradictions of this distributive limbo, which is a material and market problem made into a conundrum for literary history. As the novel also shows, however, material–historical voids can become catalysts for literary–historical mythmaking. Fooling with the oeuvre of Flann O'Brien, whose second novel, *The Third Policeman* (1967), went unpublished for over two decades until after O'Brien's death in 1966, *Mulligan Stew* acknowledges literary history's reliance on publishers' whims and the publishing industry's market imperatives. Yet Sorrentino suggests in his novel and in his personal letters that the specific correspondences and contradictions generated in literature are not to be found through market-driven or institutional optics alone. Institutional histories can indeed tell us much about literary history. But too few institutional histories tell us how institutions can also make nothing happen, thereby suspending rather than guiding literary history's uncertain succession.

The history and publishing imperatives of Dalkey Archive Press reveal alternatives to the institutionalization of literature and the creation of mainstream and academically sanctioned literary canons and histories. Sorrentino, for instance, plays a much more minor role in Mark McGurl's account of creative writing programs than he does in the history of Dalkey Archive Press. In the introduction to *The Program Era*, McGurl argues that

> the dominant aesthetic orientation of the writing program has been toward literary realism and away from . . . experimentalism . . . This is mostly accurate as a description of the programs at schools like Iowa and Stanford, which emerged from the rich descriptive regionalist literary movements of the thirties, and have generally remained committed to some version of literary realism ever since. Still, one can find obvious

82 Editing and the Institution

exceptions to this rule even at these places—for example, Kurt Vonnegut at Iowa, Gilbert Sorrentino at Stanford,

and several others.[37] While Sorrentino ended up in one of the academic institutions from which he had once encouraged John O'Brien to flee, his literary work does not fit into the institutional narrative McGurl tells. It becomes instead an unlikely exception in a story about the institutional establishment of literary likeness. The minor role of his work in McGurl's book thus tells its own cautionary tale: an eclectic or experimental body of work—as Sorrentino's most certainly is, with styles that can change dramatically from book to book—cannot be drawn easily into institutional literary history precisely because of its particularity. Dalkey Archive Press coalesces around such particularity. Its limbo-like archive calls forth literary histories that unsettle those instituted more forcefully by market strategies and dominant academic discourses.

Coda: *Interviews with Black Writers*

My argument up to this point has focused on the relationship between literary history and the material economies of literature, prizing Dalkey Archive Press for the way it holds up a broken mirror to the field of contemporary literature. Like many editorial and publishing ventures, however, Dalkey Archive can also generate voids of its own, and I dwell here in conclusion on Dalkey Archive's drift away from what had once been John O'Brien's research emphasis: African American fiction and the authors who write it. As I noted early in this chapter, O'Brien's success with *Interviews with Black Writers* (1973), which had been the basis of his PhD dissertation, prompted him to write to Sorrentino for a second book of interviews. That second volume was never produced, in part because Sorrentino's guidance redirected O'Brien's interests toward establishing the *Review of Contemporary Fiction* and Dalkey Archive Press. These became O'Brien's admirable lifelong projects, publishing and keeping in print many vital works of English-language and translated fiction. Yet both of these editorial–critical projects left *Interviews with Black Writers* as a quietly resounding remnant in the history of the formation of Dalkey Archive Press.

LIVERIGHT / L-81

Arna Bontemps

Cyrus Colter

William Demby

Owen Dodson

Ralph Ellison

Ernest J. Gaines

Michael Harper

Robert Hayden

Clarence Major

Julian Mayfield

Ann Petry

Ishmael Reed

Alice Walker

John Wideman

John A. Williams

Charles Wright

Al Young

Interviews with Black Writers
Edited by John O'Brien

Cover image of John O'Brien's *Interviews with Black Writers* (Liveright, 1973), the success of which led O'Brien to conceive of a second book of interviews that initiated an extensive correspondence between him and his friend and mentor Gilbert Sorrentino.

84   Editing and the Institution

Interviews with Black Writers sets out some of the critical interests that would later drive O'Brien and his vision for Dalkey Archive Press. Training as a scholar of twentieth-century American literature, O'Brien understood early in his career that the dearth of criticism on African American writing was a critical failure on the part of literary historians—and indicative of broader discrepancies of power and visibility as they operated in the field of literary studies. Years before the height of the canon wars of the 1980s, O'Brien saw that the failure to engage deeply with writing by Black authors skews the critical understanding of American literary history as such. *Interviews with Black Writers* therefore moves provocatively across a wide spectrum of twentieth-century African American literary history, with O'Brien's interviews pursuing questions of tradition, innovation, and the editorial and publishing impediments that made African American fiction (in)visible to the contemporary reader and critic. Arna Bontemps, who died just a year after O'Brien interviewed him in the spring of 1972, had firsthand experience of the Harlem Renaissance and chronicled and eventually archived the movement's literary and intellectual history as a writer and a librarian. Ralph Ellison stands in as a giant of mid-twentieth-century fiction. Julian Mayfield represents politically radical authorship of the civil rights era. He had published his most political novel, *The Grand Parade,* in 1961, just before fleeing from the FBI to Ghana, where he worked for Kwame Nkrumah for several years. In 1962 Mayfield edited THE WORLD WITHOUT THE BOMB: *The Papers of the Accra Assembly,* which chronicles a major event in what Jean Allman calls "the struggle against 'nuclear imperialism' that emerged out of the Pan-African struggle for freedom in the late 1950s and early 1960s."[38] Ishmael Reed, just on the verge of publishing *Mumbo Jumbo,* dazzles with his iconoclasm and his vociferous charges against Western aesthetics and idealism in terms that call Charles Olson's skepticism of Ideal metaphysics from chapter 1 to mind.

Despite the range of their aesthetic and political practices, each of these writers comments critically on the anti-Black structures of publishing.[39] O'Brien asks Arna Bontemps, for instance, why Jean Toomer

Editing and the Institution 85

and Claude McKay did not initially reach a broader readership. Bontemps responds that

> the time wasn't right. Even if they had written different things, the American culture was such that it would not have accepted them. They couldn't have written anything that would have been wholly acceptable as long as they were identified as blacks. Our first attacks had to be directed against the closed doors; just as the generation of the sixties had to be preoccupied with getting into restaurants, theaters, and trains, so the writers of the Renaissance had to be concerned with trying to get published by standard publishers.[40]

Here, Bontemps addresses the cultural obstacles Black writers faced in attempting to publish their work in the first half of the twentieth century. Even if a Black writer wrote traditional or commercially oriented fiction—let alone the kinds of radical innovations in narrative seen in the works of Toomer and McKay—the odds of getting it published by a mainstream publisher were slim. At a very practical level more troublesome and demanding than the diegetic void at the center of Flann O'Brien's *The Dalkey Archive,* editorial and publishing institutions can create cultural–material voids through a refusal to publish certain literatures, traditions, and indeed countertraditions. Bontemps's charge that the "time wasn't right" for Black writers saddles this chapter with a new variation of Sorrentino's claim that "'contemporary literature' is only certain people." For Bontemps and his contemporaries, "certain people" were almost certain to be White.

Ishmael Reed falls back on a more tested metaphor to describe the situation. "Two-thirds of American literature is the part of the iceberg you don't see," he says in his interview with O'Brien. "I think that there's so much of American literature that we don't know. It's been hidden and suppressed."[41] In context, Reed's observation expresses his desire for the public and critics to read outside of established canons, particularly African American writing and other forms that draw on American folkloric and vernacular traditions.[42] In response to a question O'Brien

86   Editing and the Institution

poses about Reed's forthcoming *Mumbo Jumbo* and about creating an African American literary tradition, Reed says that "'to create our own fictions' has caused quite a reaction. The book is really artistic guerilla warfare against the Historical Establishment. I think the people we want to aim our questioning toward are those who supply the nation with its mind, tutor its mind, develop and cultivate its mind, and these are the people involved in culture."[43] This comment moves in two directions. First, Reed aims his criticism at the public and at the "Historical Establishment" that tutors the public's mind. And second, Reed addresses his answer to an academic attempting to uncover "hidden and suppressed" traditions within American literature—specifically the histories and traditions of African American writers. If Reed's answer includes O'Brien in its "we," it suggests that Reed, like Sorrentino after him, finds a critical companion in O'Brien. Nearly five decades later, this is borne out in the fact that Dalkey Archive keeps nine of Reed's works in print today and is now his primary publisher.[44] In this passionate conversation between a writer and a critic who would become a publisher, we can glimpse a vision of how literature, literary studies, and literary publishing ought to work. For Reed and O'Brien after him, it ought to make hidden histories visible in American culture whether it achieves this through narratives such as Reed's own *Mumbo Jumbo* or through editing and publishing projects such as John O'Brien's Dalkey Archive.

And yet, of the seventeen authors the young John O'Brien interviewed for *Interviews with Black Writers*, Ishmael Reed is the only one he has published with Dalkey Archive Press. When Sorrentino wrote to O'Brien in 1974 listing the "certain people" who make up "contemporary literature," Ishmael Reed and Amiri Baraka were the only two Black writers on the list. "Outside those two," Sorrentino wrote, "you're not too cool." Granted, some of the writers O'Brien interviewed have had little trouble keeping their work in circulation. *Invisible Man* has never gone out of print. Ernest J. Gaines's, John Edgar Wideman's, and Alice Walker's works are mostly available, even if some are offered only through Amazon's Kindle or print-on-demand services such as Lulu. John O'Brien also distances himself from some of the authors he interviewed even in the introduction to the collection. He writes, for instance,

Editing and the Institution 87

that "Ann Petry, Julian Mayfield, and Cyrus Colter are really outside of [the African American] tradition and are better understood if seen in the mainstream of American realistic fiction,"[45] a genre and style of American fiction in which O'Brien has never shown much interest, particularly as a publisher. For O'Brien, the African American literary tradition is "defined . . . by literary styles, themes, myths, heroes, structures, and influences. . . . The sources of the black literary tradition are clear enough: folk stories, spirituals, and blues songs that came out of the slavery experience" (vii). Petry, Mayfield, and Colter do not fit this description for O'Brien. But Arna Bontemps, William Demby, Michael S. Harper, Clarence Major, John A. Williams, and Charles Wright do, and often in the formally demanding ways O'Brien has promoted with his publishing. The great majority of works by the authors in this last list remain out of print.

Here I run up against a critical problem: a near void. Black writers are not completely absent from Dalkey's list, but they are notably few.[46] In their edited volume *Against a Sharp White Background: Infrastructures of African American Print* (2019), Brigitte Fielder and Jonathan Senchyne note that there remains a "predominant tendency of book history and studies of print and digital cultures to ignore their intersections with race and, more specifically, with African American craft and expression."[47] They insist that scholars of print culture need to explore "how race and racialization are constructed and encountered within information infrastructures ranging from digital databases of early black print to the visual and material cultures of contemporary black artists" (9). I would add that it is also imperative to extend these critical observations to editorial practices and publishing houses generally deemed unengaged with questions of race because of their emphasis on publishing White writers.[48] This has largely been the case with Dalkey Archive Press despite O'Brien's well-intentioned beginnings in *Interviews with Black Writers*. It is broadly the case for other otherwise admirable, independent publishing houses as well. If we think about the reissue alone—since the majority of Dalkey's American Literature list has been reissues—Fran Ross's rereleased *Oreo* (1974; 2017) found its place in a prestigious book list (New Directions) that

88   Editing and the Institution

has only since the 2000s really become home to increasing numbers of Black American writers, including Will Alexander, John Keene, and Nathaniel Mackey. In 2017, Ross was among the only Black women published by New Directions, though the press did add Marcia Douglas's *The Marvelous Equations of the Dread: A Novel in Bass Riddim* in 2018, two years after its initial publication with Peepal Tree Press in the UK.[49] To add another quick reissue example, New York Review Books has recently (2019) reissued Darius James's *Negrophobia* (1992), a searing book about the mediated hypervisibility of anti-Blackness. Given its subject matter, the book stands out conspicuously in a list with a very small handful of Black American writers.[50] What do we do with these palpable absences?

In the January 29, 2018, issue of the *New Yorker*, staff writer Kathryn Schulz published an essay titled "The Lost Giant of American Literature," which begins with Schulz recounting a spontaneous trip to a rural junk shop somewhere near the Chesapeake Bay. On a small cart of books she finds a clothbound copy of Langston Hughes's *Ask Your Mama: 12 Moods for Jazz* (1961) dedicated by the author himself to "William Kelley—on your first visit to my house."[51] William Melvin Kelley, the titular lost giant, then becomes the subject of the essay's unfolding. Schulz narrates Kelley's fascinating life and examines the five works of fiction Kelley published, first to great acclaim and subsequently to increasing obscurity, over the course of nine years from 1962 to 1970. Part of the purpose of Schulz's piece is to answer the question the essay's subtitle asks: "A major black novelist made a remarkable début. How did he disappear?" The hidden riddle in this question—and a reason Schulz's essay is so compelling—is that Kelley himself did not in fact disappear. He lived and worked and taught and wrote in Jamaica and Harlem until the end of his life in 2017. His work, however, did largely vanish from sight.

So, how *did* Kelley's work disappear, even as this "giant of American literature" continued to write, with at least two unpublished novels still in the family's personal papers? Schulz acknowledges that "it's difficult to say; both present-day fame and posthumous reputation are elusive, mercurial, and multifactorial."[52] She does suggest, however, that Kelley's

Editing and the Institution   89

typical approach, which was to explore the life and mentality of White America via White characters—and as a Black writer—was perhaps too far ahead of its time. Schulz observes that Claudia Rankine set up the Racial Imaginary Institute for studying Whiteness, in part, only after the fact of a landmark book (*Citizen*, 2014) and her subsequent receipt of a MacArthur Foundation Grant in 2016. Kelley's novels do the kinds of critical work the Racial Imaginary Institute pursues— but fifty years in advance and without the kinds of structural supports Rankine had at a more established point in her career. Still, in Schulz's essay the reason for the disappearance of Kelley's works remains guesswork—even if we can all guess its cause.

Kelley's wife, Aiki Kelley, names it specifically. "We made a revolution and we lost," she says, a sentiment William Melvin Kelley seems to have shared.[53] According to Schulz's contextualization of this statement, the Kelleys felt that after heightened interest in writing by Black writers through the 1960s the sense of urgency (and the sales) diminished, making the year of Kelley's final published novel, 1970, look like both an augur and a confirmation. Even if one can name the exceptions— Baldwin, Morrison, Reed—they begin to look much more like the "certain people" Sorrentino identifies just a few years later in 1974 and that Amiri Baraka warns against in his essays on Black writers and big press publishers in the early 1960s.[54] Having one or two Black writers on a list becomes a reason for not having any more—regardless of how different those writers' interests might be.

I conclude with this story about William Melvin Kelley for a couple of reasons. First, I think it helps to contextualize O'Brien's own turn away from the writers in *Interviews with Black Writers,* a project that emerged during a period of heightened interest in African American writing in the 1960s and early 1970s. As much as O'Brien railed against the structural biases of the publishing industry, and as much as Dalkey Archive has fought to change the conversation about writing in translation, O'Brien's press was nevertheless subject to those biases and also perpetuated them. So did—and does—the publishing industry more broadly, with some exceptions, to this day. And second, when I took on a three-month editorial fellowship at Dalkey Archive Press in

90 Editing and the Institution

March 2016, I mentioned to John O'Brien that Dalkey Archive had not published any of the writers from his 1973 volume, save Reed, and that it would be great to republish some works by them and others. He immediately agreed to the project and told me to get a list of four to six books together that would create a kind of publishing event that could be thoroughly publicized and marketed. This way the books would at least stand a chance of remaining outside the out-of-print void from which we would try to take them.[55]

At the top of my list: William Melvin Kelley. I had learned about his final, most formally demanding book, *Dunfords Travels Everywheres* (1970), from Nathaniel Mackey's introduction to his own critical volume, *Discrepant Engagement* (1993).[56] There, Mackey groups Kelley with a handful of writers that he says demand to be read and studied for their formal experimentations and innovations—perhaps pushing criticism on Black writers and writing in new directions and beyond discussions of racism and oppression that, for Mackey, framed much of Black literary studies at the time (18). When I read Mackey's introduction in 2012, old copies of *Dunfords* were already selling for over fifty dollars online—a good sign of reader interest, potentially, for someone wanting to reissue the book—but I managed to find one in a bookshop in Buffalo, New York. I read and loved *Dunfords,* puzzling through its phonetic spellings. And I kept the novel in mind as one of those ideal republishing projects should one ever get the chance. About a month after my conversation with O'Brien about reissuing works by Black writers, I also happened to be heading to the archives of Columbia University to conduct some research in the Amiri Baraka and Dalkey Archive archives. William Melvin Kelley was living in New York, and when I sent an inquiry to Kelley's Sarah Lawrence email address, he and his daughter Jess replied immediately.

I met William Melvin Kelley in his daughter's apartment in the Sugar Hill neighborhood of Harlem in mid-April 2016.[57] Kelley's daughter and Kelley himself were immensely gracious and unfailingly kind. Kelley noted that he was excited about the prospect of publishing with Dalkey in part because Dalkey had put out a book by his friend, mentor, and colleague at Sarah Lawrence, Joseph Papaleo, whose *Italian*

Editing and the Institution 91

Stories Dalkey Archive had published in 2002. Kelley himself had grown up in a predominantly Italian American neighborhood of the Bronx, which Papaleo's stories fictionalize and bring to life. Kelley spoke about his influences, especially Joyce and the Bible, both later confirmed in Schulz's *New Yorker* essay.[58] He also spoke of his unpublished work—using some of the same characters from his already published fiction. All of these details were dotted with the playful charm of Kelley himself, who showcased some of the dialects of American English he had perfected—an ear for the sound of language that is in large part the formal focus of *Dunfords*—and even a bit of song. Kelley was captivating and kind—and clearly adored by his family (a grandson wandered through while I was there as well—and Kelley's Facebook page, still maintained by his family, remains the primary source for all news related to Kelley and his work). When the time came to discuss contracts later on, I was allowed to offer $1,000 to $1,500 to reprint the book. The sum seemed small for this "giant," but Jess's response was that they were happy with this and only wanted what was fair for her father. Their only condition: that Aiki Kelley's artwork be used for the cover of the Dalkey Archive edition.

Upon my return to the Dalkey offices in Illinois in May 2016, I had the green light from John O'Brien to republish *Dunfords,* but just beyond it a series of roadblocks. Although John agreed we should republish *Dunfords* and maybe even more of Kelley's work depending on outcomes, we could not write up a contract for Kelley until we had settled on some further books for the publishing event. I'd had some in mind to begin with, and so did John, but some were not available: Baraka's *Tales* and *The Systems of Dante's Hell* were being redone by Akashic Books. John Edgar Wideman's *Hurry Home* was still available via print-on-demand. The rights to reissue William Demby's *The Catacombs* were available, but only for lease, which was a nonstarter for any Dalkey Archive book and a good way for a large publisher to keep a book out of print. While we did this work and followed up on rights availability, my time at Dalkey was running out.

In the end, I left Dalkey Archive without a contract for William Melvin Kelley's book, despite my hopes. It was a great disappointment and

92   Editing and the Institution

is still a keen regret, especially given Kelley's death in 2017. This regret is mitigated somewhat by the publication of Schulz's article, which has led to a newfound and international readership for Kelley's work, but which appeared only after Kelley's passing. In light of Schulz's essay, Penguin has republished all of Kelley's novels, including *Dunfords Travels Everywheres*. I cannot say what John thought of the rest of list I had written up by the time I left Dalkey Archive. I filed it away though. To put some names and titles to authors whose work might remain out of print and in a literary historical void, these were the books I had hoped to republish when I departed Dalkey Archive in early July 2016:

> Robert Boles, *Curling* (1968)
> William Melvin Kelley, *Dunfords Travels Everywheres* (1970; republished 2020)
> Vincent O. Carter, *The Bern Book: A Record of a Voyage of the Mind* (1973; republished 2020)
> Carlene Hatcher Polite, *Sister X and the Victims of Foul Play* (1975)
> Xam Wilson Cartier, *Be-Bop, Re-Bob* (1987)[59]

I am finishing this manuscript in August 2020. According to Amazon, Dalkey Archive Press reissued Vincent O. Carter's *The Bern Book* on July 21, 2020.[60] It includes an introduction by the writer and scholar Jesse McCarthy. McCarthy's own first book, *Who Will Pay Reparations on My Soul?*, will appear in 2021 with Liveright, the same publisher that still keeps John O'Brien's *Interviews with Black Writers* in print.

3

Editing and the Ensemble

Nathaniel Mackey's Hambone

"Hambone, Hambone, where you been?"
"Around the world and I'm going again!"

—African American vernacular poem and song

In a 2004 essay on "The Knowledge of Freedom," Fred Moten asks how enslaved people could have a knowledge of freedom. To answer this question Moten advances a theory of "ensemble"—a collective mode of being and knowing—that works at "the intersection of the knowledge of language (as prayer, curse, narrative [*récit* or recitation]) and the knowledge of freedom."[1] Hambone, the figure of an African American call-and-response rhyme whose origins remain obscure, emerges at this intersection. Hambone is a figure of ensemble who speaks and is spoken on behalf of an incoherent collective he cannot fully define, articulate, or encompass, but to whose knowledge of freedom his own existence attests. This chapter proposes that the writer and editor Nathaniel Mackey locates his literary journal *Hambone* at this same intersection, making the journal a locus of ensemblist theory that generates incoherence and discrepancy—as lines of flight—by way of its invitation to collective making, what I am calling in this chapter Mackey's ensemblist and editorial poetics.

In a 1998 essay titled "Editing *Hambone*," Mackey looks back on the history of the literary journal he has edited and published since early

94 Editing and the Ensemble

in his career. The journal was founded as the publishing outlet for the Committee on Black Performing Arts at Stanford University while Mackey was a graduate student there in the early 1970s.[2] When the initial editor left Stanford before the first issue was completed, Mackey took over the editorship and published the inaugural issue in the spring of 1974. He published that first issue under a new and noteworthy title, *Hambone*, not only the figure of a call-and-response rhyme but also the name of an improvisational musical practice and the title of an Archie Shepp jazz composition released on *Fire Music* in 1965. Despite assembling an exciting first issue that included a handful of writers who are well known today—Michael S. Harper, Gloria Watkins (bell hooks), Ishmael Reed, and Al Young—the Committee stopped publishing the journal following Mackey's own departure from Stanford shortly after the appearance of *Hambone* 1. Mackey considered reviving the journal for several years before he returned to it in the early 1980s, this time as its sole editor and publisher (244). *Hambone* had called him back.

Since the publication of *Hambone* 2 in the fall of 1982, the journal has appeared regularly, with intervals of about one year in the 1980s and early 1990s that have since lengthened to two or three years. The widening frequency of publication has had a close correspondence with the development of Mackey's own writing career. Although he had published a chapbook (*Four for Trane*, 1978) prior to resuming his editorship of *Hambone*, his first book-length works did not appear until the mid-1980s. *Eroding Witness*, his first book of poetry, was selected by Michael S. Harper for the National Poetry Series and published in 1985 by the University of Illinois Press. *Bedouin Hornbook*, volume 1 of Mackey's ongoing epistolary fiction about an avant-garde jazz ensemble—now in its fifth volume—was published in 1986 as part of the Callaloo Fiction Series. Mackey's distinct contribution to American letters has since become increasingly visible, signaled in more recent years by his receipt of the National Book Award for *Splay Anthem* in 2006, a Guggenheim Fellowship in 2010, the Ruth Lilly Poetry Prize in 2014, and the Bollingen Prize in 2015. These last two were awarded for lifetime achievement and encourage us to consider how Mackey's editorship of

Editing and the Ensemble

Hambone—now in its twenty-second book-length volume—forms a practice-based point of departure for the decades-long development of his poetics.

Exploring Mackey's editorial work with *Hambone* shows how his editorial practice participates in his poetics of "discrepant engagement." But it also extends our and Mackey's conceptualization of discrepant engagement by developing practice-based theories of ensemble, creative labor, and hospitality. In the introduction to *Discrepant Engagement*, a book that focuses broadly on "dissonance, cross-culturality, and experimental writing," as its subtitle tells us, Mackey describes discrepant engagement as constituted by "practices that, in the interest of opening presumably closed orders of identity and signification, accent fissure, fracture, incongruity, the rickety, imperfect fit between word and world. Such practices highlight—indeed inhabit—discrepancy, engage rather than seek to ignore it."[3] Mackey's emphasis on practices that "inhabit" discrepancy and thereby open up "presumably closed orders of identity and signification" invites closer consideration of the editorial practices that configure the singular *Hambone*. These too seek to open closed orders of signification in American letters, particularly those that establish and enforce notions of race and ethnicity in relation to what Mackey dubs simply "experimental writing." Mackey has noted, for instance, that his journal became "significantly different upon resuming publication" in 1982,[4] and a close look at the table of contents for each issue shows the difference. *Hambone* 1 features work of African American writers, composers, and artists almost exclusively.[5] *Hambone* 2 and all subsequent issues, by comparison, publish numerous African American writers, but always alongside a variety of other writers, most often Euro-American and Caribbean authors, though not exclusively. This change in emphasis shows how cross-culturality became central to Mackey's thinking about poetics long before he penned his well-known statement on "discrepant engagement." As early as 1982, *Hambone* gave voice to Mackey's later-developed proposition that experimental writing in the United States inhabits the terrain of the cross-cultural, making Mackey's editorship of the journal a noteworthy point of departure for exploring his broader poetic theory.

96 Editing and the Ensemble

The writers included in *Hambone* 2 provide a glimpse into the kinds of interests and discrepant engagements that Mackey fostered with the journal. Mackey includes poems by American poet Susan Howe and the Barbadian cofounder of the British Artists Movement, Kamau Brathwaite, that speak to one another through their investigations into the linguistic and affective ramifications of the colonization of the Americas. Howe's contribution, which eventually appeared in *Defenestration of Prague* a year later, weaves together "sylvan imagery"[6] from Edmund Spenser, archaic English such as "flasket" and "cratch,"[7] and reports of early colonial contact with Indigenous peoples of North America. Her sequence activates "Tiny words of substance [that] cross / the darkness"[8] in order to reflect allusively on languages and the histories of colonialism.[9] In "Manchile," a poem from Brathwaite's 1976 collection *Black + Blues,* Brathwaite examines how the history of colonial conquest invades even the most intimate scenes of domestic life:

> and she arching, glowing closer, closer
> curving as the world curves
> the wind like a soft fresh of showers
> her almond of silence
>
> she enters your soul
> displacing your anger, the days' useless lumber
> she lets it explore you
> converting you prone to columbus[10]

For Brathwaite, the poetic language of erotic love operates in the shadow of New World conquest: Columbus's insistence that Earth is curved infiltrates the poet's description of a woman's body, eventually making the poet's subject "prone to columbus" in the scene.[11] Whereas Howe investigates colonial history by way of archaic language and fractured lines and syntax, Brathwaite takes an alternative approach. He asks how colonial history and the linguistic associations it generates inhabit contemporary domestic life. The two poets share interests in the history of colonial conquest and in poetry's capacity to engage with that history, but their approaches in these poems diverge, with Howe's

Editing and the Ensemble 97

more conceptually distanced and Brathwaite's more intimate. Such characterizations might not hold true for Howe's and Brathwaite's work more broadly, but in the pages of *Hambone* 2 their close proximity encourages an examination of the points not only of convergence but also of discrepancy, where their differing methods help to make conceptions of colonization creak.

Elsewhere in the volume, surprising con- and disjunctions take shape between Sun Ra's Christian-inflected cosmic philosophy and the religious tracts of colonial Puritans such as Cotton Mather, assembled in a selection from Paul Metcalf's *Golden Delicious* (1985). Metcalf himself responded to the variety of writers in the issue with delight. In a congratulatory letter to Mackey, Metcalf ponders "How could anybody include [John] Taggart and [Ishmael] Read [*sic*] in the same magazine? Well, Nate Mackey could, that's how/who."[12] Metcalf's comment hints at the way that categorical containers come unbound in *Hambone,* where John Taggart's spare and repetitive lines of poetry take their unsettled place beside Ishmael Reed's rhetorically bombastic interview addressing an ongoing feud with Amiri Baraka. Yet the opening lines of each contribution offer unexpected connections. Taggart's poem begins, "Very slow from very far away child in slow motion / child not red angel child ignited."[13] Reed, by comparison, launches his attack with "Mr. Baraka's primitive European God–Devil system needs to conjure a satanic force, and so for many years he's been trying to paint me into a conservative corner."[14] A close reader such as Metcalf could be left to wonder whether Taggart's "child not red angel child ignited," which the reader comes to realize is not a satanic image (red angel) but rather the atrocious image of a child aflame in American napalm,[15] results from the "primitive European God–Devil" system that Reed sees Baraka conjuring. Such an unlikely point of correspondence in writers who might not otherwise be read side by side—with Taggart most often associated with Objectivist poetry and Reed with African American and postmodern fiction—exhibits the kinds of rickety fit made possible through Mackey's editorial poetics of discrepant engagement.

As a printed manifestation of discrepant engagement, *Hambone* displays the imperfect fit not only between the word and the world, as

98   Editing and the Ensemble

Mackey states explicitly, but also between the word and the world of letters, by which I mean the nebulous constellation of practices, outlets, apparatuses, and discourses that constitute literary culture in the United States. In this, Mackey's editorial project joins a range of editorial interventions that have sought to reshape the contexts and aesthetic commitments of postwar American literary culture. In his essay on editing *Hambone*, Mackey acknowledges several of his literary forebears, including "*Coyote's Journal, Credences, Io, Isthmus, Montemora, New Wilderness Letter,* and *New World Journal.*"[16] The idiosyncratic effects these journals had on American literary culture—and anti- and postcolonial literary culture in the case of *New World Journal,* which was a significant publication for cross-Caribbean politics and poetics from 1963 to 1972[17]—were enough to encourage Mackey's later editorial efforts. Like each of these journals, *Hambone* forms from a "particularist undertaking . . . with a certain drive, which every magazine should have, toward ensemblist identity and definition."[18] Each editorial project, that is, maintains its own stylistic and operative peculiarities while also welcoming its own ensemblist dis-organization. *Hambone* is a materially bound printed object and also a conceptually bound "literary journal" whose formal protocols remain largely intact. *Hambone* still looks and reads like a well-produced literary journal: carefully laid out and edited; featuring visual art on the covers from *Hambone* 2 onward, and internal visual art as early as issue 3. As such, *Hambone* is not in a different category of literary editing and experimentation than those journals Mackey mentions, and researchers could profit from examining the specific aims and methods of those publications in the future. What interests me with *Hambone* is the way that the writing the journal publishes has a two-pronged effect that helps Mackey develop his thinking on cross-cultural poetics and literary experimentation. On the one hand, the materials Mackey selects and publishes make *Hambone* a singular journal. The kinds of writers it brings together, as Eliot Weinberger puts it in a response to *Hambone* 2, "is worth a 100 *Conjunctions* or *Callaloos,*"[19] a reference to two experiment-oriented journals that at that time published mostly White and mostly Black writers, respectively. On the other hand, the writing that the journal brings together strains

Cover image of *Hambone* 2 (1982), edited and published by Nathaniel Mackey.
A small musical ensemble—a trio—moves away from the viewer.

100 Editing and the Ensemble

against Mackey's own organizing rubrics as well as those of the world of letters he seeks to test. When Mackey leads off *Hambone* 3 with a twelve-page selection from the Palestinian poet Mahmoud Darwish—a poet whose writing Mackey had not known before a translator read *Hambone* 2 and sent Mackey some of his translations[20]—how does that placement encourage a reconsideration of the primarily U.S. American and Caribbean coordinates Mackey had set out with *Hambone* 2?

These observations coalesce in a provocative contradiction that Mackey exploits by way of his ongoing editorial poetics: *Hambone*'s singularity is contingent on its ensemblist form. The journal is worth studying not only because of the specific writers it brings together but also because the editorial practices that bring them together form a theory of ensemble that is central to Mackey's world-testing poetics of discrepant engagement. This chapter argues that for Mackey the creative labor of editing, which gives rise to "ensemblist identity and definition," helps to confound often racialized divisions of intellectual labor and creative expression that continue to structure the literary field.[21] Mackey set up his journal in Hambone's name as a cross-cultural undertaking that tracks Hambone's fugitive flights into the world and back again. Yet as the initial sections of this chapter make clear, Hambone is the figure of an incoherent ensemble: a group of people whose physical labor and freedom were stolen from them, but whose creative labor remained in flight to contest the forms of being and knowing that slavery and White-supremacist culture sought to impose. Mackey draws on this intellectual history to advance a theory of ensemblist form that makes Black history, experimental practice, and creative labor the meeting grounds for a cross-cultural poetics and politics at the outset of the canon wars in the 1980s and into the 1990s.

Hambone's History

The Hambone with whom most Americans would be familiar is the figure of the vernacular rhyme, which has had various iterations in popular song. In response to the initial question "Hambone, Hambone, where you been?" Hambone replies, "Around the world, and I'm going again." The origin of the rhyme remains irretrievable. Its structure and

Editing and the Ensemble

figure, however, derive from the traditions of African and African American music and the cultural legacies of enslavement. In the opening chapter of *African American Music,* the editors write that "by the third decade of the seventeenth century, accounts of New World music-making by African slaves, as observed by slaveholders, travelers, and missionaries began to surface. Sources such as diaries, journals, reports, and memoirs provided firsthand documentation of the activities of Blacks, noting the use of antiphony as a recurrent musical structure."[22] In a marginal gloss the authors define antiphony as "a performance practice in which a singer or instrumentalist makes a musical statement which is answered by another soloist, instrumentalist, or group. The statement and answer sometimes overlap. Also called call-response; call-and-response" (8). Antiphony is thus among the earliest recorded Black[23] musical forms in America. It is also an important point of reference for Mackey, who concludes his essay on editing *Hambone* remarking that, "as in the music the journal's name refers to, this is what one wants: that the call not go without response."[24]

Like so many African cultural traditions, antiphonal music adapted quickly to the conditions of living under enslavement. Lawrence W. Levine writes on the topic of "African American Music as Resistance" in the antebellum period, reporting that

> the overriding call-and-response pattern that Blacks brought with them from Africa . . . placed individuals in continual dialogue with each other. The structure of their music presented slaves with an outlet for individual feelings even while it continually drew them back into the communal presence and permitted them the comfort of basking in the warmth of shared assumptions that permeated the slave songs.[25]

Individual expression in the service of communal solidarity—which calls to mind Mackey's characterization of *Hambone* as a particularist undertaking with an ensemblist identity—paints a warm picture here. Yet Levine goes on to remind his reader that the reciprocity inherent in antiphony forms a protest against enslavement. "In no other expressive medium," he writes, "were the slaves permitted to speak so

102   Editing and the Ensemble

openly of the afflictions of bondage and their longings for freedom. In this sense, there was always an element of protest in the slaves' religious songs" (590). The figural Hambone's flight around the world appears to be more secular than the religious songs to which Levine refers, but its protest is equally persistent. What better figure to oppose enslavement, forced labor, and involuntary travel than one who moves around the world unfettered? Although Hambone's mysterious reappearance—which prompts the question "Where you been?"—at first implies a returning home and a potential reincorporation into the lifeworld he left behind, his return always anticipates another departure: "and I'm going again." This carefully struck balance embeds the protest that Hambone's departure entails within a musical form that has itself been a conceptual vessel for creative dissent.

In addition to being the figure of an antiphonal rhyme, hambone is also a musical practice. Burnim and Maultsby define hambone as "a form of rhythmic body percussion that involves slapping the hands against the thigh and hipbones."[26] Also known as "pattin' juba," hambone's origins are as murky as those of the rhyme. In a documentary called *The Human Hambone* (2005), the historian Margaret Washington acknowledges that hambone almost certainly stems from African traditions, but she also gives a reason for its unique persistence in the United States. In the Province of South Carolina in September 1739, some of the enslaved initiated what became known as the Stono Rebellion. The largest slave rebellion of the eighteenth century in North America, the revolt and its eventual suppression by a local militia led to the death of "more than sixty people . . . fewer than twenty-five white."[27] The legal consequences of the rebellion were severe. Margaret Washington reports that the Rebellion "created the Negro Act of 1740. They [the slaves in Carolina] lost the *de facto* right to learn to read and write and they lost the right to use their own African instruments."[28] In the context of the film, Washington's point here is that hambone persists in the United States as a response to dispossession. With the complete ban of drumming and literacy, enslaved Blacks turned to traditional and improvisational forms such as hambone to signal an ongoing rebellion against the imposed orders of signification that dispossession meant to set in place.

Editing and the Ensemble 103

Whereas hambone adapted as a creative and oppositional response to forcibly closed orders of signification in colonial and antebellum America, *Hambone* asks how the repercussions of such creative protest reverberate in the world of contemporary letters. In *Bedouin Hornbook* (1986), Mackey calls on this history of musical dispossession but sets it out in the language of his fiction's theoretically adept characters. The narrator, N., writes letters to the "Angel of Dust" to tell him about his experiences as a member of an experimental jazz ensemble. Nearly three years after N. begins writing to Angel of Dust, the band has begun to consider adding a drummer. Two of N.'s bandmates, Lambert and Penguin, hold different opinions about whether the band needs a drummer, and if it does, about how to select one. Lambert takes a strong position on including a drummer, suggesting that the band's current methods are rather makeshift. Penguin makes an impassioned rebuttal, narrated after the fact by N.:

> He went on to say that the more crucial point he wished to make was that the approach Lambert had referred to as makeshift, disparaging it on historical grounds, was not without historical precedent, not without a certain sanction from the past. He reminded us that in this country, unlike places like Trinidad, Cuba and Brazil, the drums had been taken away during slavery. . . . This theft, however, he encouraged us to recall, had given rise to a tradition of oppositional, compensatory or, if we would, makeshift practices, a making do with whatever came to hand whose inaugural "moment" was marked by more emphatic recourse to such things as footstomping, handclapping and the-body-used-as-drum in general. . . . He took this "moment" to be the seed of such subsequent developments as the tendency to reinstate, as it were, the outlawed or abducted drum by taking a percussive approach to ostensibly non-percussive instruments.[29]

Although Penguin does not refer to the Stono Rebellion in particular here, his argument hinges on that history of subsequent musical dispossession and also shows Mackey's close consideration of this history. The passage also insists that "historical precedent[s]" and "sanction[s] from the past" form the foundation for thinking about creative practice

104　　　　　　　　　Editing and the Ensemble

today. Hambone is "the seed" of *Hambone,* which records the creative repercussions of historical dispossession that Mackey himself outlines in his fiction. The journal's call is to "reinstate . . . outlawed or abducted" histories of creative practice and signification by way of the "makeshift practices" of editorial poetics.

Hambone's Expeditions into Wholeness

Mackey's decision to change the name of the Stanford-based journal to *Hambone* in 1974 was one of his first significant editorial interventions in a career now filled with them.[30] We have seen that the title situates the journal in a history of protest and creative practice. The world-traveling Hambone—the figural Hambone—additionally prefigures two of the journal's primary emphases: first, on the cross-cultural dynamics of American literary culture, where African American, Caribbean, Euro-American, and translated literature meet; and second, on what Mackey has called "centrifugal poetics," which he associates most closely with Black creative expression and which opposes narratives of "incorporation" that often define theories of the avant-garde.[31] On the first point, Mackey has been resolute in publishing and promoting work by Caribbean writers in the pages of *Hambone* and has regularly included selections from Fred D'Aguiar, Kamau Brathwaite, Édouard Glissant, Wilson Harris, Mark McMorris, and M. NourbeSe Philip, among others. Some of these writers have also been guiding figures for Mackey's own conceptualization of his editorial project. When Mackey describes *Hambone* as promoting "cross-cultural work with an emphasis on the centrifugal," for instance, he adopts the critical idiom of Glissant and Harris (245), who advanced theories of cross-cultural writing and centrifugal poetics as critical concepts for understanding Caribbean and more broadly American letters. This section sets Mackey's own theory of editorial poetics alongside these collaborators, mentors, and forebears in order to show how *Hambone* functions as an apparatus for centrifugal poetics in Mackey's thought.

Nathaniel Mackey began corresponding with the British Guyanese writer Wilson Harris in the late 1970s. Nearly thirty years Mackey's senior, Harris had established himself as a major writer by the time

Editing and the Ensemble 105

Mackey began his professional academic and authorial career. Harris's first book, *Palace of the Peacock,* had been published in the UK by Faber and Faber in 1960 and was followed closely—a book per year—by the remaining three volumes in what became the Guyana Quartet. Harris's productivity hardly slowed. By the time Mackey sent Harris a copy of his academic article on *The Eye of the Scarecrow* sometime in 1978 or early 1979, Harris had published fifteen books of fiction and a range of other critical works, short stories, and interviews.[32] In a letter from Harris to Mackey written on April 29, 1979, the first that I found in Mackey's papers at Emory University, Harris thanks Mackey for "the brilliant essay [he] wrote on *The Eye of the Scarecrow*"[33] and goes on to offer trying to place another of Mackey's critical articles on his work in *Commonwealth Letters* in Denmark.

"The Unruly Pivot: Wilson Harris's *The Eye of the Scarecrow,*" the article Mackey sent to Harris in the late 1970s, was itself a pivotal point for Mackey because it helped to introduce him to, and impress, the writer who became his closest literary mentor. He and Harris continued to exchange letters and phone calls up until Harris's death at age ninety-six in 2018.[34] This early article, among Mackey's first published works, also shows Mackey's developing critical interests in the dynamics of cross-cultural and centrifugal poetics, even if he did not name those interests as such at this early stage. Nevertheless, the critical perceptions that Mackey pursues and elaborates on in his essay can be seen to sketch the conceptual terrain that Mackey would work in for years to come, including with his editorship of *Hambone.* Mackey notes, for instance, that *The Eye of the Scarecrow,* Harris's sixth novel, is of a piece with his five previous novels insofar as "all six have to do with journeys beyond the boundaries of conventional consciousness, journeys into a jungle representing the marginality of authentic thought."[35] According to Mackey's reading of Harris, these journeys are compelled by a philosophical and spiritual "unruliness" common to much of Harris's writing. The fragmentary form that *The Eye of the Scarecrow* takes "has to do with a religious unwillingness to invest entirely in the things of the empirical world, a recognition of the empirical realm's inability to retain—to *contain*—the spirit. The impossibility of reducing even

106   Editing and the Ensemble

empirical reality to some static, fixed representation testifies to an indomitability or an unruliness which intimates the spirit's domain" (193). What Mackey identifies as an indomitable "unruliness" here encapsulates the disruptive and discrepant function of cross-cultural and centrifugal poetics as both Harris and Mackey later discuss them. In the final passage of this early essay on Harris, Mackey also offers a conclusion that points forward to his editorial work, writing that Harris's fiction is after "an open dialogue within which a free construction of events will emerge in the medium of phenomenal associations all expanding into a mental distinction and life of their own" (196). This, too, could aptly describe Mackey's approach with *Hambone,* a figure borne of dialogue and antiphony, and a journal that forms a "medium of phenomenal associations."

Mackey revisits Harris's notion of centrifugal poetics more directly fifteen years later in his introduction to *Discrepant Engagement.* The introduction is a provocative and persuasive argument that largely reflects on and defends the opening sentence: "These essays address work by a number of authors not normally grouped under a common rubric."[36] Common rubrics form the "closed orders" that Mackey's discrepant engagement seeks to open up. They also shape the terrain on which histories of American literature play out. A product of the canon wars in some ways, but more accurately a product of Mackey's long-held interest in Caribbean literature and cross-cultural poetics, *Discrepant Engagement* calls out the institutional formations that led to "the frequent assumption that black critics are to write only about black writers and that black writers are to be discussed only in relation to other black writers" (3). In lieu of common rubrics and the institutionalization of an African American canon to sit neatly alongside the sanctioned American canon, Mackey offers discrepant engagement, as we have seen. He also offers "creative kinship," whose "lines of affinity . . . are much more complex, jagged, and indissociable than the totalizing pretensions of canon formation tend to acknowledge" (3).

It is in thinking through the jagged forms of creative kinship as a counterinstitutional model that Mackey turns to his mentor Harris. In a 1985 interview with Jane Wilkinson that Mackey quotes at length

Editing and the Ensemble 107

in his introduction, Harris outlines his understanding of "the partial image, the therapeutic work of a play of images around the acknowledgment of a partiality one strives to overcome" (5). This theory of the partial image becomes central for Mackey's elaboration of centrifugal poetics. In response to a question about identity, wholeness, and the broken individual as figuring centrally in Caribbean writing,[37] Harris replies:

> Well, as I tend to see it at this point in time, there is a kind of wholeness, but one can't structure that wholeness. One knows it's there and one moves into it ceaselessly, but all the time one moves with partial images. Now the partial image has within it a degree of bias but it also represents a part of something else, so that there is a kind of ceaseless *expedition* into wholeness which has to do with the ways in which one consumes— metaphysically consumes—the bias in the partial image and releases that image as part of something else which one may not be immediately aware of in that context—one may not be immediately aware of how the partial image links up with another partial image until the centre of being in an imaginative work breaks or moves and the illusory centrality of the partial image is enriched in creative paradox.[38]

The process Harris describes here wavers between the centrifugal and the centripetal. We see this most clearly in the contradictory positionality of his phrase "ceaseless *expedition* into wholeness." The prefix "ex" connotes a movement outward and is the mark of the centrifugal in the process Harris describes. Yet the partial image prompts an expedition *into* wholeness, suggesting an irrevocable complementarity between a centrifugal expedition and centripetal consolidation. Similar to Mackey's observation that there is a certain unruliness of spirit in *The Eye of the Scarecrow* as the book tests "phenomenal associations," the partial image moves endlessly outward and thereby moves into new provisional forms that one cannot entirely structure. As the final lines of the passage indicate, provisional wholeness breaks down only to enrich the partial image "in creative paradox." With its illusory wholeness revealed, the partial image once again launches outward from its compromised totality in its ongoing "*expedition* into wholeness."

108 Editing and the Ensemble

Harris's notion of a partial image's ceaseless expedition remains conceptual in Harris's interview. Yet its description characterizes the vernacular Hambone's journey into the world, creating a point of cross-cultural correspondence that momentarily situates Harris's theory in the history of American literature and culture, broadly conceived, that Mackey investigates. Consider the etymology of "expedition." It derives from the verb "expedite," which comes from a Latin verb meaning "'to free (a person's) feet from fetters' . . . hence, to free from difficulties, to help forward, to get (a work) out of hand, to dispatch, send off, etc."[39] The etymology is provocative when considering Hambone as a figure of African or African American provenance. Hambone's urge to travel can be read as a response to having one's feet fettered—impeded—as a result of enslavement. In response to forced travel, an oral tradition makes Hambone into a figure of free expedition, traveling around the world on a whim. The "world" Hambone travels around, moreover, stands in for the imagined wholeness to which Harris refers. His vision of a centrifugal poetics compelled by the "partial image" that seeks wholeness finds a related figure in Hambone, whose feet are freed for his journey into a wholeness he might not achieve but continues to strive after.[40]

The Martinican writer Édouard Glissant is a more fleeting but nevertheless significant point of reference for Mackey's thinking about cross-cultural poetics.[41] Although there is no archival record of correspondence between Glissant and Mackey, a selection from Glissant's *Black Salt* (1983) opens *Hambone* 4 in a translation by Yusef Hamid Toraia. And while Glissant's work garners less engagement than Harris's or Brathwaite's in Mackey's critical writings, Glissant's essay on "Cross-Cultural Poetics" (1973) is the primary counterpart to Harris's theory of centrifugal movement in Mackey's introduction to *Discrepant Engagement*. Mackey is specifically interested in the concept of the "new man" in an "Other America" that Glissant discusses in the essay:

> The issue . . . is the appearance of a new man, whom I would define, with reference to his "realization" in literature, as a man who is able to live the relative after having suffered the absolute. When I say relative, I mean

Editing and the Ensemble   109

the Diverse, the obscure need to accept the other's difference; and when I say absolute I refer to the dramatic endeavor to impose a truth on the Other. I feel that the man from the Other America "merges" with this new man, who lives the relative; and that the struggles of peoples who try to survive in the American continent bear witness to this new creation.[42]

Glissant's word choice here lays out the terrain in which Mackey also works. With the "Other America" he refers to "the Caribbean and South America" to oppose the tendency to identify "American" as U.S. American.[43] And by "the Other" he refers to those who have been considered the Others of Western modernity—that is, non–Western European, enslaved, and colonized peoples. The two converge in Glissant's thought to offer up a "new man" who "is able to live the relative after having suffered the absolute." This "new man" again bears a striking resemblance to Hambone, who flees from Western modernity's violent "endeavor to impose a truth on the Other."

Hambone represents the failure of this endeavor: the Other cannot be subsumed under the absolutes of Western modernity. Hambone instead works in opposition to those who seek to incorporate him under the rubrics of Otherness. Like the new man and the partial image, Hambone tracks an outward-moving freedom by finding lines of flight within the totality that Western modernity supposed itself to be. As Glissant notes further on in his essay, "The collective 'We' [an Other American 'We'] becomes the site of the generative system, and the true subject. Our critique of the act and the idea of literary creation is not derived from a 'reaction' to theories which are proposed to us, but from a burning need for *modification*" (149). For Glissant and for Mackey, the generative system that emerges from the collective work of cross-cultural poetics puts modification in motion. In forming a generative system that remains operative in practices such as Mackey's ensemblist, editorial poetics—as it draws on cross-cultural histories of political and philosophical protest—Other American literature provokes a centrifugal impulse in the heart of Western literary modernity.

While Hambone becomes a figure of unruly freedom and protest in the above reading, Mackey's journal asks how to make Hambone's

110   Editing and the Ensemble

ongoing expedition into a centrifugal force in American literature. Glissant proposes that a "new man" finds his "realization in literature." The vernacular Hambone likewise finds one realization in the pages of his namesake journal. The journal records Hambone's excursions and asks what we could learn from his ongoing returns. Might Susan Howe's urge "to move forward into unknown / Crumbling compulsion of syllables,"[44] or bell hooks's "ancestral bodies . . . surfacing in the watery passage / beyond death,"[45] or Don Byrd's figure who "believe[s] myself to be speaking, / speaking pages and not speaking / pages voices crises, / thinking meaning into words"[46] hold some clues to Hambone's flight, or share in his compulsions? Or might he be found among the Haitian refugees who are the subject of Kamau Brathwaite's sixty-two-page contribution to *Hambone* 12 published in 1995?[47] When Mackey describes *Hambone* as performing "cross-cultural work with an emphasis on the centrifugal," the cross-cultural is also cross-medial: a printed articulation for a vernacular figure—"speaking pages"—whose obscured yet reverberating history voices the centrifugal force of cross-cultural expression.

In the context of the U.S. poetry scene of the early 1980s, *Hambone*'s cross-cultural approach had exactly the kind of rubric-breaking effect that Mackey later conceptualized with "discrepant engagement." The effect registers especially strongly in a letter Eliot Weinberger wrote to Mackey in response to *Hambone*'s first two issues in late 1983. Around the time *Hambone* 2 came out, Weinberger, who was the editor of *Montemora* literary journal, had published an essay in *Poetry East* lamenting the absence of writers of color in avant-garde circles. Mackey in fact cites this essay in his brief statement on editing *Hambone*. He quotes Weinberger saying, "On the aesthetic Left, the magazines are publishing many more women than they used to, but are not attracting young writers from the minorities, despite the presence of major avant-garde minority figures."[48] Weinberger picks this thread back up in his 1983 letter to Mackey:

> The most disastrous effect of the post-1970 apartheid policy is that it has created separate channels of communication. The black small presses and

Editing and the Ensemble 111

magazines are simply not seen outside of the network of black writers. They are rarely in the literary (white) bookstores; no press or magazine ever sent *Montemora* review or exchange copies; etc. Rather than fostering a pluralistic society, we have a situation where the various groups are talking to themselves in isolated rooms.

This is where I see *Hambone* making a tremendous difference. As a black writer, you are clearly plugged into networks that I or Clayton [Eshleman] or [Robert] Bertholf are not. And you are obviously interested in some of the best writing done by white writers at the moment. *Hambone*—for the first time in 20 years—is a magazine where black and white writers can read each other. For me at least, this is worth a 100 *Conjunctions* or *Callaloos*.[49]

In its reference to a "post-1970 apartheid policy," Weinberger's letter anticipates Aiki Kelley's observation in chapter 2 about the post-1960s publishing environment for Black writers by drawing an implicit connection between the waning of the protest and revolutionary movements of the late 1960s and the seemingly segregated world of letters that emerged in the 1970s.

In this, the letter provides insight into an avant-garde-oriented segment of the small press scene in the United States in the 1970s and 1980s. Editors like Weinberger (*Montemora*, 1975–82), Eshleman (*Caterpillar*, 1967–73; *Sulfur*, 1981–2000), and Bertholf (*Credences*, 1975–85) make up an important part of that scene, but according to Weinberger they are not in touch with writers of color, at least not to the extent that they ought to be. And whereas *Callaloo*, at that time, published primarily Black experimental writers and *Conjunctions* primarily White ones, *Hambone* brought these groups together in a way that profited—"worth 100 *Conjunctions* or *Callaloos*"—American writing in general. It bridged the "apartheid" Weinberger perceived by introducing a Caribbean-influenced cross-cultural poetics to a U.S. scene where its absence hinted at the "closed orders of identity and signification" that Mackey's editorial poetics has sought to open up. As Weinberger puts it, "We have a situation where the various groups are talking to themselves in isolated rooms." Such closed orders structure the field of

112   Editing and the Ensemble

letters whether an editor intends them to or not. Weinberger clearly
wishes he could edit otherwise. He nevertheless critically identifies
that closed orders—whether they are homosocial groupings or mostly
White or Black poetic circles—define the limits of the "literary" in the
1970s and early 1980s. Mackey's cross-cultural and editorial poetics
works within these limits and makes them creak.

Ensemblic Hospitality

Since its inception, *Hambone*'s conceptual terrain has shifted around
Mackey's understanding of the call his journal puts forth. The contributors and their poetic and political interests form the bassline for
Hambone's poetic refrain. "As in the music the journal's name refers
to," we have seen Mackey comment, "this is what one wants: that the
call not go without response."[50] Mackey was careful in directing the
initial call and solicited all the work for *Hambone 2* when he resumed
publishing the journal in the early 1980s. His "aim in composing the
issue entirely of solicited work was to delineate the magazine's intended range and reach, to sketch out some of what I intended to be its
defining dispositions and concerns" (248). The result was a set of contributors who draw a literary map and establish a range of interests not
exclusive to the United States. The physical range of the journal was
limited to U.S. circulation primarily, even if Mackey shipped copies to
Harris and other international contributors. Its conceptual range, however, elicits a collection of cross-cultural engagements.

A 1980 letter from Mackey to the poet Robert Kelly hints at the
cross-cultural interests that Mackey sought to establish with *Hambone 2*.
In the letter, Mackey tells Kelly about the journal he wants to relaunch
and then invites him to contribute some of his writing. Yet it is not a
completely open invitation. Mackey specifies:

> I'm especially interested in some poems you read in Boulder back in the
> fall of 1977 and which I heard on the public library's videotape of the
> reading. I recall you introducing them by remarking on your sense of
> rapport between Black and Irish investments in eloquence, which you
> carried back to Egypt as a common source . . . You say at one point, "And

Editing and the Ensemble 113

we were black, two spurs of Egypt, Celts and Bantus." . . . Can't offer much of an overture as far as the thrust I want to give the mag is concerned. "Crossings" is a word which comes to mind, as does the much more widely worked expression "New World poetics"—but I wouldn't push either one of them beyond what particular work gives substance to.[51]

This solicitation provides a valuable glimpse into Mackey's thinking about *Hambone* and his own editorial role in guiding the journal's direction. On the one hand, the specificity of Mackey's request lets the prolific Robert Kelly know that Mackey is not equally interested in any poem Kelly has recently written. This is not a solicitation for a poem by Robert Kelly, who was a well-established poet by 1980, but whose prolific nature allowed him to pursue a variety of poetic interests. Rather, it is a request for a specific piece of Kelly's writing that foregrounds Kelly's engagement with cross-cultural poetics. Here we see again the "particularist undertaking" that Mackey understands editing to be, with Mackey seeking out certain material to relaunch the journal. On the other hand, when it comes to specifying the aims of the journal Mackey's letter becomes much more hesitant. The two keywords or phrases that Mackey provides—"crossings" and "New World poetics"—are put into scare quotes to set them lightly under erasure as organizing rubrics for the journal. Mackey proposes instead that *Hambone* is to be "what particular work gives substance to."

Despite Mackey's editorial hand guiding the project, then, *Hambone*'s itinerary—the work it will ultimately include over the course of its run, and the range of its interests—remains open and unforeseen. Most of the contributors to *Hambone* 2 continued to publish in the journal's pages and some still do. These poets are "all the birds [that] sing bass" for the journal.[52] They give it a sense of consistency across the various issues. And yet in reflecting on his editorial work Mackey also appreciates the unexpected responses that *Hambone* 2 provoked:

That issue was a call, a summons, an invitation to those who located themselves in the terrain it mapped to submit work . . . I've been especially gratified to receive a good deal of unsolicited work that fit, to be

114   Editing and the Ensemble

introduced to the work of writers I wasn't previously aware of but who, in some cases, have become regular contributors, to be taken, especially by the work of such writers as Anne-Marie Albiach, Max Aub, Julio Cortázar, Mahmoud Darweesh [sic], and Alejandra Pizarnik, submitted by translators, in directions I hadn't planned or foreseen. As in the music the journal's name refers to, this is what one wants: that the call not go without response.[53]

While Mackey has editorial control of his journal, he notes that opacity also guides editorship and that he was "gratified . . . to be taken . . . in directions I hadn't planned or foreseen." Much of what he had not known—at least according to this list—is due to the limitations set in place by languages, limitations overcome only in part by translators and their translations. Lodged in Mackey's comment on the emergence of the unforeseen is a practical and conceptual reflection on editing as ensemblic literary work: an editor cannot know all authors and languages and so a journal and its ensemble think more openly than any sole editor possibly could.

Mackey's diction in the above passage also initiates a reflection on the function of hospitality in *Hambone*'s call. Words such as "call," "summons," "invitation," "terrain," and "gratified" call to mind hospitality as it was theorized in Jacques Derrida's late essay "Hostipitality." Derrida begins by pointing out the paradox of hospitality in Kant's theory of perpetual peace. There Kant claims that "Cosmopolitan Right shall be limited to Conditions of Universal Hospitality."[54] The paradox, which Derrida terms an aporia, is that "universal hospitality" is in fact "limited" because Kant conceives of it as a "law." This aporia—between universality and conditionality—makes hospitality a threshold within Derrida's late thought, and it leads him to the claim he reflects on for most of the essay: "We do not know what hospitality is [*Nous ne savons pas ce que c'est que l'hosptitalité*]. Not yet" (6).

Mackey's editorial poetics and Derrida's theorization of hospitality converge on the condition of "not knowing," but where not knowing speaks to the distinction between subjective knowledge and intersubjective or "ensemble" forms of knowledge. Derrida works through his

Editing and the Ensemble 115

aporetic axiom—we do not know what hospitality is, not yet—by way of four "acceptations." The acceptations belong to the discourse of hospitality and denote "the action of receiving, the welcome given, the way one receives" (7). I focus here on his first acceptation: "This not-knowing is not necessarily a deficiency, an infirmity, a lack. Its apparent negativity, this grammatical negativity (the not-knowing) would not signify ignorance, but rather indicate or recall only that hospitality is not a concept which lends itself to objective knowledge" (7). Such not-knowing bears on Mackey's conception of *Hambone*'s call, because the journal makes not-knowing a condition of literary receptivity.[55] Like Derrida's theorization of hospitality, Mackey refrains from outlining his journal's purpose in negative terms. He instead suggests that the call a journal puts forth elicits a response, thereby configuring the co-constitutive mode that articulates *Hambone*'s receptive form. Mackey's co-constitutive conception of *Hambone* thus elucidates a key aspect of Derrida's theory: hospitality does not lend itself to objective knowledge in part because it is a mode of coarticulation or even polyvocal articulation, where the ground of knowledge takes on ensemblist form.

While Mackey has remarked that he sees *Hambone* as a "personal undertaking,"[56] he also undercuts that observation immediately by adding "yet with a certain drive, which every magazine should have, toward ensemblist identity and definition" (246). The personal aspect of his editorship is apparent in Mackey's archives at Emory. Nearly thirty archival boxes are dedicated to the correspondence, editorial notes, and issue proofs related to Mackey's work on *Hambone* volumes 2 (1982) through 20 (2012), though these exclude the digital correspondence from later years. All aspects of the archive, from personal letters to edited proofs, speak to his personal devotion to editing the journal and to the contributors that send him their work. Mackey's meticulous reading and editing practices are apparent throughout these documents.

His editorial care when working with manuscripts by Will Alexander, for instance, whose writing often works by way of conceptual abstraction, neologism, and opaque scientific and technical diction, illustrates Sarah Blackwood's observation that editing is carework and not merely a form of mastery or learned curation.[57] Alexander has been a regular

116   Editing and the Ensemble

contributor to *Hambone* since its earliest issues and his manuscripts are often dotted with typos, with Alexander stating simply in a note with a submitted manuscript from 1992: "P.S. check for typos."[58] In a note on a separate manuscript that was fairly heavily edited by Mackey mostly with regard to typos but also with subtle changes in word choice— "yes men watching out for profit of the parent monster" becomes "yes men seeking money for the parent monster" after Mackey's edits— Alexander responds to a note by Mackey saying, "I don't find the corrections obnoxious. On the contrary they seem to make an improvement. Writing at white heat, typing at precarious moments of the day combined to create the errors."[59]

It is a recurring theme. When Alexander submitted the manuscript excerpt from *Diary as Sin* that leads off *Hambone* 19 (2009), he once again requests, "If this text works, check me for typos."[60] Alongside the standard typo corrections on the manuscript, one also sees light squiggly underlining marking phrases that require a second look. These light lines are legible as marks not of correction, but of editorial care and of the thinking that Mackey puts into his reading of Alexander's work. When Alexander submits a sentence that reads, "Certainly war has been waged against me, but I, the sovereign dice player always carries in her seeming culpability sigils beatific with distraction,"[61] Mackey quietly modifies it. In the published version, it reads, "Certainly war has been waged against me, but I, the sovereign dice-player, always carry in my seeming culpability sigils beatific with distraction."[62] In a text that switches between the pronouns I and her throughout and whose syntax demands a reader's full attention, catching such a slip is a mark of the care and labor that Mackey puts into his editing. Such examples fill the archival record, making apparent why Alexander, in his contribution to *Callaloo*'s special issue on Mackey's work (2000), says that "Mr. Mackey's creative largesse is riverine, charismatic," a characterization under which Alexander specifically discusses "the superior skill [Mackey] exercises as the editor of the journal *Hambone*."[63]

And yet as much as the above exchanges with Alexander are examples of Mackey's personal devotion to the journal, they are also examples of the collaborative nature of editing and of the "ensemblist identity and

Editing and the Ensemble 117

definition" that emerge from it. In this sense, the marks Mackey leaves on the pages of manuscripts are marks of thinking in common. They connote a mode of thinking together in such a way that one might see the editorial encounter as an encounter of hospitality. Judy Platz, who contributed five poems to *Hambone 2*, makes the connection between ensemblist form and literary hospitality in a letter she wrote to Mackey after reading *Hambone 2*. Platz writes:

Dear Nathaniel Mackey,

I need to tell you that I feel truly privileged to be included in your magazine, *Hambone*. You and *Hambone* are the most sincerely appreciative audience I have found. Most people are struck by something in my poems, but aren't sure just what it is. That "something" is a certain conclusion about this country in its karmic place NOW in the world, this planet. And, you know, from THERE I build the poem. The majority of small press mags, so far, have not picked up on these vibrations, so a lot of my poems continue to be misinterpreted. You are a careful, thoughtful reader though. I have gathered this from your letters. Yet, I never dared believe you were putting together a magazine like this!!

For me to read the other writers/musicians/artists in this issue is like coming home. To say "thank you" seems to be a ludicrous cheapening of the energies *Hambone* generates. The magazine is beyond this, in my opinion. I am pleased and impressed, to say the least . . .

Well, *Hambone* is a real, concrete, energy force now . . . you have done something to be very proud of. You are, you know, MAKING your own "Crossroads Choir."[64]

Hospitality and ensemblist form converge here. Platz initially notes that not just Mackey but *Hambone* itself are "the most appreciative audience" she has had, turning the letter at the outset away from the strategic rituals of thanksgiving.

Indeed, although Platz notes that she is "pleased" about being included in *Hambone*, she refuses to say "thank you." For her, saying

118   Editing and the Ensemble

"thank you" would be "a ludicrous cheapening of the energies *Hambone* generates." Here she recognizes that her thanks cannot be directed at Mackey alone. This would follow an exchange-like economy of patronage that Platz declines to acknowledge. She instead insists that any thanks would have been directed at *Hambone* and the energies it generates. Even still, Platz refuses to offer thanks. This refusal, I propose, is an acceptance or acknowledgment of the indeterminate form of ensemblist hospitality. Platz's refusal, after all, stems from her statement that "for [her] to read the other writers/musicians/artists in this issue is like coming home." Derrida's theory of hospitality suggests that hospitality cannot be conceived as emerging from instrumental exchange. Its conditions exceed that logic. Platz sees that clearly in this letter, which is not a thank-you letter but a theory of ensemblist identity and literary hospitality. Like Mackey, she links this theory to other aspects of Mackey's work, noting Mackey's "careful" reading practices and concluding her letter by invoking Mackey's own writing: "You are, you know, MAKING your own 'Crossroads Choir.'" This reference to Mackey's own contribution to *Hambone* 2 is apt, because in the context of that piece, the Crossroads Choir is a band with which N's own band, the Mystic Horn Society, wishes to collaborate. N's band has recently begun a fruitful collaboration with the Boneyard Brass Octet, but the Crossroads Choir has been quiet. Mackey thus concludes his selection for *Hambone* 2 with N saying, "Now, if I could only hook up with The Crossroads Choir."[65] We have seen Mackey reading Will Alexander's work carefully. Here, Judy Platz gives the same meticulous attention to Mackey's writing. Is this final sentence not, after all, another expression of *Hambone*'s call, an ongoing search for a "crossroads choir" with which to form an ensemble? Platz reads it that way, seeing in N's search for the Crossroads Choir Mackey's own search for ensemblist identity and definition with *Hambone*. This ensemblist form ultimately makes her feel "at home" and gives rise to her theory of literary hospitality in the form of a personal letter.

Yet as Platz also acknowledges in the last sentence of her letter, Mackey himself has some hand in "making" this Crossroads Choir, returning us once again to Derrida's theory of hospitality, particularly

Editing and the Ensemble

as it struggles to conceptualize intellectual labor as a component of the discourse of hospitality. Derrida's conception of hospitality at first helps to clarify how intellectual labor generates the "not-knowing" on which hospitality depends. In his discussion of the first acceptation of hospitality mentioned earlier, Derrida writes that "hospitality, if there is such a thing, is not only an experience in the most enigmatic sense of the word, which appeals to an act and an intention beyond the thing, object, or present being, but is also an intentional experience which proceeds beyond knowledge toward the other as absolute stranger, as unknown, where I know that I know nothing of him."[66] Derrida sets the movements of hospitality in two directions here. On the one hand, hospitality is an enigmatic experience which "appeals to" an act beyond "the thing, object, or present being." This is the call of hospitality, which invites the emergence of nonobjective knowledge within its experiential parameters. On the other hand, hospitality is an "intentional experience which proceeds beyond" the parameters of objective knowledge toward the "absolute stranger." In this second formulation, hospitality prompts outward movement, an "intentional experience" that proceeds beyond things as they are currently thought to exist. Taken together, the two halves of Derrida's claim configure hospitality as both centripetal and centrifugal. The appeal calls outward and invites the "beyond" to it. The "intentional experience," by comparison, moves with the call and proceeds beyond its initial knowledge. While intention compels the latter experience of hospitality, the experience proceeds beyond its instigating intention, thereby becoming an outward-moving force lodged within hospitality's appeal. Derrida never mentions labor as such in his article on hospitality—perhaps its discourse is too different from the one he seeks to examine. Yet his "intentional experience" that proceeds beyond knowledge nevertheless reflects on the practices that give rise to hospitality. Understanding Derrida's intentional experience in such a way allows us to reflect on intellectual labor—and in the context of this chapter, forms of literary practice—as a generative locus of hospitality.

Allow me to rephrase, then, by thinking with Mackey and *Hambone*: the condition of possibility for the unforeseen to emerge is intellectual labor cognizant of the not-knowing it itself cocreates. This is what

120   Editing and the Ensemble

I would call the labor of hospitality: it accepts and even invites not-knowing as the return on that labor, though even using the language of "returns" is inadequate and false here. Intellectual labor—such as editorial care and making a Crossroads Choir—becomes a practice of hospitable receptivity and ensemblist theory. It is a method of discrepant engagement that subtly pries apart closed orders of identity and signification through its open engagement with, and championing of, co-constituted forms of working, knowing, and being. *Hambone's* ongoing call, emitted in part by Mackey's editorial labors and in part by an ongoing tradition of creative expression as a protest against divisions of labor, creates a literary terrain in which the concept of hospitality becomes imaginable if not entirely realizable. It is not realizable because the call proceeds beyond knowledge, keeping the concept of literary hospitality in flight and keeping the search for the Crossroads Choir ongoing. Mackey describes *Hambone* as "cross-cultural work with an emphasis on the centrifugal,"[67] an encapsulation of his journal that joins "work"—the labors of literary practice—with a flight that proceeds beyond knowing.

"Destination Out": On Centrifugal Inconclusion

In *Paracritical Hinge*, Mackey groups his brief essay on editing *Hambone* with two other short essays that weigh centrifugal and marginal forces in contemporary experimental writing. These three essays make up only ten pages of a 350-page book. Yet they offer some of Mackey's most lucid statements concerning divisions of intellectual labor as they relate to experimental writing in general and Black experimental and "innovative"[68] writing in particular. "Destination Out" (2000), for instance, is a three-paragraph polemic that links centrifugal poetics with divisions of labor and identity as they take shape in and shape the cultural field. In the essay that follows "Destination Out," titled "Expanding the Repertoire," Mackey writes, "Racialized dichotomies between content and form, accessibility and difficulty, conventionality and innovation, and the like rest on a division of cultural labor black experimental writing has to contest and overcome."[69] Mackey pursues

Editing and the Ensemble 121

this line of argument in "Destination Out" as well, but puts the essay in contention with discourses of the avant-garde. The polemic's sequence of declarative statements and its provocative brevity (three short paragraphs) recall the avant-garde manifesto.[70] However, like *Hambone*, whose title is meant to connote a "suggestive meeting of the vernacular and the avant-garde," "Destination Out" advances an argument that establishes "Black centrifugal writing" as a form of creative practice that is in discrepant engagement with the discourse of the avant-garde.

Although the avant-garde as an artistic formation has historically exploded neat divisions between art and not-art and between art and politics, it has also been described extensively as serving an incorporating function.[71] The avant-garde and the discourses that theorize it, that is, bring radical and alternative art forms into the fold of both the institution and the economy. Paul Mann describes his book *The Theory-Death of the Avant-Garde* (1991) as a "disturbed glimpse of the centripetal currents of even the most marginal and transgressive projects."[72] Mann does not discuss race extensively in his book. But the incorporating function of avant-garde discourse that he connotes with "centripetal currents" has often reinforced and exacerbated the racialized divisions of creative labor that Mackey seeks to address.[73] In "Destination Out," Mackey's theory of centrifugal writing engages with discourses of the avant-garde in two key ways. First, it seeks to engage with experimental forms of Black intellectual and creative labor—and to emphasize their capacity to work cross-culturally—in such a way that their recuperation need not be bound to narratives of cultural or economic incorporation. And second, he proposes that centrifugal poetics refuses to reproduce the often racialized divisions of intellectual and creative labor on which certain delineations of the "avant-garde" have operated.

Mackey begins by placing the keywords of his polemic front and center: work and centrifugality. "Centrifugal work," he writes,

> begins with good-bye, wants to bid all givens good-bye. It begins with what words will not do, paint will not do, whatever medium we find ourselves working in will not do. Amenities and consolation accrue to a

122   Editing and the Ensemble

horizon it wants to get beyond, abandoning amenities and consolation or seeking new ones. It will, of course, suffer marginalization, temporary in some cases, unremitting in most.[74]

The declarative opening—"centrifugal work begins with good-bye"—is immediately qualified by the clause that it "wants to bid all givens good-bye." This qualification is significant because the "want" here arises from working within the context of "all givens." Like Charles Olson's observation that "limits are what any of us are inside of" discussed in chapter 1, Mackey situates "centrifugal work" in medias res, with any given medium serving a limiting function that nevertheless gestures beyond its own givenness and affordances (239). Yet media gesture beyond themselves only insofar as one perceives medial limitation in the process of doing work. Both the perception of limitation and the want to go beyond such limitation originate in creative labor, in working with(in) the limits of one's media and discursive formations. Stating that centrifugal work "begins with good-bye," Mackey makes work into the condition of possibility for proceeding beyond the given.

He insists on this point for a specific reason: the work of Black experimentalism is often conflated with the task of constructing Black identity. This sleight of hand—from creative work to identity—results from specific divisions of intellectual labor and categorizations of creative expression, particularly those resulting from academic discourse. In the second paragraph of his tract, Mackey argues that

> black centrifugal writing has been and continues to be multiply marginalized. Why would it be otherwise? At a time when academic and critical discourse battens on identity obsession (even as it "problematizes" identity), black centrifugal writing reorients identity in ways that defy prevailing divisions of labor. In the face of a widespread fetishization of collectivity, it dislocates collectivity, flies from collectivity, wants to make flight a condition of collectivity. (239)

Mackey's dissatisfaction with the terms of the conversation is apparent here. Black centrifugal writing works by the logic of neither identity

Editing and the Ensemble 123

nor fetishized collectivity. Its disposition instead critically assesses and flies from the structures that seek to locate its positionality and coherence. As Mackey notes, these structures can be reinforced through academic discourse, as the institution battened on "identity obsession" in the 1980s and 1990s. Yet he acknowledges elsewhere in his body of work that the fetishization of identity and collectivity, specifically with regard to "prevailing divisions of labor," is not without historical precedent.

Mackey's poem "On Antiphon Island" provides a poetic illustration of the issues Mackey theorizes in "Destination Out." In the poem, however, he addresses the historical rather than contemporary divisions of labor and identity that Black centrifugal writing seeks to upend. The poem's title recalls the antiphony that structures Hambone's rhyme while the poem itself relates a narrative of the Middle Passage. Mackey has his speakers—a plural we—conclude:

The world was ever after, elsewhere,

no

way where we were
was there[75]

Here Mackey's speakers respond to a violent dislocation with a critical-creative disposition that rejects the terms of that imposed dislocation. The collective we instead imagine an "elsewhere" as an alternative world to the one they now inhabit. Stefano Harney and Fred Moten see this poem as evidence of "flights of fantasy in the hold."[76] These speakers "in the hold" take expeditious flight by way of fantasy, speaking to the centrifugal force of collective creative labor even when physical labor and freedom have been violently stolen from them. Moten also finds in this poem a rejection of the forms of identity and subjectivity that slavery and the Middle Passage seek to impose. Following Frank B. Wilderson III, Harney and Moten argue that these speakers—in their unwillingness to be easily located—announce "the void of our subjectivity. And so it is we remain in the hold, in the break, as if entering again and again the broken world, to trace the visionary company and join it"

124   Editing and the Ensemble

(94). Far from fetishizing a collective "we" in this poem, the choral voice—choral in its antiphonal response to historical dispossession—speaks on behalf of a collectivity that cannot be properly identified or located, a "visionary company" that remains in flight from attempts to find it and define it. This is an imaginative flight created by unknown multitudes, the unnamed we, who speak the poem, and it is one source from which centrifugal poetics forms as a protest against divisions of labor.[77]

Like "On Antiphon Island," *Hambone* is a poetic apparatus that "trac[es] the visionary company" of a collective constantly in flight. But it does so not by imagining an irrecoverable historical collective, as the poem does, but rather by publishing a cross-cultural ensemble of artists and poets who follow *Hambone*'s call. Mackey, we have seen, does not work alone. He instead initiates a particularlist undertaking that gives way to ensemblist identity and form. Perhaps it should be unsurprising, then, that the figural Hambone is repeatedly twinned in the literary corpus that his call helps to create. Take, for instance, Al Young's contribution to *Hambone 2*. In a poem titled "What Is the Blues?" a speaker uncannily similar to Hambone starts out,

> Far away, I suppose you could say,
> Is where I'm always coming back from.
> In any event, it's where I want to be
> —naked, undressable, inaccessible,
> at the tip edge of the vanishing point.[78]

Like Hambone, this figure's address wavers between return and departure, making "the tip edge of the vanishing point" a commentary not only on his imagined destination but also on the poem itself as an unsettled node of transition. Mahmoud Darwish, whose work was unknown to Mackey before the poet and translator Stephen Kessler submitted a selection to him after the publication of *Hambone 2*, also reflects on itinerancy and poetic departure. The speaker of his poem travels among Palestinian refugees:

Editing and the Ensemble

> we walk in the direction of a distant song
> we walk toward the first freedom
> and we touch the world's beauty for the first time[79]

The provocative overlap between Young's blues and Darwish's refugees hints at the cross-cultural connections taking shape between *Hambone*'s covers and across its issues. As if responding to the desire to be "at the tip edge of the vanishing point," bell hooks's contribution to *Hambone* 3 offers a more grounded consideration of poetic expression. She writes:

> the earth
> it is round
> there is no edge
> there is no way to fall off[80]

The figural Hambone and Young's speaker already know this: Hambone continually returns from his trip; and "far away" is where Young's speaker "is always coming back from." Yet having "no way to fall off" does not undercut the centrifugal work of *Hambone*'s call and the itinerancy it charts. It rather rearticulates Mackey's desire to show how flight and collectivity converge, and how this provisional convergence gives one a place to depart from again and again.

Hambone provides such a point of departure. It recuperates a history of creative labor that maintains its disruptive potential in its capacity to lead us elsewhere. Hambone is a critical figure—and *Hambone* a vital journal—for considering creative work historically and at present. Hambone emerged as a figure of intellectual freedom from those unknown and unnamed who had their physical freedom taken from them. Their creative labor, however, remained in flight from, yet in engagement with, the impositions of Western modernity. We glimpse this ongoing flight in *Hambone*'s call, which calls so that we may meet him elsewhere, among some ensemble, near "the tip edge of the vanishing point."

4

Editing and Eros

Chris Kraus, Semiotext(e), and I Love Dick

> Love stories are stories of form, and . . . every act of
> solidarity is an act of sphere formation.
>
> —Peter Sloterdijk, *Bubbles: Spheres I*

Toward the end of the preceding chapter on *Hambone*, this chapter's subject was quietly introduced: the operations of desire in literary work. *Hambone*'s call-and-response structure struggles against the centripetal currents of avant-garde discourse by tracking Hambone's creative flight. Desire motivates this flight—the desire to go beyond givens; the desire to exceed the affordances of one's expressive media; the desire to fly from, and reconfigure conceptions of, collectivity. Centrifugal work "wants to bid all givens goodbye," just as it "wants to make flight a condition of collectivity."[1] It longs to abandon familiar objects, histories, collectivities, and subject categories, and it is propelled by a desire whose object and destination remain emphatically unknown.

Desire's inconclusive destinations also drive the editorial and written work of Chris Kraus, who became an editor at Semiotext(e) in the late 1980s before publishing her own first book, the comically explicit *I Love Dick*, with the series in 1997. At first glance, *I Love Dick* is a "study in female abjection"[2] in which the protagonist, Chris, becomes infatuated with the titular Dick, widely known to be based on the cultural theorist Dick Hebdige.[3] Chris writes voluminous love letters to Dick—sometimes at the prompting of, or in collaboration with, her husband

128   Editing and Eros

Sylvère—amassing an epistolary narrative of erotic obsession that Kraus ultimately edits into *I Love Dick* not only by collecting the dated letters in order but also by forming these into a coherent narrative by adding third-person linking narratives. Indeed, while the narrative may begin as a study of female abjection, Eileen Myles proposes that Kraus reroutes her abject desire through her narrative, and especially through her talent for editing. Myles writes that, in the end,

> [Chris's] *living* is the subject, not the dick of the title, and while unreeling her story she deftly performs as art critic, historian, diarist, screenwriter of an adult relationship, performance artist. Even her much vaunted "failed" filmmaking career bequeaths her one mighty tool. Chris really knows (like Bruce Chatwin knew) how to *edit*. Which is the best performance of all. To go everywhere imaginable in a single work and make it move. All at the service of writing an entirely ghastly, cunty exegesis.[4]

In Myles's reading, editing redistributes desire from Dick to living itself, a link Myles reinforces with their typographic emphasis on both *living* and *editing*. Kraus's editing allows Chris to move around her object of desire—Dick/dick—and toward a mode of living in which desire might be more radically distributed.

The redistribution of desire that Kraus undertakes in *I Love Dick* has a practical and theoretical antecedent in the formation of Semiotext(e), which the French-born critic Sylvère Lotringer founded as a journal in 1973 before it also became a publishing house over the following two years. According to Lotringer, the journal was purpose-built to reroute the American academic desire around French semiotics.[5] Its nominal purpose, to begin, was to translate and publish key works of French semiotics for a U.S. audience. Its critical purpose, however, was to question the fashionable position that semiotics held in the American academy. The journal was remarkably successful in its subversion of desire for structuralism, but desire itself did not abate. Rather, it redirected itself—and was redirected with the help of both the journal and the publishing house—to poststructuralist writers who established a new fetish discourse in turn. By its second year of publication the *Semiotext(e)*

Poster for Semiotext(e)'s Schizo Culture colloquium from 1975. The first quotation at upper right reads: "'One does not desire revolution, desire is revolutionary'—G. Deleuze and F. Guattari." Copyright and courtesy of Semiotext(e).

130   Editing and Eros

journal was publishing works by Jacques Derrida and early translations into English from *Anti-Oedipus* by Gilles Deleuze and Félix Guattari. Publishing such figures put Semiotext(e) at the forefront of French poststructuralism in the United States so that by the time Chris Kraus launched her Native Agents series for Semiotext(e) in 1990, Lotringer's own Foreign Agents series had published significant and now classic works of French critical theory by authors such as Jean Baudrillard, Deleuze and Guattari, Jean-François Lyotard, and Paul Virilio, among many others.[6]

Despite its success as a publisher of French theory, an unsettling figure remained in Semiotext(e)'s formation: the visible, gendering, and unpronounced "(e)" in the press's name.[7] Semiotext(e) set out to subvert academic desire and helped to usher poststructuralist theory into the position that semiotics once held. When Lotringer met Chris Kraus in the 1980s, however, Kraus criticized the male-dominated Foreign Agents list that Lotringer had assembled, later calling it a "huge embarrassment . . . that all 25 Foreign Agents authors [at the time] were white males!"[8] As savvy as Lotringer had been about the redirection of desire, what he had dubbed Semiotext(e)'s "schizo-culture,"[9] his Foreign Agents series had not addressed that riddling (e) in the press's name. The academic desire for French theory, it seems, was a largely male homosocial desire that worked by way of friendship, mentorship, rivalry, and camaraderie, mostly to the exclusion of women.[10] Still, the (e) remained a mark of the visible yet unpronounced operations of gender and erasure in critical theory, academic work, and creative practice more broadly. And for Kraus, it was a quiet solicitation to deconstruct the masculine façade that Semiotext(e) had erected.

In response to the lack of women writers in Semiotext(e)'s list, Kraus launched her Native Agents series with the press in 1990. She began by publishing women and nonbinary writers almost exclusively, including, in roughly their order of publication, Cookie Mueller, Ann Rower, Eileen Myles, Kathy Acker, Lynne Tillman, David Rattray, and Barbara Barg. As its name suggests, Native Agents responded to Lotringer's Foreign Agents by publishing works written in English by North Americans,[11] but Kraus saw the books doing more than merely

Editing and Eros 131

responding to the existing Semiotext(e) list. In a lively interview with Henry Schwarz and Anne Balsamo conducted in 1994, Kraus argues that "French theory is reinvented in this fiction—in the United States, gay and women's writing was the 'place' in which those theoretical issues were being worked on or over."[12] She adds to this that the books she had edited and published by 1994 were written with "a polemical, not an introspective, I," and that taken together they are "aggressive and funny and they don't see the personal as a final closed destination. Everything is in flux" (212). These books eschew the monadic, coherent, and introspective I, turning outward instead and moving away from any "final closed destination." The Native Agents series, in turn, keeps the personal open and in flux by putting it forth and making it public, that is, by editing and publishing it. Kraus's Native Agents series thereby participates in the redistribution of desire that Lotringer had designed Semiotext(e) to undertake, but by looking where Lotringer had not: to a host of writers, artists, performers, and visionaries who had been living and working in plain sight.

This chapter focuses on these figures by studying Kraus's early work with the Native Agents series alongside Kraus's own writing on redistributed desire in *I Love Dick* and in her many essays of art criticism. Together these writings record the movements of the roving public I that Kraus often points to in essays and interviews. Yet to focus solely on the development of an outward-directed I in the early Native Agents books, including *I Love Dick*, would be to overlook how Kraus's written and editorial work interests itself equally in affective modes of affiliation, with love, empathy, and friendship primary among them.[13] My reading of *I Love Dick*, for instance, shows that, although the infatuated love letters to Dick appear to form the through line for the book, the letters themselves are also addressed to ghosts of lost friends and unknown artists. Kraus's public I might move through the world with no final closed destination in mind, but she nevertheless makes loving and empathetic affiliations on her journey. In the first book of his *Spheres* trilogy, which Semiotext(e) published in 2011, Peter Sloterdijk outlines the aim of his initial volume with the assertion that "love stories are stories of form, and . . . every act of solidarity is an act of sphere

132 Editing and Eros

formation."[14] This chapter seeks to show how Kraus's written and editorial work anticipates Sloterdijk's polemical and theoretical claim. Editing, like writing, can be an act of eros.

For Kraus and her Native Agents, sphere formation is often intimate. It is a mode of affective affiliation that Kraus makes explicit throughout her body of work, from *I Love Dick* to the Native Agents books that preceded it and made it possible. In Kraus's 2014 account of how she came to write *I Love Dick,* Kraus comments on the debt her first book owed to Native Agents writers:

> After publishing five or six of these books [with Semiotext(e)], I realised they had something in common. *Yes* they were all written by women— *yes* they were all written in the first person—and like practically all books and films of their time, they included writing about sex . . . What seemed most important to me was not the fact of the "I" but the way it moved through the text and the world. It was an active, public "I"—the "I" of American realist fiction, from Mark Twain to Melville to Burroughs and Kerouac and Alexander Trocchi. I did not begin writing myself for another few years, but I learned how to write largely by reading and editing the first Native Agents books.[15]

By Kraus's own account, she comes to recognize the "public I" that she admires precisely because the books she published had it "in common." This commonality attests to more than Kraus's personal interest in a particular kind of writing. It hints at the way that Kraus's "public I" moves in and toward commonality and connection. Many of the early books that Kraus learned from, including Cookie Mueller's *Walking through Clear Water in a Pool Painted Black* (1990), Ann Rower's *If You're a Girl* (1990), and David Rattray's *How I Became One of the Invisible* (1992)—all of which I discuss later in this chapter—not only adopt a polemical and public I; they are also written by Kraus's friends and acquaintances and track modes of affiliation and sphere formation at work in creative practice. Like the series they are a part of, a result of both editing and eros, these books loop back to friends, lovers, and forgotten artists. Their loving loops—sometimes nostalgic, and nearly

Editing and Eros 133

always empathetic—create the fragile spheres of connection and collectivity to which this chapter attends.

Chris Kraus is most known today as a writer of fiction and art criticism and only indirectly as an editor and filmmaker. Her reputation as a writer rests on the four autobiographical fictions that she has published since 1997, all with Semiotext(e): *I Love Dick* (1997); *Aliens and Anorexia* (2000), which chronicles the failure of Kraus's film *Gravity & Grace* (1996); *Torpor* (2006), which narrates "Sylvie and Jerome's" 1991 journey across former communist states in a failed attempt to adopt a child in Romania; and finally *Summer of Hate* (2012) about "Catt Dunlop's" romantic relationship with a working-class man who is a former inmate and who helps her to manage her properties in the American Southwest. *I Love Dick*, Kraus's best-known work, tells the story—first in epistolary form with interludes of third-person linking narration—of Chris's infatuation with Dick. Chris feeds her obsession by writing many lengthy love letters, most of which she does not send. Dick, in turn, does not respond to any of the letters he does receive until the final pages of the narrative, where he chastises Chris and her husband–collaborator Sylvère for making him an unwilling participant in their "bizarre game."[16] Chris's desire to become a writer, which overlaps with her desire for Dick himself, intrudes on what Dick perceives to be his inalienable right to privacy. In his single letter of response, which he addresses only to Sylvère in an act of epistolary revenge, he concludes, "I do not share your conviction that my right to privacy has to be sacrificed for the sake of [Chris's] talent" (260). Even so, Chris's talent prevails, with her story bringing into focus the fraught relations between desire, privacy, and publishing in a contemporary economy of letters.

The few reviews *I Love Dick* initially received were mixed. In the flowing metaphors not only of Deleuzian theory but also of misogyny, David Rimanelli of *Bookforum* quipped that *I Love Dick* was "not so much written as secreted" and that the book "reads like straight spillage."[17] Despite this, or as likely because of it, Rimanelli finds it "unexpectedly riveting" (7). A *New York Magazine* article described the book as "a stream of fawning love letters so intrusive that what [Chris]

134 Editing and Eros

refers to as 'abstract romanticism' seems more like epistolary stalking."[18] Although it did not receive widespread critical acclaim, *I Love Dick* acquired a cult following and Kraus's later works—three fictions and three books of art and cultural criticism—gained her further recognition, leading to the republication of *I Love Dick* in 2006. This edition includes a foreword by Eileen Myles as well as an afterword by the critic Joan Hawkins and has now gone through several printings. The British Tuskar Rock Press, a boutique imprint headed by Colm Tóibín and literary agent Peter Straus, published the first British edition of *I Love Dick* in late 2015. Writing in *The Guardian,* the author Joanna Walsh gives it a glowing review and notes that "a whole generation of writers owes her."[19] Walsh singles out younger authors such as Sheila Heti and Ben Lerner, both of whom write first-person fictions that draw on their own lives for inspiration and fictional experimentation. In 2015 the *New Yorker* also published an effusive retrospective on Kraus and her work by the writer Leslie Jamison. And in 2016, Sarah Gubbins and Jill Soloway adapted *I Love Dick* as a critically acclaimed Amazon Prime Original series. Twenty years after its initial publication, Kraus's work had found a wide and passionate readership, with many writers among its devoted followers.

I Love Dick begins, however, at a very different moment in Kraus's life and career. The initial third-person narrator notes that it is December 3, 1994, and "Chris Kraus, a 39-year-old experimental filmmaker and Sylvère Lotringer, a 56-year-old college professor from New York, have dinner with Dick _____, a friendly acquaintance of Sylvère's, at a sushi bar in Pasadena."[20] Over the course of the book, we learn that Chris has just completed a film version of Simone Weil's *Gravity & Grace* and its prospects look bleak. The film's editors in New Zealand, where Kraus spent most of her adolescence and also attended university, are delaying the project and demanding more money. Meanwhile, the prestigious film festivals to which Chris has submitted the film have all rejected it. Chris writes to "Dick, Sylvère, Anyone" on December 17, 1994, that "it's clear that the film has no chance in movie terms. I may as well own it but ohhh, I thought there'd be more movies after *G & G*. If there are no movies I need to figure out what it's gonna be"

(83). A couple of days later, Chris writes to Dick that "once I accept the failure of *Gravity & Grace* it won't matter anymore what I do—once you've accepted total obscurity you may as well do what you want" (88). There is possibility in obscurity here, for these letters show Kraus doing what she wants: they record her midlife shift from screenwriter and filmmaker to writer of books and arts criticism.

I Love Dick thus presents a transitional moment, framed as a re-direction of desire, in Kraus's intellectual, personal, and artistic life. It charts her movement from filmmaker to writer while also tracking her transition from what she sees as a dependent wife to an "American artist" (97). The two transitions go hand in hand, for *Gravity & Grace* had been financed in part by Sylvère's professorship in New York and the various additional talks he gives as an expert on French psycho-analysis, semiotics, and poststructuralism. When Chris tells a regional curator that she funds her films by "tak[ing] money from Sylvère" (86), she consequently notes "it occurred to me that I was suffering from the dizziness of contradictions" (87). Chris plays the role of the exper-imental filmmaker while agonizing over her financial dependence on Lotringer; her love for Dick leads to despair rather than elation; she wanted to be a filmmaker, but has inadvertently, at least according to the book's logic, become a writer. Together these contradictions and transformations make *I Love Dick* into a variety of Künstlerroman where the Künstlerin begins in the midst of things as a struggling filmmaker and dependent wife. The encounter between Chris and the curator, however, leads to an epiphany several pages later. The third-person narrator, who aligns to a degree with the author–editor Kraus, remarks that "Chris was not a torture victim, not a peasant. She was an Ameri-can artist, and for the first time it occurred to her that perhaps the only thing she had to offer was her specificity. By writing Dick she was offer-ing her life as Case Study" (97).

I Love Dick as Vulgar Telling? Another Turn of the Screw

Chris's "case study" is a Künstlerroman insofar as it tracks her tran-sition from filmmaker to writer; it is also one in the sense that this transition is mediated through other works of criticism, literature, and

136   Editing and Eros

art. Some of the work Chris draws on is the writing of friends and contemporaries such as the poets Barbara Barg, David Rattray, and John Wieners, the first two of whom Kraus published early in her Native Agents series. Some is writing from twentieth-century authors with whom Chris feels some special affinity; Patricia Highsmith, Jane Bowles, and Chris's fellow New Zealander Katherine Mansfield appear several times.[21] Still others appear repeatedly throughout Chris's story, working as points of reference that guide her narrative. Chris meets Dick on December 3, and on December 9 she and Sylvère begin writing letter after letter addressed to him. By December 12, with dozens of pages already written, Chris remarks that "writing this has been like moving through a kaleidoscope of all our favorite books in history: *Swann's Way* and William Congreve, Henry James, Gustave Flaubert. Does analogy make emotion less sincere?" (70). Of these, Flaubert's *Madame Bovary* receives the most extended references in the text, with Chris and Sylvère even signing one of their cowritten letters as Charles and Emma Bovary.

And yet, Henry James's *The Turn of the Screw* is an equally telling point of reference for understanding how desire, literary economy, and affective attachments operate in Kraus's novel.[22] James's novella provides Kraus with a literary precedent in which obsession and love underwrite a tale acutely aware of its own modes of telling. Like *I Love Dick,* *The Turn of the Screw* fixates on how love stories are told and how they are stories of form and sphere formation. James's novella, after all, opens on the scene of a story being told publicly around a fire with multiple frames and narrators setting up the eventual coming to light of the Governess's tale. Whereas *The Turn of the Screw* is famous because the Governess's tale ultimately "*won't* tell, not in any literal vulgar way,"[23] *I Love Dick* revels in explicit telling, with Chris offering her life as a case study in desire. *The Turn of the Screw's* narrative strategies, which rely on the limits imposed by first-person perspective, make it difficult for readers and critics to resolve the riddle of the text: what happens to the Governess at the Master's estate? *I Love Dick,* by comparison, proposes that making one's story explicit through an effusive first-person narration might engender new modes of narrative inquiry for contemporary writers.

Editing and Eros

Even if James crafts his novella so that the Governess's story *won't* tell, *The Turn of the Screw* nevertheless coalesces around affiliations made possible through telling. The narrative begins with a small group of people, including an unnamed first-person narrator, sitting around a fire telling and listening to ghost stories on Christmas Eve. The tale opens as one story about a haunted child concludes, a story that "had held us, round the fire, sufficiently breathless" (1). This initial story elicits a "reply" from a man named Douglas who says he knows a story in which not one but "two children" are haunted by ghosts (1). The news arouses curiosity among the group and so Douglas sends away for a manuscript of the story that he has kept locked in a drawer elsewhere for years. While the small group awaits the arrival of the manuscript, Douglas narrates its history. It was written in "a most beautiful hand. A Woman's"—and the woman was his sister's governess who has been dead for twenty years (2). Douglas shows his deep admiration for this woman and when he attempts to clarify how the manuscript came into his possession he explains the scenario, focusing specifically on the unnamed first-person narrator of this initial frame:

> "I liked her extremely and am glad to this day to think she liked me too. If she hadn't she wouldn't have told me. She had never told anyone. It wasn't simply that she said so, but that I knew she hadn't. I was sure; I could see. You'll easily judge why when you hear."
>
> "Because the thing had been such a scare?"
>
> He continued to fix me. "You'll easily judge," he repeated: "*you* will."
>
> I fixed him too. "I see. She was in love."
>
> He laughed for the first time. "You *are* acute. Yes, she was in love. That is she had been. That came out—she couldn't tell her story without its coming out. I saw it, and she saw it; but neither of us spoke of it." (2)

This exchange at once revels in and reveals the desire and affection attendant to the act of telling. The tale's circulation and eventual publication—being told around the fire by Douglas and eventually being published by the first-person narrator in this scene to whom Douglas leaves the original manuscript on his own deathbed—hinges on love. Douglas says that the Governess was in love, and the audience is led to believe that this love leads to the frightful narrative we are about to read. Moreover, it is the Governess's later admiration ("she liked me"), perhaps even love, for Douglas that leads her to tell her story at all rather than taking it silently to her grave. Douglas's singling out of the first-person narrator in this frame—"You'll easily judge . . . *you* will"—implies yet another budding friendship on which the tale's print publication and circulation depends. In the logic of James's novella, then, the Governess's tale circulates according to the pathways of love and friendship, where, as Sloterdijk observes in this chapter's epigraph, "every act of solidarity is an act of sphere formation." The tale's "publication" depends on these relationships, solidarities, and spheres, but these in turn take shape and shift around the telling of the story itself.

Even with the complexity of affective affiliation dramatized in the opening frame of the story, some critics have fixated on the Governess's love for the Master in their critical assessments of the work. Edmund Wilson's now dated Freudian reading of the novella in "The Ambiguity of Henry James" is exemplary here, and proposes that the love Douglas mentions in the framing narrative is the love that the Governess feels for the Master but cannot express. For Wilson, *The Turn of the Screw* is about the Governess's "inability to admit to herself her sexual impulses and the relentless English 'authority' which enables her to put over on inferiors even purposes which are totally mistaken and not at all to the other people's best interest. . . . *The Turn of the Screw*, then, on this theory, would be a masterpiece—not as a ghost story—but as a study in morbid psychology."[24] In her "Turning the Screw of Interpretation," Shoshana Felman argues that Wilson's reading "follows [the] interpretative pattern of accounting for the whole story in terms of the governess's sexual frustration: she is in love—says Wilson—with the Master, but is unable to admit it to herself, and thus obsessively, hysterically projects her own desires upon the outside world, perceives them as exterior to herself in the hallucinated form of fantasmatic ghosts."[25] Felman then quotes Wilson, who writes, "The theory is, then, that the governess who is made to tell the story is a neurotic case of sex repression, and that the ghosts are not real ghosts but hallucinations of the governess" (103). According to Wilson's logic, the Governess's tale is legible only in the context of her obsessive and even hysterical desire for the Master, with all other plot elements—the ghosts and the Governess's relationship with the children—subordinated to her primary fixation.

A central scene from *The Turn of the Screw*'s framing narrative, however, cautions the reader against simple conclusions about the distribution of desire in the Governess's narrative. When Douglas confesses that the Governess "was" or "had been" in love, a member of his audience asks:

> "Who was it she was in love with?"
>
> "The story will tell," I took it upon myself to reply. . . .
>
> "The story *won't* tell," said Douglas; "not in any literal vulgar way."[26]

This reticence—that the story emphatically *won't* tell whom the Governess loved—forms the enticement of James's tale and has induced many critics to answer for it, whether from a position of mastery (Wilson) or one that champions non-mastery (Felman). In this story that won't tell the name of the loved one—or even more radically, that suggests that there is no singular *one* to love—James effectively develops a narrative of desire without a final or closed destination. Yet as we see in James's narrative framing, to conceive of desire without a final destination is not to imagine a desire without attachments. Instead, James's novella, like Kraus's "Dumb Cunt's Tale"—her Jamesian name for *I Love Dick*—scrutinizes how desire gives rise to a multitude of attachments and forms. Its opening scene stages the affective acts of solidarity that storytelling entails. Kraus explores such acts throughout her body of written work, beginning with *I Love Dick* but initiated in editorial acts of empathy and affection.

Love Stories and Ghost Stories: From James to Kraus

The narrative of *I Love Dick* takes place in two parts: "Scenes from a Marriage" and "Every Letter Is a Love Letter." At the end of "Scenes from a Marriage," which comprises the letters Sylvère and Chris write

140 Editing and Eros

to Dick, Chris decides to leave Sylvère and live on her own. She makes this decision not because her relationship with Dick has become more intimate, but because her letter writing has brought her to some realization about her own desires and interests beyond Dick and Sylvère. "Every Letter Is a Love Letter" is also made up of letters to Dick, but these are written primarily by Chris, are much longer, and read more like critical essays on a range of topics: artists, filmmakers, or writers Chris admires; the possibility of publishing the letters as a book; and reflections on Chris's adolescence and early adulthood in New Zealand. Whereas "Scenes from a Marriage" presents Chris at a low point in terms of her film career and marriage—the run-up to which Kraus covers in detail in *Aliens and Anorexia* (2000)—"Every Letter" sees Chris turn toward art in this midlife Künstlerroman. This turn toward art hinges critically on Chris increasingly addressing the work of dear and dead friends, forgotten artists, and even some of the writers Kraus published as the editor of the Native Agents series. "Every Letter Is a Love Letter" is motivated by love. Yet as its broad title suggests, Chris's love proliferates into and draws its pathos from other areas of her life; she begins to find other attachments and to form other affiliations. The second half of Kraus's fiction thus turns from a singular infatuation with Dick to a more peripatetic and restless love, one that helps Chris to examine love, art, and artistic practice as related modes of creative affiliation.

The striking first letter of "Every Letter Is a Love Letter" shows a shift in Chris's attention: from emphatic infatuation with Dick to empathetic reflections on art and attachment. The letter is dated two months after Chris and Sylvère initially met Dick for sushi. Chris tells Dick that she has just moved to Thurman, New York, a "community of exiles" where "no one asks me any questions 'cause there's no frame of reference to put the answers in."[27] Although Chris lives in Thurman, she is not entirely detached from the New York arts community where she made many of her early connections in and around the St. Mark's scene in the 1970s. Now, in the 1990s, the art she takes interest in attempts to recall and excavate such scenes from artistic and literary history. She writes, "For several days now I've been wanting to

Editing and Eros 141

tell you about an installation I saw last week in New York. It was called *Minetta Lane—A Ghost Story*, by Eleanor Antin, an artist/filmmaker who I don't know very much about. The installation was pure magic" (122). Chris goes on to describe the physical approach to the installation: "You entered it through a sharply cornered narrow corridor—the white sheet rock of the gallery abruptly changed to crumbling plaster, rotting slats and boards, rolls of chicken-wire and other prewar tenement debris" (122). The entryway places her in a mock-up version of Greenwich Village decades earlier. Eventually, Chris exits the corridor into something like a foyer with a semicircular wall with three windows: "Three films played simultaneously in each of the three windows, rear-projected against the window panes. The corridor'd led you to this point so you could attend a kind of séance, becoming a voyeur" (122). The description of the installation is at once simple and rich, setting up themes that become central to the second half of Kraus's book. Chris imagines to be both an attendee at a séance—which relies on a medium to communicate with figures from the past—and a voyeur, a ghoul who watches, fixed primarily on what is present. In effect, the description of Antin's installation launches Chris into a meditation on art, its histories, its forms and apparatuses, and its ghosts.

One such ghost emerges from the depths of Antin's installation in the form of a solitary figure: a lone woman, painting in a room, rear-projected on one of the three screens. This painting figure leads Chris to an epiphany wrapped in nostalgia and longing, and it serves as a fulcrum in the narrative where infatuation with Dick morphs with and into Chris's desire for other modes of affiliation and other outlets of desire:

> Through the far-left window a middle-aged woman was painting on a large canvas. We saw her from behind, rumpled shirt and rumpled body, curly rumpled hair, looking, thinking, drawing on a cigarette, reaching down onto the floor to take a few drinks from a bottle of Jim Beam here and there. It was an ordinary scene (though it's [*sic*] very ordinariness made it subversively utopian: how many pictures from the 50s do we have of nameless women painting late into the night and living lives?).

142   Editing and Eros

And this ordinariness unleashed a flood of historical nostalgia, a warmth and closeness to a past I've never known—the same nostalgia that I felt from seeing a photo exhibition at St. Marks' Church a few years ago. There were maybe a hundred photos gathered by the Photographic / Oral History Project of the Lower East Side of artists living, drinking, working, in their habitat between the years 1948 and 1972. The photos were meticulously captioned with the artists' names and disciplines, but 98% of them were names I didn't know. The photos tapped into that same unwritten moment as Antin's show—it was the first time in American art history, thanks to allowances provided by the GI Bill, that lower-middle class Americans had a chance to live as artists, given time to kill. Antin recalls: "There was enough money around from the GI Bill to live and work in a low-rent district . . . Studios were cheap, so were paints and canvases, booze and cigarettes. All over the Village young people were writing, painting, getting psychoanalyzed, fucking the bourgeoisie." Where are they now? The Photographic / Oral History Project show transformed the streets of the East Village into tribal ground. I felt a rush of empathetic curiosity about the lives of the unfamous, the unrecorded desires and ambitions of artists who had been here too. What's the ratio of working artists to the sum total of art stars? A hundred or a thousand? The first window did the job of shamanistic art, drawing together hundreds of disparate thoughts, associations (photos in the exhibition; lives; the fact that some of them were female too) into a single image. A rumpled woman paints and smokes a cigarette. And don't you think a "sacred space" is sacred only because of the collectivity it distills? (122–24)

Chris's "flood of historical nostalgia" and the subsequent "rush of empathetic curiosity" are aroused here not by Dick, but rather by an installation and photography exhibition that seek to document the often "unrecorded desires" of art's history and the lives entangled in it. A middle-aged woman painting alone in her room elicits Chris's empathetic response, with her empathy and memory then reaching out further still to a collection of photographs of mostly unknown artists, the great majority of whom will remain unknown to a wide public. Chris acknowledges that her empathetic experience mixes nostalgia

Editing and Eros

143

with voyeurism. But her empathy with the lost and little known rings no less true for its proximity to these. Like Antin's installation, Chris turns her empathetic gaze toward "the only thing that gives [passing] moments any meaning: history and time passing through other people's lives" (124). One means of recording such passing, as Chris's own epistolary range makes clear, is through documentation as a method of empathy and affiliation.

In light of Chris's epiphany, an earlier moment in her story comes back into focus, one that makes this love story—*I Love Dick*—also a ghost story. The day after Chris and Sylvère meet with Dick for sushi, and ultimately sleep at his house because of bad weather, Chris finds herself moved to write her first short story in five years. She calls it "Abstract Romanticism." Although her desire to write this story is provoked by her "Conceptual Fuck" with Dick, Dick is not its subject nor its addressee. It is addressed instead to David Rattray, Kraus's close friend whose work she was editing for publication with Native Agents (*How I Became One of the Invisible*, 1992) when Rattray was diagnosed with a brain tumor that led to his early death in 1993. Kraus's second book is also "dedicated to the memory of David Rattray."[28] In this scene of Kraus's return to writing, the third-person narrator notes that

> [Chris] addresses this story, intermittently, to David Rattray because she's convinced that David's ghost had been with her last night for the car ride, pushing her pickup truck further all the way up Highway 5. Chris, David's ghost and the truck had merged into a single unit moving forward.
>
> "Last night I felt," she wrote to David's ghost, "like I do at times when things seem to open onto new vistas of excitement—that you were here: floating dense beside me, set someplace between my left ear and my shoulder, compressed like thought."
>
> She thought about David all the time. It was uncanny how Dick had said somewhere in last night's boozy conversation, as if he'd read her mind, how much he admired David's book. David Rattray had been a reckless adventurer and a genius and a moralist, indulging in the most improbable infatuations nearly until the moment of his death at age 57.

144   Editing and Eros

And now Chris felt David's ghost pushing her to understand infatuation, how the loved person can become a holding pattern for all the tattered ends of memory, experience and thought you've ever had. So she started to describe Dick's face, "pale and mobile, good bones, reddish hair and deepest eyes." Writing, Chris held his face in her mind, and then the telephone rang and it was Dick.[29]

Eileen Myles praises Kraus for "marching boldly into self-abasement and self-advertisement, not being uncannily drawn there."[30] And indeed, much of the interest in *I Love Dick* derives from its explicitness, its publicness, with both Myles and the scholar Anna Watkins Fisher describing Kraus's book as a public "performance."[31] Kraus turns infatuation inside out by making it public and publishing it. Yet this passage shows that the uncanny has its own role to play in Chris's tale. Enfolded in her explicit narrative about Dick, we find the story of a lost friend. David Rattray's ghost haunts Chris, leading her to identify the uncanny precisely when Dick mentions his admiration for Rattray's book, which Kraus collected, edited, and published in 1992.

The uncanny coincidence between Dick and David shows how Chris's infatuation mingles with her desire to reconnect with a dead friend. Her desire for Dick and David also converges with her desire to tell her story, with this scene showing us Chris's return to writing. The comingling of erotic desire and empathetic and mournful longing compels much of Chris's narrative, particularly in "Every Letter Is a Love Letter." Rattray's ghost pushes Chris to understand how "the loved person can become a holding pattern for all the tattered ends of memory, experience and thought you've ever had." Initially, this observation appears to apply most readily to Rattray, whose ghost Chris addresses in the passage. Yet Chris reports that she writes the story to and for David only "intermittently," a word that implies the sporadic nature of directed written address while also evoking etymologically something that is sent (in Latin, *mittens*) between (*inter*). It is precisely such intermittency—the itinerant nature of loving address—that allows for Chris to arrive at her conclusion, in which an equivocal "loved person" enables her to form a "holding pattern" into which she brings "all the tattered ends of

Editing and Eros   145

memory, experience and thought." This holding pattern is not merely conceptual; it is the very structure of *I Love Dick*. Intermittent address ensures that the love that structures the narrative is not addressed to Dick alone. It is also addressed to David. It is also addressed to the figures of Eleanor Antin's *Minetta Lane: A Ghost Story*. It is also addressed to the largely unknown figures in the photographs at St. Mark's. As Kraus concludes her touching essay memorializing the artist Julie Becker (1972–2016), "the gallery is a place where things are held."[32] So, too, is *I Love Dick*. Its scenes of affiliation are forms of loving embrace that recall Kraus's own editorial shaping of the Native Agents series.

Kraus's Native Agents: Looping Desire and Loving Form

Kraus launched her Native Agents series of Semiotext(e) in 1990 as an "'antidote' to the male-dominated, primarily French Foreign Agents series to explore American, primarily female, voices and issues of subjectivity."[33] Cookie Mueller's *Walking through Clear Water in a Pool Painted Black* and Ann Rower's *If You're a Girl* initiated the series in 1990, followed closely by Eileen Myles's *Not Me* and Kathy Acker's *Hannibal Lecter, My Father* in 1991, and then Lynne Tillman, David Rattray, Barbara Barg, and Fanny Howe, among others, in following years. The series published sixteen books between 1990 and 2002, when Hedi El Kholti joined Semiotext(e) and began to collaborate with Kraus on the fiction list. The list has since expanded "to encompass sexual politics in general (regardless of gender), ranging from super-masochist Bob Flanagan's diaries to the fiction of the only openly gay man in Morocco, Abdellah Taia."[34] In an interview conducted in 2014, Kraus comments on this change in direction: "After the first twelve of fourteen titles, I figured I was finished with editing Native Agents as a heavily female first-person series. We'd done what we set out to do, and it was fine. Hedi and I work closely together on the fiction list. While it's no longer exclusively female, neither does it posit the straight middle-class white male as the ultimate subject."[35] Given the size and range of the current Native Agents list—seventy-one books as of this writing in June 2020— I want to focus in this section on several of the "first twelve or fourteen" titles that Kraus published with the series. These form a provisionally

146   Editing and Eros

finished set of sorts, and they also form a holding pattern that allows us
to observe the interests, desires, and affiliations that activated Kraus's
Native Agents. If Chris's story in *I Love Dick* touches on "the lives of
the unfamous, the unrecorded desires and ambitions of artists who
had been here too,"[36] then the Native Agents series was, from the very
beginning and in anticipation of *I Love Dick,* designed to be a record of
such lives and unrecorded desires.

The Native Agents series prioritizes women's movements over a
singular women's movement, and each of the first several books in the
series takes artistic or countercultural scenes as the milieu through
which its roving protagonist moves. Ann Rower's *If You're A Girl* includes Rower's "transfictions," or transcript fictions, that provide a fictional and personal documentation of the New York poetry and art scene
in the 1970s and 1980s. Given the personal dimension of Rower's documentary process, however, the documentation of these scenes often
rubs against personal desire. On the occasion of attending a fundraiser
poetry reading at the Marlborough Gallery on Fifty-Seventh Street, for
instance, Rower strikes a flippant tone: "I didn't even care about hearing the reading: Ted Berrigan, Allen Ginsberg, Anne Waldman, the
usual. I was there for the social rub."[37] Rower's glib treatment of the
poetry and art scene as the backdrop of her personal agenda exemplifies the kind of slant approach to cultural documentation that many
of the Native Agents books take. Documentary here becomes a record
of personal interests, acknowledging how desire spins the documentary impulse, sometimes in the direction of fiction. The final seventy
pages of Rower's book, for example, provide the reader with an actual
transcript. Rower explains that it is the transcript of a conversation she
held with a theater group. They had interviewed her about her experiences with Timothy Leary while she was living in Newton, Massachusetts, when Leary was beginning his work at Harvard. The theater group
then edited and rewrote the transcript—fictionalizing it to degree—
leading Rower to re-present the original edited manuscript in *If You're
a Girl.* "Once the play opened," she writes, "the original group interview from which the text came was forgotten, which I think is a shame.
The variance between it and the edited text which precedes it is also

Editing and Eros

something like the tension between real life and invention that I use to write stories" (202). *If You're a Girl* does not provide the play's text. Yet Rower offers a brief glimpse of the tension between documentary and invention at work in her writing, always situating this tension also at the intersection of art scenes, countercultural scenes, and personal desire.

What we glimpse in Rower's transfictions takes fuller form in Cookie Mueller's *Walking through Clear Water in a Pool Painted Black*. The book similarly uses autobiographical fiction to recount Mueller's experiences as a working artist and mother moving through various art scenes from the late 1960s to the mid-1980s, and from Haight-Ashbury to the Lower East Side. Mueller is perhaps most well known now for her appearances in John Waters's *Pink Flamingos* (1972) and *Female Trouble* (1974), among other films, but Kraus had gotten to know her, as with most of the other Native Agents writers, in the New York poetry and art scene in the 1970s and 1980s. Kraus writes:

> When I started the Native Agents series, I had just heard Cookie Mueller read at the Poetry project [*sic*]. Cookie was this great, legendary New York figure: she'd been a star of the early John Waters movies, this great Baltimore new age biker girl who "took notes" on her life by writing these perfect stories. Everyone loved Cookie, and the readings that she gave in New York for five or ten years before that were real high points. So it seemed incredible that no one had done a book of Cookie's work. Obviously her book should have been done by Random House or Harper Collins [*sic*], but it seemed all the major publishers she'd seen wanted so many changes that Cookie couldn't be bothered. So we published her book, *Walking through Clear Water in a Pool Painted Black* (1990), verbatim, as the first in the series and it's sold out several editions.[38]

This recollection brings the formation of Native Agents more clearly into focus in several ways. First, it is a testament to the scene in which Kraus and Mueller's collaboration took place. Mueller was a regular reader in New York and a legend beloved by all. The very fact that Mueller's book was published by Native Agents is itself a record of the

148   Editing and Eros

operation of certain sphere formations constantly taking shape in that scene at that time. At a more formal level, and in retrospect of what Native Agents was to become, this early Native Agents publication brought Kraus's vision for the series into focus. Mueller's stories take shape as "notes" on her life that she transfigures into "perfect stories." A variation on this transition—from notes to stories (or from life to poems in the case of Eileen Myles's *Not Me*)—characterizes much of the Native Agents list up until 2002.

Mueller's story "Haight-Ashbury—San Francisco California—1967" illustrates the intersection of journal-like note-taking and fictional storytelling. The story's title is typical for the collection, with "Haight-Ashbury" nestled between "Two People—Baltimore—1964" and "The Pig Farm—Baltimore and York, Pennsylvania—1969." With the place and time vaguely set, Mueller leaves the stories themselves to wander toward the unreal. "Haight-Ashbury" starts out as an apparent journal entry on a day in Mueller's life:

> An earthquake rolled me off the mattress onto the floor. It woke me along with the rest of San Francisco. It was nothing too unusual considering the San Andreas fault [*sic*]; there were a lot of houses all over the city that were crooked from past tremors. This one was 5.6 on the Richter scale at 10 a.m., an uncivilized hour.[39]

Mueller's subtle opening nods to a degree of historical accuracy—a magnitude 5.6 earthquake did take place on December 10, 1967, but it struck a couple of hours later than Mueller notes—while the syntactic strategy in the first two sentences places Mueller as the direct object of external occurrences. Similar to the Richter scale she references, Mueller measures cultural shifts taking place around her.

After this jolting start, Mueller's story proceeds in a series of unexpected aftershocks. We learn that Janis Joplin lives just across the courtyard: "On some mornings I could see her rattling her pots and pans in her kitchen. Sometimes we'd talk across the concrete abyss like housewives" (6). The sleepy narrator wanders down into the street, where a stranger invites her to a van to smoke a joint. The van is filled with young women who ask the narrator to join them on a trip up and

Editing and Eros

down the coast. She declines. The women push a little harder: "You should really wait for Charlie to come back from the store before you decide" (7). The narrator leaves anyway and then reports, "Those girls were Squeaky Fromme, Susan Atkins, Mary Brunner . . . I just missed meeting Charlie Manson by five minutes" (7–8). Leaving the van, the narrator overhears a woman "extolling the virtues of Jimi Hendrix, after having fucked him the night before." She casually adds, "I'd fucked him the night before she had" (8). Soon she's on the Grateful Dead's flatbed truck, filled with gear for a concert at San Quentin (10). After the show, she runs into a friend who talks her into visiting Anton LaVey, "America's foremost demonologist and devil worshipper of the moment" (11). This leads to a botched satanic ritual in the mountains north of San Francisco. The narrator then rounds out her day by going to see Jim Morrison play in Berkeley, after which she's raped at gunpoint—a point she does not dwell on, but still records—before returning home to an apartment filled with high roommates:

> They offered me some cocaine and methadrine [*sic*] and we ushered in the dawn talking about aesthetics, Eastern philosophy, Mu, Atlantis, and the coming apocalypse. We recorded the conversation, not realizing we were all making the same points five or six times. It would sound foolishly cyclical the next day. But it was already the next day . . . time for me to go back out on Haight Street and have some more fun. (17)

I enumerate this list of occurrences to show how what begins in a journal-like mode concludes as an expertly stylized fiction in which numerous experiences are condensed into the narrative of a single day. The story operates in a mythical, circular pattern—ending more or less exactly where it begins—in order to encompass not a day-in-the-life story, but rather something akin to the mythos of a famed American subcultural scene, its violent dangers for women not excluded.

Mueller's story is a masterpiece in miniature. It documents a scene—"Haight-Ashbury—San Francisco—1967"—while also formally enacting the loops and cycles that inhabit methods of documentation, storytelling, and mythmaking. The appearance of Mu and Atlantis in the tape-recorded conversation—an appearance that recalls Charles Olson's

150   Editing and Eros

recognition of the proximity between acts of documentation and acts of imagination from chapter 1—signals Mueller's recognition that documentation and mythmaking correspond with one another. The lost worlds are not diacritics of a new sought-after utopia but rather markers of the creative and critical generations taking place in the act of documentation itself, especially as that act is driven by desire. In an essay on the Austrian conceptual artist Elke Krystufek, who had been developing art projects on the mythology surrounding the disappearance of the artist Bas Jan Ader in 1975, Kraus makes the pithy observation that "myth never comes free of its documentation."[40] Mueller flips this observation: documentation carries myth with it. Stories and lives alike turn back on themselves, creating mythic and narrative form. The looping form of Odysseus's nostalgic return thereby corresponds, intermittently, with Mueller's tape-recorded conversations and her similarly looping story that chronicles life in Haight-Ashbury—San Francisco—1967.

Narratives of artful looping and nostalgic returns appear with notable frequency in the first set of Native Agents books, often in relation to past artists and friends. In a 2002 critical essay on the artist Andrea Bowers, Kraus comments on the effect of looping in the creation of art and artistic affiliation. Describing Bowers's *Mouth to Ear* exhibition from 2002, Kraus writes that

> Bowers memorializes twenty of the dead people in 20th century culture who've enabled her—a female artist born in Wilmington, Ohio in 1965—to be. *After you've gone / And left me crying . . . Your heart will break like mine . . .* Bessie Smith's voice resounds around the gallery. . . . And it's like this in *Battlefields, Gardens, and Graveyards,* Bowers's 50-frame wallpiece in the *Mouth to Ear* show. Janet Jackson samples Joni Mitchell, Nina Simone covers Bessie Smith, Lori Twersky creates a magazine to memorialize the best of female rock & roll—each of these fifty images shows how people loop back to find inspiration from others who made their lives possible. It is the essence of culture.[41]

It would be a mistake to think of Kraus as a sentimental writer. Yet in this essay titled "Sentimental Bitch"—adopting the title of Bowers's

Editing and Eros 151

piece memorializing the editor Lori Twersky—sentiment leads Kraus to the kind of grandiose claim she usually refrains from making: "It [i.e., people looping back] is the essence of culture." This sentimental slip, where a grand claim emerges from emotional acuity, hints at the centrality of memorialization, looping back, and drawing on friends and artists to Kraus's projects, both written and editorial. Consider, for instance, that Kraus commissioned Mueller's book not long before Mueller's death from AIDS in 1989. Mueller died just four months before Kraus was able to publish the book as the inaugural title of Native Agents. Kraus similarly commissioned and edited David Rattray's *How I Became One of the Invisible* (1992), during which Rattray discovered he had an inoperable brain tumor. Like Bowers's *Battlefields, Gardens, and Graveyards,* the Native Agents series forms a loop: an artistic sphere shaped by Kraus's turning to and drawing inspiration from the artists and friends who make her work possible.

The books Kraus publishes all similarly circle back. They intensify Native Agents' operations of loving and empathetic recursion by also making friends—and lost friends—central to the stories they tell and the ways they tell them. Although Mueller begins her book with a wonderful and funny and violent story about her experiences in and around Haight-Ashbury, for instance, she concludes on a more intimately personal and devastating note. The final section is a three-page piece called simply "Last Letter—1989." But this is a last letter twice over. It is Mueller's literary "last letter" that creates a closing frame for her book as her health deteriorated; but it also includes a reproduction of an actual last letter that Mueller received from a close friend before he died of AIDS in 1982. "Last Letter—1989" is split roughly between Mueller's reflection on the HIV/AIDS crisis in the 1980s and a transcription of her friend Gordon's last letter to her. In Mueller's section before she gives the last letter over to Gordon's writing, Mueller laments:

> Perhaps there is no hope left for the whole of humankind, not because of the nature of the epidemic, but the nature of those it strikes. Each friend I've lost was an extraordinary person, not just to me, but to hundreds of people who knew their work and their fight. These were the

152   Editing and Eros

kind of people who lifted the quality of all our lives, their war against ignorance, the bankruptcy of beauty, and the truancy of culture. They were
people who hated and scorned pettiness, intolerance, bigotry, mediocrity,
ugliness, and spiritual myopia; the blindness that makes life hollow and
insipid was unacceptable. They tried to make us see.
    All of these friends were connected to the arts.[42]

Mueller reminds her reader here of the devastation caused by HIV/
AIDS in the 1980s, all the more heartbreaking given that her book was
published shortly after her own death in November 1989, and that as
her biography in the book notes, her husband, Vittorio Scarpati, had
died of AIDS just months earlier in September 1989.

Instead of facing this devastation alone, Mueller turns to Gordon.
Similar to "Haight-Ashbury," where Mueller concludes by returning
to friends to share stories and talk about Mu and Atlantis after being
raped at gunpoint, here she turns back to Gordon's "last letter" for
solace and care. Her friend, in turn, concludes,

I KNOW, I KNOW , I KNOW that somewhere there is a paradise and
although I think it's really far away, I KNOW, I KNOW , I KNOW I'm going
to get there, and when I do, you're gonna be one of the first people I'll
send a postcard to with complete description of, and map for locating . . .
    Courage, bread, and roses,
    Gordon (150)

Given that Mueller herself offers no reading of the letter, it would be
wrong to speculate about her own feelings about a utopian afterlife. She
does not discuss it elsewhere in the book. Mueller's looping back to
her lost friend is itself a hopeful if not fully utopian gesture, however,
because it is a gesture underwritten by love, admiration, and care, even
if also by mourning. Turning back to her friend allows her to glimpse
a "hope for humankind" she feels is being devastated and perhaps ir-
retrievably lost by HIV/AIDS. It is heartbreaking, as Mueller continues
her fearless and loving documentation of life; and it is also hopeful, as
Mueller's book—*Walking through Clear Water in a Pool Painted Black*—

Editing and Eros

provides her with an opportunity to correspond with friends, both living and dead. Facing her own death with incredible grace, Mueller shows her reader that friendships with people like Gordon made her life—and also her art—possible.

Kraus's admiration for artistic acts of solidarity is distributed across her range of practice, from her publication of Mueller's work as the inaugural text of the Native Agents series to her own more recent writing on the visual arts. In a 2010 essay on the work of the Canadian and New York–based visual artist Moyra Davey, Kraus responds to Davey's solo exhibition *My Necropolis* at the Murray Guy Gallery in New York in 2009. According to the gallery description, *My Necropolis* "pairs footage of cemeteries with attempts at interpreting an enigmatic line from a letter that Walter Benjamin wrote to his friend Gershom Scholem in 1931. Benjamin, living in difficult financial circumstances, mentions a clock outside his window which increasingly becomes a luxury that 'it is difficult to do without.'"[43] According to Kraus, a "loop" of this video played on a box-set television in the center of a gallery room.[44] On the walls of this room were Davey's additional 32 *Photographs from Paris*, in which Davey made poster-sized prints of photographs she had taken in Paris and then folded these prints in order to mail them to friends in North America. For the exhibition, she got permission from these friends to gather the mailed images and hang them on the walls of the gallery. Kraus reports that her initial response to Davey's show was "excitement" and then offers her reader some of the notes she made on first visiting the show (97). It is characterized, Kraus writes, by "a movement outward. The view of the dead she shoots through a window [*My Necropolis*] and the 32 faux-tourist photos she sends through the mail to her friends are both ways of travelling out: in the first case [of the film], she / the artist is traveling outward towards something—but in the second [the sent photographs], she / through the object is traveling also, to friends" (104). Traveling, through art, to friends is fundamentally generative for Kraus's work. Indeed, Kraus arrives at conclusions about Davey's work that could equally apply to her own, writing that "Davey offers herself as protagonist to lead us towards recognitions that arise in a heightened intellectual/emotional

154   Editing and Eros

state through *correspondence*" (104). Echoing the critical scene from *I Love Dick* noted above, Kraus identifies art and writing—and I would add editing and publishing as practices that initiate "a movement outward"—as modes of affective correspondence. They respond to and shape fragile spheres of solidarity. Their forms derive from the empathetic affiliations so often at work in the work of art.

In an essay from ten years earlier, Kraus arrives at a similar conclusion but stated differently. Addressing the work of the artists Christiana Glidden and Julie Becker, both of whom devise systematic works of art that constantly gesture to the "deep chaos" from which they emerge, Kraus concludes that "they are faltering and grasping at emotion, the place to which all systems lead."[45] This aphoristic announcement—another theory of art—also describes Kraus's artistic practice. Native Agents, after all, forms a loose system that not only leads to emotion but also derives from it. In the looping correspondences of art, affection, and affiliation, there is no singular point of origin. There is instead documentation and remembrance and invention and play, all ongoing. Like Kraus's own books, Native Agents and the books it publishes are systems grasping toward emotion, whether in the funny and devastating stories of Cookie Mueller, or in the powerful and sometimes metaphysical story of a struggling female filmmaker in Fanny Howe's *Indivisible* (now published as one of five books in Howe's *Radical Love* series, 2006).

David Rattray provides a psychedelic version of grasping toward emotion in *How I Became One of the Invisible* (1992). The book collects numerous short pieces on a variety of subjects, but it is held together by stories that recall Rattray's friendship with Alden Van Buskirk, "or Van for short."[46] Buskirk and Rattray became close friends in their early twenties and undertook some Beat-inspired travels before Buskirk died from a rare form of kidney disease in 1961, aged twenty-three.[47] His illness became frighteningly apparent during his travels with Rattray, after which Buskirk was eventually hospitalized in Oakland. A mutual friend wrote to Rattray, now elsewhere, that there would have been no point in his coming to Oakland to visit Buskirk. Rattray's immediate response: "I took peyote and had a vision of Van with tubes in him on

Editing and Eros

a hospital bed, yet somehow also outside time in a heightened, eternal here-and-now state that the peyote made me feel was one in which everything in the universe past, present, and future is alive and simultaneous. From the experience I made a poem and sent it to Van. It now seemed to me that every word we exchanged had a special weight, and the power to cross immeasurable distance."[48] Affection and correspondence once again merge, with Rattray developing an acute sense that correspondence might hold the possibility of crossing "immeasurable distance." Correspondence is in fact the form their love takes at this late stage in Buskirk's illness. He and Rattray continue to exchange postcards from coast to coast. Buskirk then plans to travel back to the East Coast on December 18. But, as Rattray reports, "on the morning of December 11th, my sister knocked at the door where I was staying to tell me someone had phoned with the news that Van had died the night before" (28).

Like Mueller's Native Agents book, Rattray's is attentive to friends who went before him and to the ways that art, affection, and affiliation work hand in hand. Mueller's book ends with a "last letter," and Rattray's begins with stories of lost poets and friends: the first recounts Rattray's tragic encounter with the poet Stephen Jonas (1921–1970), whose struggles with mental health form the story's tragic end; its second is the tale of "Van." We have to look elsewhere, however, for Buskirk's own last letter. After Buskirk's death in December 1961, Rattray edited and published a collection of his poems under the title *Lami* (1965). The first poem, "Oakland 1961," offers an uncanny and anticipatory echo of Kraus's reading of Moyra Davey's work. Setting the tone for the volume, the poem begins

> in another mental universe whose
> associations orbit outward into infinite
> theory while bodies
> decay in Oakland furnished rooms[49]

In four lines, Buskirk outlines some of the interests that coalesce in the Native Agents series, above all the relation between associative theory

156   Editing and Eros

and the particularity of experience. Here, Buskirk's body decays while
his mind and writing orbit outward. The last entry in *Lami* is a letter
Buskirk wrote in November 1961, shortly before his death. It is a last
letter of sorts, which Buskirk called an "open letter to all former contacts (i.e. loves) sech [*sic*] as you, Dave" (87). Buskirk's letter orbits outward to "Dave," who includes it as the concluding entry in *Lami*. The
letter, however, is not conclusive. Rattray's story "Van" forms a response
to this friend who can no longer answer, but to whom Rattray nevertheless writes. Buskirk's last letter is a love letter, and "Van" is a loving
letter addressed, in return, to a friend.

By tracking the connections that structure Kraus's writing as well as
the writing she publishes in her Native Agents series, I have tried to
show how Kraus and her correspondents develop a theory of affective
sphere formation that takes shape through looping and loving affiliation. Reflecting on the formation of Native Agents in 2014, Kraus
writes that "what seemed most important to me was not the fact of the
'I' but the way it moved through the text and the world. It was an active,
public 'I.' . . . I did not begin writing myself for another few years, but
I learned how to write largely by reading and editing the first Native
Agents books."[50] In Kraus's final sentence, her essayistic "I" loops back
to an earlier one: the one who wrote *I Love Dick* by reading and editing
the first Native Agents books, a loop even further back. It is easy to
characterize *I Love Dick* as the result of erotic obsession. Yet Kraus's
constant attentiveness to other artists—seen here in the credit she
gives to writers who went before her—reminds us that *I Love Dick*
issues from and addresses different kinds of loving affiliation: erotic,
certainly, but also love and empathy for her friends and fellow writers;
for lost friends; for artists that have been largely forgotten. *I Love Dick*
is a record of desire. The desire it records, however, is the desire that
operates in art and through its practices. The Native Agents series similarly records this desire. It shows how forms of art are bound up in
various love scenes that are also art scenes. While Kraus stresses her
interest in the way the I moves "through the text and the world," this
chapter has shown that it does not move alone. Its movement arcs

LAMI

THE LAST POEMS OF A POET
WHO DIED IN 1961 IN HIS EARLY 20s

BY

COLLECTED FROM HIS WRITINGS
BY DAVID RATTRAY

ALDEN

WITH AN INTRODUCTION
BY ALLEN GINSBERG

VAN

THE AUERHAHN SOCIETY
SAN FRANCISCO : 1965

BUSKIRK

Cover of *Lami* (Auerhahn Society, 1965) by Alden Van Buskirk, edited by
David Rattray and published after Buskirk's death in 1961. Courtesy of
EclipseArchive.org.

158   Editing and Eros

toward the formation of spheres. And, most often for Kraus and her Native Agents, it is traveling via love toward friends.

In the Event, and After

In January 2016, New York University's Fales Library and Special Collections announced the acquisition of Chris Kraus's personal archive.[51] The news appeared nineteen years after the initial publication of *I Love Dick* and exactly twenty after a lesser-known event in Kraus's history: Chance, an "antiacademic theory-fest"[52] that she organized in 1995–96. When I set out to revise this chapter in light of reader reports in early 2020, the coronavirus pandemic made it impossible for me to travel to NYU to visit Kraus's now-available papers. My subsequent search through the archive's finding aid and through Kraus's own itinerary for the past several years led me to a book based in part on materials in Kraus's archives and so allows me access to them at a remove. Becket Flannery's artist's book, *The Chance Event, wherein* . . . , draws on Kraus's archive at Fales Library to revisit the Chance Event and to dwell on the structures and media of chance in contemporary artistic practice.[53] Framed as an archival and essayistic investigation into an event that exists only partially in the material archive, the first half of Flannery's book combines four critical essays written by himself and three "archival texts": the manuscript for Jean Baudrillard's keynote; an essay written by Kraus eight years after the event and revised for Flannery's book; and a recollection written by the poet and Chance participant Luis Bauz specifically for Flannery's book. As Flannery notes in his prologue, "Bauz's piece is written like a flowing archive of affects and impressions, and as such we have presented it as another kind of documentation."[54] Most of the second half of *The Chance Event, wherein* . . . comprises around seventy photographs of the event from both the NYU archive and the personal collections of the event photographers, Reynaldo Rivera and Julia Scher; twenty film stills from video taken at the event; and finally, a two-page spread of the Chance Event's advertising poster with art by Mike Kelley and designed by Mark Stritzel.

The structure of Flannery's book at first suggests a kind of accounting in reverse. The promotion poster ends the book while a prologue

Editing and Eros 159

titled "Tape Delay" introduces it with an acknowledged sense of belatedness joined with nostalgia. Flannery's careful structuring of the work, however, is designed less to submit to teleology than to challenge it through the forms of affective looping I have been exploring in Kraus's own written and editorial work. His description and loose classification of Bauz's contribution as a "flowing archive of affects and impressions" that forms "another kind of documentation" insists on the essay's significance as an affective, archival form in itself. That is, Bauz's essay, unlike Flannery's brilliant and somewhat more distanced critical interventions, accesses an affective archive that remains elsewhere than the Fales Library at NYU or even the personal archives of the photographers Rivera and Scher.[55] Acknowledging this elsewhere archive in the scope of his own project—indeed even as the most provocative and productive locus of his project—Flannery writes, "Chance was videotaped, photographed, and reviewed, but almost all of this material ended up exclusively in physical archives. Outside of these repositories, there is only the retelling, which turns up now and again."[56] Retelling is a circling back. In Flannery's own words, the essays in the book "are not interpretations of the event, but, rather, alternative tours through experiences and histories that still seem sensitive" (9). Aligning with Kraus's own written and editorial work as forms of assembling fragile collectives, *The Chance Event, wherein* . . . remains sensitive to lived experiences by keeping the archival artist's book open to the affective reverberations rippling out from the event itself.

To keep his book open to affective aspects of the Chance Event is, for Flannery as for Kraus when she organized the event, to acknowledge the structural and human dimensions of what might otherwise be the cold logic of chance. Chance is shot through with risk and opportunity, and these are unequally distributed. Flannery begins this discussion with a quick example from Chance itself: "Doug Hepworth, a Wall Street trader versed in chaos theory, offered advice to aspiring gamblers at Chance: bet everything on the first roll, because the odds eventually average out in the house's favor" (39). This observation initiates one of the most profound and indeed affecting discussions in Flannery's book, where "the house" of Hepworth's example—drawing

160 Editing and Eros

on the event's location at a casino just on the Nevada side of the California–Nevada border—quickly morphs into broader structures of power that not only tilt the balance in the house's favor but also expose others to greater risks of harm in the process. "For Kraus," Flannery writes, "chance is not a neutral framework of random occurrences, but inflected by discrepancies of power" (42). Kraus sought to embed some of these discrepancies in Chance's programming, inviting Calvin Meyers, for instance, "an advocate for the Moapa Band of Paiute Indians," to speak on ecology and tribal rights and to lead an early morning walking tour.[57] While Baudrillard was the keynote speaker in part because of the way his famous formation of the "desert of the real" resonated with the physical geography of Primm, Nevada, and the irreality of the casino, "Calvin Meyers would describe an alternate view of the terrain: at this site of Baudrillardian emptiness, Meyers saw a sacred land of rock formations, animals, and tribal history."[58] In Meyers's own words responding to both the Chance Event and the then-proposed Yucca Mountain nuclear waste repository finally scrapped by the Obama administration in 2011, "It's easy for Las Vegas to say okay to nuclear waste, Las Vegas can move. But my people can't move, this is our home . . . I've got a driver's license, but I won't renew it. I'm not going anywhere."[59] It was not chance that led to a nuclear waste repository being proposed for this region. Nor was it chance that Kraus invited Meyers to the Chance Event. She knows—and Flannery recovers it beautifully—that the deck is often stacked against those with the most to lose. To engage with chance is also to engage with structural inequalities and violence and with the stories of those who experience it most acutely.

The unequal distribution of risk and harm roils beneath many Native Agents books. If we think back to Cookie Mueller's vivid story about life in Haight-Ashbury in the mid-1960s, the sequence of chance events leads to a quickly passed over but horrific rape at gunpoint before Mueller ends up in her home, held in the collective embrace of her friends as they speak about Atlantis and Mu.[60] A Native Agents book from later in Kraus's sole editorship of the series, Shulamith Firestone's *Airless Spaces* (1998), narrates stories of women on the edge of

Editing and Eros 161

poverty, with mental institutions always looming, doors gaping, behind them. As Eileen Myles writes in their blurb for Firestone's book, "In the century I'm most familiar with, the 20th, the explosion was never-ending, the pieces tinier and tinier. Shulamith Firestone, in her radical insider's tale, informs us repeatedly . . . that all of us are vanishing in a century of institutions that take and take until everyone has gone away and there's no one left to shut the door."[61] Myles speaks here of the extensive violences of the twentieth century, the latter half of which Kraus and a handful of writers document in the Native Agents series. The explosion is ongoing and the doors wide open. In the "structured precariousness of American life," Flannery writes, "the odds are not impersonal, and we put ourselves at stake."[62]

When Chris addresses David Rattray in the early pages of *I Love Dick,* she feels Rattray's ghost encouraging her to understand "how the loved person can become a holding pattern for all the tattered ends of memory, experience and thought you've ever had."[63] The Native Agents series serves a similar purpose. It is a holding pattern and a space of affectionate embrace. It is an act of solidarity and the formation of a sphere—of spheres. These fragile spheres cannot shore up completely against the depredations of twentieth- and twenty-first-century life. Nor should they renew a culture of redemption. They nevertheless offer some respite—some space for rage and resilience—from the experienced discrepancies of power across academia, publishing, the arts, and beyond. They are forms and records of desire just as certainly as their continued emergence is an affirmation of desire's changing destinations.

CODA

Editing and *Entropy*

The Editor Function has explored various iterations of Peter Gizzi's proposition that "editing, like writing, is fundamentally about composing a world."[1] At times, the world takes shape as an ensemble from which Hambone emerges and to which he takes flight once again. Other times, it forms as a coterie of lovers and friends as with Chris Kraus's editorship of the Native Agents series. Charles Olson's conception of editing addresses the world-composing function of editorial labor most directly. Although we know that Olson never edited much himself, at least not formally, he nevertheless wrote voluminously to his editors and conceptualized editing as a burst of energy that establishes print–poetic dwellings in the shape of literary journals and little magazines. Call it hubris, call it machismo, or call it faith in the world-building *poiesis* in editorial practice: Olson firmly believed that new collectives, new political formations, and even new worlds (of letters) could be formed by way of the editor function. Jump ahead sixty-three years to 2014, the year that writers and editors Janice Lee and Peter Tieryas Liu establish *Entropy*, an online magazine and community space for the arts. Academia has gone through its postwar boom; the program era has been firmly instituted; the canon wars from decades earlier reverberate into the present. More discussed and disruptive still: we are six years after the 2008 recession and the contraction of the market for stable academic employment continues to intensify; people with MFAs

163

164 Coda

or PhDs—or both—vastly outnumber the jobs advertised on the MLA job list; precarity is the condition under which much academic and para-academic labor is done; and it is the condition that makes nearly all academic labor possible, with those few available tenure-track and research-focused jobs often dependent on contingent labor to keep teaching loads down while appeasing management's imposed budgetary constraints.

I end this book with a brief coda on Janice Lee and *Entropy* because *Entropy*'s organizational structure is shaped by and responds to the working conditions of many writers, critics, editors, and publishers at work—and out of it—today. Like other popular humanities and arts sites such as *Los Angeles Review of Books* (2012–), *Public Books* (2012–), and *Literary Hub* (2015–), along with smaller and more academic-facing online publications such as *sx salon* (2010–), *Post45 Contemporaries* (2011–), and *ASAP/J* (2017–), *Entropy* emerged amid the fallout of the 2008 recession and the intensified implosion of the academic job market in the United States.[2] I take this context and *Entropy*'s specific response to it as a means for reflecting on the conditions of editorial practice at present, when editing can at once provide a way out of precarity—in the form of greater visibility, networking potential, professional experience for the CV, and the general accrual of cultural capital—and a greater entanglement with it. Much editorial labor, including that of Lee and countless others, is uncompensated in terms of actual pay or even institutional acknowledgment. Instead of conceptualizing editing in such instrumental terms, however, Lee makes it a means of continually addressing a question that informs all of her creative practice: "how do we hold space open while maintaining intimacy?"[3] By examining the editorial formation of *Entropy* alongside Lee's writing on the filmic long takes of the Hungarian filmmaker Béla Tarr, this coda proposes that Lee and her collaborators develop a corresponding editorial long take directed toward openness and intimacy. Such openness and intimacy attend to the working conditions of many editors, academics, writers, and artists today, creating spaces of camaraderie and care in an increasingly precarious present.

Lee's editorship of *Entropy* is also a suitable endpoint for this book in the way that it shadows the book's starting point: Charles Olson's conception of editing and the open field in the immediate postwar period, especially in his letters to the editor of *Origin* that I examined in chapter 1. As their names hint at, *Origin* and *Entropy* respond to two distinct moments of institutional uncertainty: the early boom just prior to the consolidation of "the program era," when starting something new in an institution was on the cusp of being possible;[4] and the post-2008 recession and its shrinking academic job market when entropy, or, "broadly: the degree of disorder or uncertainty in a system,"[5] continues to increase. And each journal adopts metaphors of *energy* and *force* in order to reflect on the conditions of editorial practice and intellectual labor in their time.[6] In a particularly compelling letter to the young Cid Corman, who edited *Origin* from the 1950s to the 1980s, Olson urges Corman to see editorial work and the volumes it puts forth as a method for collective expression and a measure of creative force:

> that THE DEMAND
> ON YOU, CID CORMAN, is, to accomplish each issue—to see it, always
> clearly, exhaustively, as—A
>
> FIELD OF FORCE
>
> that is, that, as agent of this collective (which ORIGIN is going to be) the
> question is larger than, yr taste, alone: it has the same sort of
> confrontation as—in any given poem—a man faces: how much energy
> has he got in, to make the thing stand on its own feet as, a force, in, the
> fields of force which surround everyone of us, of which we, too, are
> forces: to stand FORTH
>
> This is getting to sound altogether too much like a P[rojective] V[erse]
> thing![7]

Individualist and masculine ideologies of labor still haunt Olson's statement, with Olson using a variation of the "pull oneself up by one's bootstraps" metaphor to propose that intellectual labor results in a journal or a poem "stand[ing] on its own feet." Yet Olson also conceptualizes

166   Coda

editing as a creative and collaborative force that could be the basis for establishing new collectives. The literary journal must provide a record of human energy and intellectual labor across a broad field, and this human energy must be the advanced guard of a new postwar poetics and a renewed politics of collectivity. In this reading, Corman the editor becomes a bonding "agent of this collective (which ORIGIN is going to be)."

The critic Robert von Hallberg has noted how Olson brought the energy he had for bureaucratic organization in the Office of War Information to bear on his postwar poetic project.[8] I want to redirect that observation here to suggest that the "force" Olson names in his letter to Corman is directed in part toward the labor of institution building, whereby the work that gives rise to a journal foretells how intellectual labor can create new institutions.[9] While Olson's letter to Corman emerges from the institutional uncertainty of the immediate postwar period, when most writers were not yet part of the program era,[10] the letter itself nevertheless imagines a future in which such uncertainty could be overcome through the organizational efforts of editors and other cultural workers. There is a utopian dimension to Olson's conception of editing as an expression of world-composing energy. Hallberg would ascribe this to Olson's "New Dealer" mentality. Such a utopian dimension remained available to Olson in the postwar and indeed post–New Deal environment in which he worked. Editorial and intellectual labor could still make things cohere. They could still form the foundations for building.

Over sixty years later that utopian drive still operates in many editorial projects, but some take a slant approach to it in order to acknowledge the increasingly difficult and uncompensated conditions under which much intellectual work takes place. When Janice Lee and Peter Tieryas Liu launched *Entropy* in 2014, they included an "About" page that resonates unexpectedly with Olson's theory of the little magazine as an energy force. Instead of the more typical editorial statement about editorial vision, Lee and Tieryas Liu begin their "About" page with two entries on entropy. The first comes from an early Thomas Pynchon story titled "Entropy" (1960); the second from a Wikipedia entry on entropy. The Pynchon quote, as rendered on the *Entropy* "About" page, reads as follows:

> [H]e found in entropy or the measure of disorganization for a closed system an adequate metaphor to apply to certain phenomena in his own world . . . and in American "consumerism" [he] saw a similar tendency from the least to the most probable, from differentiation to sameness, from ordered individuality to a kind of chaos. He found himself, in short, restating Gibb's prediction in social terms, and envisioned a heat death for his culture in which ideas, like heat energy, would no longer be transferred, since each point in it would ultimately have the same quantity of energy; and intellectual motion would, accordingly, cease. ("Entropy," by Thomas Pynchon)[11]

Unlike Olson's editorial force in a dynamic field of forces, Pynchon's metaphorical use of entropy sees consumerist-driven entropic disorder eventually resulting in a state where the exchange of ideas becomes meaningless. Each idea holds the same amount of intellectual energy and therefore ceases to transfer energy at all.

By placing this quotation at the top of their "About" page, Lee and Tieryas Liu refuse to fall back on the generic formula of editorial statements, whereby this or that journal will address this or that gap in the literary field as it exists. *Entropy* is more anarchic in its interests and less assured in cultural work's ability to effect change, or, looking back to Olson, to build institutional or organizational foundations for a utopian future. Consider, for instance, that the second quote introducing *Entropy*'s "About" page is a definition drawn from Wikipedia, famed for the collective labor that compiles it. The inclusion of a (now unavailable) Wikipedia definition of entropy instead of one from a formally sanctioned and published encyclopedia or dictionary extends Lee's and Tieryas Liu's investigation into editing and entropy, this time more subtly linking them to intellectual labor. Wikipedia, after all, operates on the abrogation of the editor function in the older gatekeeping sense. It still employs measures to ensure the accuracy of published information, but in theory at least, everyone can be a Wikipedia editor.[12] But we

168 Coda

are beyond thinking of Wikipedia as an instrument of cultural revolution, aren't we?[13]

What are we to make of the quotations that introduce *Entropy's* "About" page? Do they signal a theory of cultural production at odds with Olson's productive forces? And to the point of this book and this coda, do they suggest an organizational model in which *Entropy* refuses to retell a narrative of cultural redemption—a utopian strand central to so many editorial projects including Olson's—in favor of the more modest intention of simply existing? I explore these questions and others in the remainder of this coda by discussing Lee's editorial work in relation to her writing. Specifically, I examine her engagement with the work of Hungarian filmmaker Béla Tarr, whose films have helped Lee to develop a critical vocabulary for examining her editorship and the precarious conditions from which *Entropy,* as a collection of writing from increasingly un- or underemployed writers, artists, and academics, emerges.

Janice Lee is a self-described "Korean-American writer, editor, publisher, and shamanic healer."[14] She has published five books since 2010, with a sixth on the horizon.[15] During this time she also cofounded *Entropy* and began editing a book series called #RECURRENT with the publisher Civil Coping Mechanisms. Her several authored works have covered a range of styles—from experimental sci-fi in her debut book *Kērotakis* (2010) to the moving and brief essayistic work reflecting on her mother's death, *Reconsolidation: Or, It's the Ghosts Who Will Answer You* (2015). Most recently Lee has published a book of travel essays, many of which were originally published on *Entropy,* titled *The Sky Isn't Blue: The Poetics of Spaces* (2016). In her biographical description of herself, Lee says that her writing continually addresses a single question: "how do we hold space open while maintaining intimacy?"[16] Yet the title of her #RECURRENT book series and the editorial organization of *Entropy,* which publishes voluminously by way of its roughly sixty editors with full access and publishing rights for the website,[17] attest to the way that this question embeds itself in Lee's creative and collective practices more broadly. Her writing, editing, and publishing demonstrate how openness and intimacy often coalesce in creative acts of collaboration and extended duration.

Lee's interest in the filmmaking techniques of Béla Tarr takes on new significance in this context. In a coauthored essay titled "Apocalypse Withheld: On Slowness and the Long Take in Bela Tarr's *Sátántangó,*" Lee and Jared Woodland ask whether Tarr's use of the filmic long take results in "our inability to make meaning from our own stare[.] Or does the long take's patience imply humanity and empathy?"[18] Lee and Woodland affirm both, proposing that Tarr's technique allows for a state to emerge in which "depression becomes the norm becomes the apocalypse becomes the present moment becomes the hope of life. Slowness becomes indifference becomes generosity becomes utterly human." The viewer's inability to make meaning from their stare in fact allows them to dwell in an empathic temporality in which "depression" can become "the hope of life."

Around a year before Lee established *Entropy* and then collaborated with Woodland on slowness and the long take in *Sátántangó,* she had published a book whose title she took from another of Tarr's films: *Damnation* (2013; film 1988). *Damnation* is an ekphrastic engagement with Tarr's films—primarily *Damnation* and *Sátántangó*—that finds Lee developing textual strategies for dwelling in the films' durational modes. She describes Tarr's films at length and sometimes even transcribes the English subtitles. She also sketches scenes from the films, creating spare, after-the-fact storyboards of sorts. These descriptive, transcriptive, and visual practices anticipate Lutz Koepnick's reading of Tarr's films, where

> the ruthless duration of each and every shot eventually wears down any desire for interpretation, leaving both Tarr's protagonists and his viewers in a void in which words, concepts, metaphors, and interpretations, let alone metaphysical speculation, ring utterly hollow . . . the disenchanting logic of modern time leaves no room for transcendental thought or grandiose philosophies of meaning making.[19]

Koepnick's analysis echoes common critical refrains about Tarr's films: its duration eschews transcendence; its time is unredeemed by hermeneutic interpretation.[20] And yet Lee's *Damnation* is a record of countless

Janice Lee, scene-by-scene sketches of *Damnation* (1988), directed by Béla Tarr. Copyright and courtesy of Janice Lee and Penny-Ante Editions.

Coda   171

hours using words and images to articulate a relation with Tarr's films. It does not seek to provide a hermeneutically coherent reading of them, even as its descriptions, transcriptions, and sketches dwell on and in a relation to duration.

Established a year after *Damnation*'s publication, *Entropy* is the editorial kin of Tarr's filmic long take. It asks how disorder works within the loose coherence that the naming and functioning of an arts magazine establishes. When I first conceptualized this coda, this observation was the end point of my analysis: that *Entropy*'s wonderful and accumulating disorder exposes in full the energetic chaos that the editor function puts into the world. *Entropy*'s dozens of editors, all available for pitches and submissions via email, continually add to a site whose title becomes increasingly apt and descriptive over time. In 2020, *Entropy* typically publishes one or more new pieces a day, and the variety of genres it publishes in addition to the volume of articles overcome my critical capacity to account for *Entropy* in any coherent way. Creative nonfiction meets with music reviews, book reviews, indie press profiles, a series on birds, short fiction, an incredibly ambitious set of daily news links collectively known as *Trumpwatch*, interviews with writers and artists, and more. Broadly, then, *Entropy* is a platform for the arts with an emphasis on writing, but not only that. It is messier and more open, operating at the extreme end of the editor function. It demands new modes of criticism—perhaps doubling as description—that can dwell, like Lee's *Damnation*, in the logic of the editorial long take.[21] The entropic disorder that emerges through the journal's openness to a remarkable variety of work takes precedence in *Entropy*'s editorial structure. *Entropy* does not fully cohere because it was never meant to. In 2015, for instance, *Entropy* initiated a nonfiction accolade called the Boltzmann Entropy Award. It is meant to celebrate "new voices that add to the brilliant entropy of literature and that 'neglect internal statistical correlations in the overall particle distribution' of the chaos in writing."[22] Chaos over correlation seems to be *Entropy*'s model, if one can model disorder, with *Entropy*'s loose coherence becoming a means for dwelling in disorder.

172   Coda

And yet—and this is where correlation in chaos is in fact a method of historical analysis—dwelling in disorder is not merely a conceptual or practical disposition. It is the lived reality of most writers and researchers working today, including many on the masthead for *Entropy*. Dwelling in disorder characterizes the dysfunction of higher education in relation to its teachers and researchers, whether they are still graduate researchers and teachers fighting uphill battles to unionize, or those among the legions of contingent staff. As I continued to think about *Entropy*, the increasingly desperate working conditions of close friends, fellow editors, and colleagues led me to ask whether *Entropy*'s large-scale abrogation of the gatekeeping function of editorship was not itself a response to contemporary working conditions. As of this writing in July 2020, *Entropy* lists twenty-two editors on its masthead, under nineteen unique subsections of editorial responsibility, and a further thirty-eight contributing editors.[23] It should come as no surprise that Google searches of these editors reveal that few have tenure-track academic work even though many hold MFAs and PhDs. Lee, who is one of the few on the tenure track, started her position several years after co-establishing *Entropy*, although she appears to have had relatively stable employment at CalArts before moving to Portland State. In a 2011 essay on editors and editing that I cited in the introduction, Roxane Gay writes that there are "Too Many of Us, [and] Too Much Noise." It appears likely that the trend Gay observes three years after the onset of the recession—that "increasingly, everyone wants to be an editor"[24]—is itself a response to the intensification of production and networking required to get a stable job as a teacher of creative writing or literary studies—or even just to stay in or proximate to these fields. Gay addresses this point in her provocative conclusion: "The good news . . . is that we (writers, readers, editors) love this literature thing so much, we'll endure the tightening in our chests as long as we can" (274).

Gay's sardonic conclusion returns us to the question of duration by way of endurance. In Lee and Woodland's essay on Tarr's *Sátántangó*, they quote Jacques Rancière writing of Tarr's long take:

Coda   173

> We cannot identify ourselves with [the characters'] feelings. But we enter into something more essential, into the very duration at the heart of which things penetrate and affect them, the suffering of repetition, the sense of another life, the dignity assumed in order to pursue the dream of this other life, and to bear the deception of this dream.[25]

This observation on Tarr's films takes on new dimensions if we read it in relation to the conditions of academic labor today and to the kinds of endurance and forbearance—and suffering—it demands from those who seek reasonable compensation for it. Rancière, however, introduces a distinction between identifying with feelings (empathy) and identifying with the experience of duration. Lee and *Entropy*'s editors seek to make this distinction porous via *Entropy*'s editorial long take. In an interview for the podcast *Lit Mag Love,* the host Rachel Thompson asks what Lee has learned from editing that "informs what [she's] doing in [her] own writing." Instead of addressing Thompson's question on its own terms, Lee immediately answers: "I've learned a lot of things but I think the thing that I think about the most, especially recently, is we have learned more about the capacities for intimacy through editing."[26] The editorial long take keeps space open and intimate, offering some relief to many whose task, today, is to endure.

Editing here becomes a political, durational, and empathetic act of paying heed to new, embattled, and underrepresented voices. "Writing and editing and publishing," Lee says,

> are also connected to reading and sharing and dialoguing and thinking together and all of this is about existing together as part of the larger community. And this larger community is where the work actually exists right? It doesn't exist in a vacuum and when we write our work at home, you know, that's sort of different than when the work is received out in the world. So this whole process just allows people I think to share what they see and to see what others see. And I think especially, especially right now I think this is also political act. Even if the work that's being shared isn't political just the fact that we're reading work by different people and encountering works that we wouldn't normally encounter in

174 Coda

our every day. So how different voices, [how] marginalized voices get to articulate their everyday reality and how all of these realities can, can sort of coexist.

Thompson responds, "Yeah I often feel like just the empathy built-in [*sic*] writing is a political act. Just being empathetic is politics." And then Lee: "Yeah totally! I mean just reading something by someone that you wouldn't normally read something by, you know, I mean just, just reading and just hearing that point of view I think is such a political act."

Such intimacy and empathy, however, are always under threat. The demands of simply keeping a job or paying the bills continually encroach on editorial practice, and Lee acknowledges that *Entropy*'s openness is limited by the time constraints of its various editors. In response to a question about editorial guidance and developmental editing at *Entropy*, Lee responds:

> For the most part, I think [editing] just has to do with practical concerns like time. And so since all of our editors are volunteers and they're also all working full-time jobs already or several part-time jobs or have families, this is like the extra thing that we're all doing just because we want to be doing it. But for the most part, most of the editors don't do work that requires any heavy developmental editing. Because we're trying to write it more like a community space and less like a magazine. Also, we tend to just trust in the work. And so if we like the work, we tend to ask for very few changes if any and usually that has to do with clarity or if there's any copyright issues or proofreading and so small things like that. For me, when submissions come to me, if it's going to require, you know, like more than 20 minutes of editing, I usually just say no and I'll just usually explain why. Just because I don't have the time to sit down and edit every piece that goes up. Because we're publishing so much.[27]

This passage shows the challenge Lee and *Entropy* face in their task to hold space open while maintaining intimacy. Looming over the task are the impositions of time and questions of endurance. How long can one voluntarily work under these conditions before it is no longer tenable? How long can one await a stable and reasonably compensated job in a university (or elsewhere) before it becomes impossible? Are intimacy and empathy enough to keep an editor going? Lee is still hopeful, noting the many writers and fellow editors that she has come to know through her editorial work, and the many new voices that shape her understanding of the literary encounter.[28] But under the current conditions of intellectual labor, *Entropy*, like so many other voluntarily run editorial formations, begins to look like a time-limited labor of endurance as much as an exploration of duration and intimacy.

Nevertheless, it is worth recalling precisely why Lee emphasizes intimacy and openness in her work. In their essay on Tarr's *Sátántangó*, Lee and Woodland draw on one other quote from Rancière in which he attempts to define "the time after"—the subtitle of his book—by way of the endless waiting that is central to Tarr's films and the long takes he employs:

> The time after is neither that of reason recovered, nor that of expected disaster. It is the time after all stories, the time when one takes direct interest in the sensible stuff in which these stories cleaved their shortcuts between projected and accomplished ends. It is not the time in which we craft beautiful phrases or shots to make up for the emptiness of all waiting. It is the time in which we take interest in the wait itself.[29]

The editor function that this book historicizes, describes, and theorizes has been and will be many things. I have discussed a handful of them in this book's preceding chapters. In the context of *Entropy*, the editor function is a mode of waiting. It is a practice not only of biding time, but of holding time open—through one's volunteered labor—so that others might bide theirs as well, perhaps even in good company. Janice Lee, to my knowledge, has never published any writing that engages polemically with precarity in academia.[30] However, by structuring *Entropy* as an editorial long take, Lee and *Entropy*'s editors seek to keep the publishing formation open as a space for intimate sharing, solidarity, and care.

176 Coda

In the face of increasing precarity, intimacy and empathy cannot compensate for job security or healthcare or physical safety.[31] I do not want to propose that they do or can. But as foundational components of community building, they have roles to play in advancing the action ultimately required to bring about institutional and structural change. Here, the utopian drive of the editor function kicks in again, looping us back to *Origin* but with different ends in mind. *Entropy* envisages composing another, better world (of letters), a world that emerges from what we do here, just now, and how we attend to others in that ongoing moment. It is a process of composition, and the proposal of a world, without guarantees. And yet, as *Entropy*'s archive of endurance and empathy makes clear, it is imperative to understand how this process can build solidarity within and against precarious time so that waiting could become waiting to act. Editors and editing, in their way, might yet serve this function.

Acknowledgments

This book is guided by the idea that creative and critical conversations—written, editorial, published, or otherwise—constitute their own modes of thought. It is with great pleasure and gratitude that I see this book emerge from such conversations. Lodged within each of the chapters and subsections are discussions I have had with friends, mentors, writers, audiences, colleagues, classmates, and indeed editors. Each has helped to give this book its form and to shape its methods. I remain grateful to all of them for their generosity.

A challenge this project has always faced is how to capture in writing the kinds of thoughtful energy and care that inhere in and derive from the process of exchanging ideas. I sense that challenge again in trying to describe Jonathan Eburne's dynamism and support as a mentor and friend. He has an uncanny way of turning his deep engagement with the constitutive processes of intellectual history into advice that appears intuitive. For me and no doubt many others, he has modeled the kind of vitality and kindness that can inhabit academic work. This book would not exist without his incredible support. Robert Caserio has supported and guided my thinking, research, and reading since my first days in his graduate seminar on World War II modernism, and his own writing on the concept of literary history has been deeply influential for some of my lines of argument in the preceding chapters. I still delight in our email exchanges discussing recent reading

178 Acknowledgments

and personal relocations. Ben Schreier's office door was always open (a practice he may sometimes have regretted given the frequency of disturbances) and our conversations brought new focus to many parts of this book. I hope my engagement with Brian Lennon's most recent book in chapter 1 speaks better than I can here to the influence he has had on my thinking on publishing and media history. Nergis Ertürk's guidance in anti-colonial theory and histories of philology continues to influence my thinking about the histories and politics of writing, editing, and publishing. Aldon Nielsen pointed me to Nathaniel Mackey's *Hambone* at just the right moment, starting a new education for me within the framework of a developing project. Many others, including Janet Lyon, Kevin Bell, Daniel Purdy, Matt Tierney, and Michael Bérubé, provided support and conversations that made my work here and elsewhere better. To acknowledge one earlier mentor, Rebecca Walkowitz's remarkable teaching and advising introduced me to some of the texts and research methods that I continue to draw on to this day.

I was fortunate to receive institutional forms of support while beginning this project. The Waddell Biggart Graduate Fellowship in 2011–12 provided me research and reading time in the very earliest stages. Penn State's Center for American Literary Studies provided financial support for my first archival visit to the Dalkey Archive Press papers at Stanford in 2012. Their continued support allowed me to attend the Futures of American Studies Institute at Dartmouth College in 2013. Penn State's Institute for Arts and Humanities' Summer Residency in 2014 enabled me to read Nathaniel Mackey, Fred Moten, and every issue of *Hambone* over the course of a transformative summer; this research underwrites the reading of Mackey's editorship in chapter 3. The Center for American Literary Studies further supported this work with funding for a trip to Mackey's archives at Emory University in 2014. My thanks to Sean Goudie (CALS), Michael Bérubé (IAH), and all others who made this research possible. Columbia University Libraries awarded me an archival research fellowship to examine materials in the Dalkey Archive Press and Amiri Baraka papers in 2016, research that has influenced the Introduction and two chapters of this book. The Center for Humanities and Information at Penn State

Acknowledgments   179

awarded me a predoctoral fellowship from 2015 to 2016, which allowed me to spend substantially more time on the dissertation that became this book than I otherwise could have. My thanks to Eric Hayot, the staff of the CHI, and the other CHI fellows for providing a dynamic forum for listening to and presenting new work. My thanks also to John O'Brien of Dalkey Archive Press, who offered me an editorial fellowship at the press just as I was completing my dissertation. My time working for the press was invaluable and provides the basis for the final section of my chapter on Dalkey Archive. Finally, thanks to the College of Humanities at the University of Exeter, which has provided financial assistance in the final stages of manuscript preparation.

The University of Minnesota Press, itself an institution founded on a tremendous amount of careful editorial work, has consistently published works that expand my own thinking on media history, poetics, and publishing. My thanks to Doug Armato and Zenyse Miller for taking this book on and seeing it to its best completion. Thanks, too, to two insightful readers whose generous engagement with my manuscript improved every part of *The Editor Function*.

Starting any job in the current academic job market still feels like a stroke of pure luck. Starting a job with brilliant colleagues who are committed to organizing, protesting, striking, and picketing against the working conditions of most has transformed my relation to this profession in profound ways, and these inform the direction this book's Coda takes. Much gratitude and solidarity for and with them. Some of these same colleagues have also offered valued feedback on parts of this book. Special thanks to Beci Carver, Rob Turner, and Paul Williams.

This is a first book and many of its ideas developed in conversations with friends in graduate school—or conversely were improved by abandoning them for a while over a drink at Zeno's or walking the ridges of central Pennsylvania. Robert Birdwell, Ting Chang, Michelle Huang, Jake Hughes, Kris Lotier, Adam Lupo, Bethany and Ethan Mannon, Ryan Marks, Frank Minneci, Phil Ortmann, Matt Price, Nate Redman, Sarah Salter, Erica Stevens, Josh Tendler, Eric Vallee, Matt Weber, Susan Weeber, Paul Zajac, and of course the annual English Graduate Organization softball squad, EGOMANIAX, thank you for everything. Kim

Andrews offered excellent feedback on late drafts of the Introduction and chapter 3 and each is immensely improved because of it. Jason Maxwell's friendship from day one of graduate school made my life in State College, and this work, better. Bob Volpicelli continually inspired me to do my best work and still does.

My parents, Jerry and Kris Foley, never pushed and always supported. My sometimes roundabout journey through education would have been impossible without this love and encouragement. Finally, whether in Berlin or London or State College, Buffalo, Hamburg, Bristol, Exeter, and now Cologne, sharing this life (and currently a small kitchen table as a desk) with Alice Mitchell has been a source of constant joy and laughter. I dedicate this book to her.

Notes

Introduction

1. Peter Gizzi, "On the Conjunction of Editing and Composition," in *Paper Dreams: Writers and Editors on the American Literary Magazine*, ed. Travis Kurowski (Madison, N.J.: Atticus Books, 2013), 231.

2. For studies that examine the incorporating narrative of the creative economy and consensus politics, see Sarah Brouillette, *Literature and the Creative Economy* (Stanford, Calif.: Stanford University Press, 2014); and Loren Glass, *Counterculture Colophon: Grove Press, the* Evergreen Review, *and the Incorporation of the Avant-Garde* (Stanford, Calif.: Stanford University Press, 2013).

3. For the history of the consolidation of the U.S. publishing industry, see Dan N. Sinykin, "The Conglomerate Era: Publishing, Authorship, and Literary Form, 1965–2007," *Contemporary Literature* 58, no 4 (Winter 2017): 462–91. In using the term "literary field," I follow John B. Thompson's definition, reworked from the sociological criticism of Pierre Bourdieu: "A field is a structured space of social positions which can be occupied by agents and organizations, and in which the position of any agent or organization depends on the type and quantity of resources or 'capital' they have at their disposal." John B. Thompson, *Merchants of Culture: The Publishing Business in the Twenty-First Century* (Cambridge, UK: Polity, 2010), 3–4.

4. The index for Peter Ginna's edited volume, *What Editors Do: The Art, Craft, and Business of Book Editing* (Chicago: University of Chicago Press, 2017), shows that the subject of "editors as gatekeepers" appears in numerous contributions to the volume, specifically on pages 17, 30, 71, 188, 228–29, and 266–67.

5. In *Does Writing Have a Future?*, Vilém Flusser writes that "the transmitter stands not outside but in the center of any text. Since the invention of the

Notes to Introduction

book press, the transmitter has usually been the publisher. A publisher is a grid in the stream of texts whose duty is to block most texts from getting into print. The vast swell of printed texts in which we currently swim is just the tip of an iceberg of texts that did not succeed in passing through the grid." Vilém Flusser, "Texts," in *Does Writing Have a Future?*, trans. Nancy Ann Roth, Electronic Mediations, vol. 33 (Minneapolis: University of Minnesota Press, 2011), 40.

6. Richard Kostelanetz, "Why *Assembling?*," in *Paper Dreams: Writers and Editors on the American Literary Magazine,* ed. Travis Kurowski (Madison, N.J.: Atticus Books, 2013), 220–21.

7. See Max Horkheimer and Theodor W. Adorno, *Dialectic of Enlightenment,* trans. John Cumming (New York: Continuum, 2002), 120–67.

8. Richard Kostelanetz, "Anarchism," RichardKostelanetz.com, last modified July 28, 2014, http://www.richardkostelanetz.com/examples/book-of-kostis/anarchism.html.

9. Nicholas Thoburn, *Anti-Book: On the Art and Politics of Radical Publishing* (Minneapolis: University of Minnesota Press, 2016), 14.

10. Richard Kostelanetz, email to author, August 14, 2020.

11. Kostelanetz, "Why *Assembling*," 220.

12. Kostelanetz, 223. For a book-length study of the "anti-book" and leftist politics, see Thoburn, *Anti-Book.*

13. Michel Foucault, "What Is an Author?," in *The Foucault Reader,* ed. Paul Rabinow, trans. Josué V. Harari (New York: Pantheon Books, 1984), 119.

14. Roxane Gay, "Too Many of Us, Too Much Noise," in *Paper Dreams: Writers and Editors on the American Literary Magazine,* ed. Travis Kurowski (Madison, N.J.: Atticus Books, 2013), 276. Gay was founding coeditor with M. Bartley Seigel of *PANK Magazine* (2006–15).

15. Gizzi, "On the Conjunction of Editing," 231.

16. Nathaniel Mackey, "Editing *Hambone*," in *Paracritical Hinge: Essays, Talks, Notes, Interviews* (Madison: University of Wisconsin Press, 2005), 246.

17. Maurice Blanchot, *The Unavowable Community,* trans. Pierre Joris (Barrytown, N.Y.: Station Hill Press, 1988), 56.

18. I am indebted here to Jonathan P. Eburne's *Outsider Theory: Intellectual Histories of Unorthodox Ideas* (Minneapolis: University of Minnesota Press, 2018), particularly the introduction (see, e.g., p. 1).

19. Nathaniel Mackey to Robert Kelly, February 27, 1980, box 78, folder 3, Kelly (Robert) Collection, Poetry Collection, State University of New York at Buffalo.

20. For studies on these three contexts in which the editor function develops, see Sinykin, "Conglomerate Era"; Mark McGurl, *The Program Era: Postwar Fiction and the Rise of Creative Writing* (Cambridge, Mass.: Harvard University

Notes to Introduction   183

Press, 2009); and Sarah Brouillette, *Literature and the Creative Economy* (Stanford, Calif.: Stanford University Press, 2014). For a fascinating study of the publishing industry just before the onset of rampant conglomeration, see Evan Brier, *A Novel Marketplace: Mass Culture, the Book Trade, and Postwar American Fiction* (Philadelphia: University of Pennsylvania Press, 2010).

21. Until the past several years, some of the most well-developed scholarship to date on print culture and book history in American literary culture since 1945 had emerged from the study of Cold War cultural politics. For a wide-ranging overview of print culture and the Cold War, see Greg Barnhisel and Catherine Turner, eds., *Pressing the Fight: Print, Propaganda, and the Cold War* (Amherst: University of Massachusetts Press, 2010); for more focused considerations of print culture and cultural diplomacy, see Greg Barnhisel, *Cold War Modernists: Art, Literature, and American Cultural Diplomacy* (New York: Columbia University Press, 2015). For a reading of Cold War literary politics that reverberate into the twenty-first century, see Juliana Spahr, *Du Bois's Telegram: Literary Resistance and State Containment* (Cambridge, Mass.: Harvard University Press, 2018). Recent exceptions to this broad observation show how quickly the critical field is turning its focus toward the practices and politics of postwar editing and publishing. See, for instance, Tim Groenland, *The Art of Editing: Raymond Carver and David Foster Wallace* (London: Bloomsbury, 2019); Amy Hungerford, *Making Literature Now* (Stanford, Calif.: Stanford University Press, 2016); Kinohi Nishikawa, *Street Players: Black Pulp Fiction and the Making of a Literary Underground* (Chicago: University of Chicago Press, 2018); Sophie Seita, *Provisional Avant-Gardes: Little Magazine Communities from Dada to Digital* (Stanford, Calif.: Stanford University Press, 2019); and Richard Jean So, *Redlining Culture: A Data History of Racial Inequality and Postwar Fiction* (New York: Columbia University Press, 2020). Dan Sinykin and Laura B. McGrath also have book projects on the horizon that will historicize the conglomeration of publishing from the 1960s to the present. Jordan S. Carroll, additionally, will soon publish a book looking at the relation between editing, publishing, and obscenity in the postwar United States. Finally, this observation applies to academic literary studies. Many non- and para-academic artists, writers, editors, and publishers have engaged with the book as a form. See, for instance, Jerome Rothenberg and Steve Clay, eds., *A Book of the Book: Some Work and Projections about the Book and Writing* (New York: Granary, 2000). Or, indeed, the oeuvre of Johanna Drucker.

22. Leah Price, "The Tangible Page," *London Review of Books*, October 31, 2002, https://www.lrb.co.uk/v24/n21/leah-price/the-tangible-page.

23. Roland Barthes, "The Death of the Author," in *The Rustle of Language*, trans. Richard Howard (Berkeley: University of California Press, 1989), 49–55. Roland Barthes, "From Work to Text," in *The Rustle of Language*, trans. Richard

184   Notes to Introduction

Howard (Berkeley: University of California Press, 1989), 56–64. Lawrence Buell, *The Dream of the Great American Novel* (Cambridge, Mass.: Harvard University Press, 2014); Kathleen Fitzpatrick, *The Anxiety of Obsolescence: The American Novel in the Age of Television* (Nashville: Vanderbilt University Press, 2006); Christopher Funkhouser, "Digital Poetry: A Look at Generative, Visual, and Interconnected Possibilities in Its First Four Decades," in *A Companion to Digital Literary Studies*, ed. Ray Siemens and Susan Schreibman (Chichester, UK: Wiley-Blackwell, 2013), 318–35.

24. As Robert Darnton has famously noted in "What Is the History of Books?," the book is just one part of a "communications circuit that runs from the author to the publisher (if the bookseller does not assume that role), the printer, the shipper, the bookseller, and the reader." Mark Vareschi also notes that Darnton expands his focus to paratextual and intertextual contexts in Darnton's later "'What Is the History of Books?,' Revisited" from 2007. See Robert Darnton, "What is the History of Books?," *Daedalus* 111, no. 3 (Summer 1982): 67; and Mark Vareschi, *Everywhere and Nowhere: Anonymity and Mediation in Eighteenth-Century Britain* (Minneapolis: University of Minnesota Press, 2018), 190.

25. In *What Editors Do*, Ginna remarks that the "author" and her "track record"—that is, past sales figures—are two primary acquisition criteria for corporate editors acquiring new books (22, 24).

26. Tom Perrin, *The Aesthetics of Middlebrow Fiction: Popular U.S. Novels, Modernism, and Form, 1945–1975* (New York: Palgrave Macmillan, 2015), 3, 120.

27. Buell, *Dream of the Great American Novel*. For a brief essay advocating for our contemporary abandonment of the term, see Lynne Tillman, "A Fictional Past: The Myth of the 'Great American Novel,'" *Frieze*, May 1, 2014, https://frieze.com/article/fictional-past.

28. Literary celebrity is not new to postwar America. For a reading of literary celebrity and authorial personae in the United States from 1880 to 1980, see Loren Glass, *Authors Inc.: Literary Celebrity in the Modern United States, 1880–1980* (New York: New York University Press, 2004). His chapter on Norman Mailer is particularly useful for thinking about macho strategizing and celebrity authorship after World War II.

29. Foucault, "What Is an Author?," 110, 118.

30. Stephen G. Nichols, "Introduction: Philology in a Manuscript Culture," in "The New Philology," ed. Stephen G. Nichols, special issue, *Speculum* 65, no. 1 (1990): 2–3.

31. For another reading of the movement from philology as a form of textual scholarship to philology as a variety of formalism, see Henry Veggian, "From Philology to Formalism: Edith Rickert, John Matthews Manly, and the Literary/Reformist Beginnings of U.S. Cryptology," *Reader: An Interdisciplinary*

Notes to Introduction

Journal 54 (Spring 2006): 67–89. Veggian shows that the transition to formalism takes place much earlier than Nichols suggests, for Veggian around 1920 when John Matthews Manly was editor of *Modern Philology* at the University of Chicago. In a 1978 defense of and paean to New Criticism—"The New Criticism: Pro and Contra," *Critical Inquiry* 4, no. 4 (Summer 1978)—René Wellek notes that "a purely philological and historical scholarship dominated all instruction, publication, and promotion" prior to the arrival of the New Critics, and that the New Critics cohered as a group insofar as they took this older philological and historical methodology as that from which they distinguished themselves (614). Finally, I do not want to suggest that Auerbach and Brooks share the same critical methods, and I think that both Wellek and Veggian make clear that philology and New Criticism must be distinguished from one another. I am dealing here instead with Nichols's characterization of Auerbach, which I am claiming is in fact a better characterization of Brooks and the New Critics' general turn away from the study of the materiality of the text.

32. Wellek, 611.

33. Charles Olson, "Projective Verse," in *Collected Prose*, ed. Donald Allen and Benjamin Friedlander (Berkeley: University of California Press, 1997), 239.

34. Charles Olson to Frances Boldereff, February 9, 1950, in *Charles Olson and Frances Boldereff: A Modern Correspondence*, ed. Ralph Maud and Sharon Thesen (Hanover, N.H.: Wesleyan University Press, 1999), 154.

35. Olson, "Projective Verse," 248.

36. Wellek identifies Eliot's *The Sacred Wood* (1920) as "decisive" in the development of the New Criticism. See Wellek, "New Criticism," 613.

37. I focus my analysis on print here because of my interest in editing and publishing. Recent critics such as Raphael Allison, Lytle Shaw, Seth Perlow, and Anthony Reed, among others, have shown how debates about textuality in postwar America included considerations of speaking, performance, audio recording, and electronic and digital media as well. See Raphael Allison, *Bodies on the Line: Performance and the Sixties Poetry Reading* (Iowa City: University of Iowa Press, 2014); Lytle Shaw, *Narrowcast: Poetry and Audio Research* (Stanford, Calif.: Stanford University Press, 2018); Seth Perlow, *The Poem Electric: Technology and the American Lyric* (Minneapolis: University of Minnesota Press, 2018); and Anthony Reed, *Soundworks: Race, Sound, and Poetry in Production* (Durham, N.C.: Duke University Press, 2021).

38. See Eva Diaz, *The Experimenters: Chance and Design at Black Mountain College* (Chicago: University of Chicago Press, 2014).

39. Amiri Baraka, *The Autobiography of LeRoi Jones* (New York: Freundlich Books, 1984), 171.

40. LeRoi Jones, "Hunting Is Not Those Heads on the Wall," in *Home: Social Essays* (New York: Morrow, 1966), 173, 175.

186   Notes to Introduction

41. For Amiri Baraka's account of his various editorial roles in the 1950s and 1960s, see *The Autobiography of LeRoi Jones,* esp. 124–201. It is important to note here, however, that Jones worked with or for women on all of these projects. In *Purple Passages: Pound, Eliot, Zukofsky, Olson, Creeley, and the Ends of Patriarchal Poetry* (Iowa City: University of Iowa Press, 2012), Rachel Blau DuPlessis remarks that the mechanisms that led to the male-dominated history of twentieth-century American poetry "emerge in apparently affiliative institutions of self- and cultural production, like editing, mentoring/protégé bonds, declaring allegiance and continuing allegiance (in manifestos and works), muse/user relations, and acts of leading, cooperating, grouping, and following" (5). We see those methods of affiliation in operation in some of the relationships I am describing here, even in a situation such as with *Kulchur,* where Lita Hornick tended to appoint male associate editors such as Jones and Gilbert Sorrentino, likely for their access to male-dominated coteries. As Diane di Prima puts it bluntly in *Recollections of My Life as a Woman* (New York: Viking, 2001), "though Roi and I coedited *Bear,* and often it was he who got the credit for the whole thing, most of the actual physical work devolved upon me and those friends I could dig up to help me. Most of the time. I am sure this was also true for Hettie, for the Totem Press books, in fact, before things got so sticky between us, I often helped her and witnessed how it was she who typed the camera copy, proofed (most of the time) and pasted up (always), but it was Roi's press, and in this he was not any different from any other male artist of his day. It was just the natural division of labor and credit" (253). While Jones receives critical recognition for his early editorial work, in part because of his subsequent renown and in part because it prepared him for the organizational work he went on to do with the Black Arts Movement, the fundamental roles Hettie (Cohen) Jones (Totem Press and *Yūgen*), Diane di Prima (*The Floating Bear*), and Lita Hornick (*Kulchur* / the Kulchur Foundation) played have been best addressed in their own memoirs. For more on the work Jones, di Prima, and Hornick did in the day-to-day editorship of the noted projects, see Hettie Jones, *How I Became Hettie Jones* (New York: E. P. Dutton, 1990); di Prima, *Recollections of My Life as a Woman*; and Lita Hornick, *The Green Fuse: A Memoir* (New York: Giorno Poetry Systems, 1989). All three memoirs look back to an earlier arts scene in New York. Chris Kraus, the subject of chapter 4, began her recovery work of women's experimental writing and literary networks with Native Agents in 1990 and can be seen to take up a task similar to these three memoirs, that is, the carework of recollection and recovery, but this time by way of editing after the fact. For a contemporary reflection on the gendered economy of editorial labor, see Sarah Blackwood, "Editing as Carework: The Gendered Labor of Public Intellectuals," *Avidly,* June 6, 2014, http://avidly.lare viewofbooks.org/2014/06/06/editing-as-carework-the-gendered-labor-of-pub lic-intellectuals/.

Notes to Introduction 187

42. Len Fulton, "Anima Rising: Little Magazines in the Sixties," in *Paper Dreams: Writers and Editors on the American Literary Magazine*, ed. Travis Kurowski (Madison, N.J.: Atticus Books), 176.

43. Di Prima, *Recollections of My Life*, 244.

44. Brian McHale, "1966 Nervous Breakdown; Or, When Did Postmodernism Begin?," *Modern Language Quarterly* 69, no. 3 (2008): 403.

45. Mark McGurl, *The Program Era: Postwar Fiction and the Rise of Creative Writing* (Cambridge, Mass.: Harvard University Press, 2009), 42.

46. John Barth, *Giles Goat-Boy* (New York: Doubleday, 1966), ix–xxxi.

47. Daniel Defoe, *Roxana* (Oxford, UK: Oxford University Press, 2008), 1–3; Jonathan Swift, *Gulliver's Travels* (New York: Penguin, 2003), 9–10.

48. Ronald Sukenick, "Author as Editor and Publisher," *New York Times Book Review*, September 15, 1974, 55.

49. Larry McCaffery, "The Fiction Collective, 1974–1978: An Innovative Alternative," *Chicago Review* 30, no. 2 (1978): 109. McCaffery notes the East Coast dominance; I am noting the homosocial network.

50. Brian McHale, review of *Narralogues: Truth in Fiction*, by Ronald Sukenick, *Poetics Today* 22, no. 3 (Fall 2001): 706.

51. To take note of just one metric, Duotrope reports the addition of anywhere from 1,473 (2017) to 2,760 (2018) "art markets" in each of the past five years for which they make data available. With "art markets," Duotrope refers primarily to literary journals (print and digital) and publishing houses that are active and accepting submissions from writers and artists. It does not report stats on how many art markets go inactive each year, but the total of active art markets as of June 26, 2019, is 7,223. See "Duotrope's State of the Stats," Duotrope, accessed June 26, 2019, https://duotrope.com/stats/stateofthestats.aspx.

52. "About Us," Make Now Books, accessed September 27, 2019, https://makenowbooks.com/about-us/.

53. *The Editor Function* proceeds in mind of the observation that literary criticism—especially of postwar literature—has not yet adequately studied the relation between literary practices and the texts and theories to which they give rise. There are exemplary exceptions, of course. Brian Lennon's *In Babel's Shadow: Multilingual Literatures, Monolingual States* (Minneapolis: University of Minnesota Press, 2010) is a deeply historical-theoretical study of the limits that a primarily monolingual publishing industry places on multilingual writers. Lennon explores the limiting functions that operate within the literary field by looking to the multilingualism of "immigrants, migrants, and exiles" whose language practices "can be neither represented nor expressed by the material apparatus of U.S. trade book publication and distribution—which marks, instead, the verge of what, in contemporary literature, it is possible to write and have read" (xiv).

188   Notes to Introduction

54. For a good overview of poetry's medial positionings in the twentieth and twenty-first century, see Thomas H. Ford, "Poetry's Media," *New Literary History* 44, no. 3 (Summer 2013): 449–69.

55. Charles Olson, *The Maximus Poems*, ed. George F. Butterick (Berkeley: University of California Press, 1983), I.17.

56. Nathaniel Mackey, "Destination Out," in *Paracritical Hinge: Essays, Talks, Notes, Interviews* (Madison: University of Wisconsin Press, 2005), 239.

57. Theodor Adorno, *Aesthetic Theory*, ed. and trans. Robert Hullot-Kentor (Minneapolis: University of Minnesota Press, 1997), 26.

58. Emphasis mine. Adorno's original reads as follows: "Zweite Reflexion ergreift die Verfahrungsweise, die Sprache des Kunstwerks im weitesten Verstand, aber sie zielt auf Blindheit." Theodor W. Adorno, *Äesthetische Theorie* (Frankfurt: Suhrkamp Verlag), 47. Adorno's choice of "Verfahrungsweise," translated as "technical procedures," is itself a look back to Friedrich Hölderlin, who wrote "Über die Verfahrungsweise des poetischen Geistes" (1800), which has been translated as "On the Operations of the Poetic Spirit." I make the connection here because "Verfahrungsweise" is an uncommon German word, and it is not to be found in many German dictionaries. The link is more apparent in the subject matter itself, as both Hölderlin and Adorno seek to conceptualize the processes or operative modes of poetic and artistic expression. Robert Hullot-Kentor's reason for adding "technical" to modify "procedures" remains unclear. Considered in light of McGurl's definition of *techne*, however, where it denotes both technology and craft, Hullot-Kentor's translation makes some sense, in that "Verfahrungsweise" is a term derived from historical poetics (Hölderin) but newly considered with regard to the technical and material procedures of artmaking.

59. Price, "Tangible Page."

60. Quoted in Peter D. McDonald, "Ideas of the Book and Histories of Literature: After Theory?," *PMLA* 121, no. 1 (January 2006): 222.

61. Price, "Tangible Page."

62. McDonald, "Ideas of the Book," 226.

63. Olson, "Projective Verse," 239.

64. The establishment of the flagship journal *Contemporary Literature* at the University of Wisconsin in 1960 is a bellwether of broader changes taking place in postwar English departments. See also Loren Glass's *Counterculture Colophon*, in which he discusses the shift toward studying contemporary writing in postwar English departments.

65. My use of "bassline" here is meant to refer to Mackey's introduction to his book, *Discrepant Engagement: Dissonance, Cross-Culturality, and Experimental Writing* (Tuscaloosa: University of Alabama Press, 1993), which Mackey titles "And All the Birds Sing Bass," itself a reference to a Bessie Smith lyric in the song "Black Mountain Blues."

Notes to Chapter 1

66. Henry James, *The Turn of the Screw*, ed. Deborah Esch and Jonathan Warren (New York: W. W. Norton, 1999), 3.

67. Peter Sloterdijk, *Spheres*, vol. 1, *Bubbles: Microspherology*, trans. Wieland Hoban (New York: Semiotext(e), 2011), 12.

68. As my chapters' focus on author–editors reveals, however, the author function has a long reach. Without access to archives (and even these are largely organized and acquired by author), the author function can be difficult to move beyond. Key sections of my chapter on Charles Olson, for instance, are based on letters that Olson wrote to the poet and editor Cid Corman. In its published form, *Letters for Origin, 1950–1956*, it is a one-way correspondence, with only Olson's letters reproduced, and this privileging of the author continues to affect how research takes shape. Tim Groenland's genealogical approach in *The Art of Editing* is an interesting counterpoint to my own methods but also needs to privilege the author to a degree, even if in an intense relationship with an editor; Sophie Seita's descriptive methods, adapted from book historians and textual scholars, in *Provisional Avant-Gardes* counters the author function exceptionally well but relies on terrific access to literary networks and archives and might not be easily reproducible for many scholars.

1. Editing and the Open Field

1. George F. Butterick, *A Guide to "The Maximus Poems" of Charles Olson* (Berkeley: University of California Press, 1978), 65.

2. Charles Olson, *The Maximus Poems*, ed. George F. Butterick (Berkeley: University of California Press, 1983), I.11.

3. It is common practice for Olson to use typography and punctuation in unorthodox ways that draw attention. Parentheses that open, as in the line just quoted, often do not close. Olson's estate has requested that we reproduce his typography and spacing as accurately as possible. I, with thanks to my meticulous copyeditor Nicholas Taylor, have taken care to honor this request.

4. Rachel Blau DuPlessis, "Olson and His *Maximus Poems*," in *Contemporary Olson*, ed. David Herd (Manchester, UK: Manchester University Press, 2015), 139. As Blau DuPlessis has shown in both in this essay and in her book, *Purple Passages: Pound, Eliot, Zukofsky, Olson, Creeley, and the Ends of Patriarchal Poetry* (Iowa City: University of Iowa Press, 2012), the "few" Olson sought out were almost entirely male.

5. It is worth noting here that while Olson wrote letters 5–7 as a response to the "Fall–Winter 1952–1953" issue of *4 Winds*, he did not ultimately send the letters to Ferrini, due to either technical difficulties or because Olson felt bad about his bullying of Ferrini in those letter–poems (see Butterick, *Guide*, 30). In a letter to Cid Corman from April 9, 1953, Olson remarks that he has been at work on "a run of 4 new Max's (provoked by Ferrini's 4 whatever they

190   Notes to Chapter 1

ares [. . .] (These new Maxies rough up Vinc [sic] considerably—I was shocked by both the choice of things and their putting together / (to put chowder before a Maximus—or at least such a one, as that one, / #3!! / But this is only part of the bigger wrong. Hold his hand (tho I don't think he deserves forgiveness) / I just hate / that the necessities (at least as I take them / are bigger / than we are / only hate it, that he had to go & get caught in the wringer." Charles Olson, *Letters for Origin,* ed. Albert Glover (New York: Paragon House, 1989), 124. Ferrini, in fact, never read or heard the letter poems until Olson published *The Maximus Poems / 1–10* late in 1953, at which point Corman, who lived near Gloucester, read the poems aloud to him at a party.

6. Miriam Nichols has identified a similar movement in Olson's thought from "document" to "myth." See Miriam Nichols, "Myth and Document in Charles Olson's *Maximus Poems,*" in *Contemporary Olson,* ed. David Herd (Manchester, UK: Manchester University Press, 2015), 25–37. Rachel Blau DuPlessis sees a similarly reoccurring transition from "fact" to "theory" in Olson's writing, where Olson purports to ground his work in documents and fact while also allowing the reader to move between the "empirical and synoptic" ("Olson and His *Maximus Poems,*" 139).

7. Charles Olson, "Materials and Weights of Herman Melville," in *Collected Prose,* ed. Donald Allen and Benjamin Friedlander (Berkeley: University of California Press, 1997), 117.

8. For more on Alfred North Whitehead's influence on Olson's poetry and poetics, see Paul Jaussen, *Writing in Real Time: Emergent Poetics from Whitman to the Digital* (Cambridge, UK: Cambridge University Press, 2017); Shahar Bram, *Charles Olson and Alfred North Whitehead: An Essay on Poetry* (Lewisburg, Penn.: Bucknell University Press, 2004); Miriam Nichols, *Radical Affections: Essays on the Poetics of Outside* (Tuscaloosa: University of Alabama Press, 2010); Don Byrd, *Charles Olson's "Maximus"* (Urbana: University of Illinois Press, 1980); Robert von Hallberg, *Charles Olson: The Scholar's Art* (Cambridge, Mass.: Harvard University Press, 1978); Robin Blaser, "The Violets: Charles Olson and Alfred North Whitehead," in *The Fire: Collected Essays of Robert Blaser,* ed. Miriam Nichols (Berkeley: University of California Press, 2006), 196–228; Paul Christensen, *Charles Olson: Call Him Ishmael* (Austin: University of Texas Press, 1979); and Sherman Paul, *Olson's Push: Origin, Black Mountain, and Recent American Poetry* (Baton Rouge: Louisiana State University Press, 1978).

9. Olson, *Maximus Poems,* I.17. I try my best to be true to Olson's typographic layout. Still, within the limits of the academic page, there might be slight variations.

10. David Herd, "Introduction: Contemporary Olson," in *Contemporary Olson,* ed. David Herd (Manchester, UK: Manchester University Press, 2015), 3.

Notes to Chapter 1   191

11. George F. Butterick, "Editor's Introduction," in *Charles Olson and Robert Creeley: The Complete Correspondence,* ed. George F. Butterick, vol. 1 (Santa Barbara, Calif.: Black Sparrow Press, 1980), ix. Olson and Creeley were first put into contact by Vincent Ferrini in March 1950. Olson had sent Ferrini some poems after seeking him out the year before (a meeting we have just seen dramatized by Maximus in "Letter 5"), and Ferrini then sent two of Olson's poems on to Creeley, who was planning to start a poetry journal in New Hampshire. Olson and Creeley's early letters are dotted with discussions of and plans for Creeley's new journal, and when those plans fell through, much of the work Creeley had assembled ended up in Cid Corman's *Origin.* See Butterick, "Editor's Introduction," ix–x; and Jonathan Creasy, "The Active Nucleus: Robert Creeley's *Black Mountain Review,*" Black Mountain Research, last accessed September 27, 2020, https://black-mountain-research.com/2015/01/26/the-active -nucleus-robert-creeleys-black-mountain-review/. When Olson sought to establish the *Black Mountain Review* to advertise the work being done at Black Mountain College, he invited Creeley to Black Mountain to be the editor. Creeley subsequently edited *Black Mountain Review* from 1954 to 1957, with Allen Ginsberg coediting the seventh and final volume. Finally, Creeley was the editor of Olson's *Selected Writings* (New York: New Directions, 1966), among the first of now many edited volumes dedicated to Olson's writing.

12. Quoted in Butterick, ix.

13. Charles Olson, "Projective Verse," in *Collected Prose,* ed. Donald Allen and Benjamin Friedlander (Berkeley: University of California Press, 1997), 239.

14. Charles Olson, "Human Universe," in *Collected Prose,* ed. Donald Allen and Benjamin Friedlander (Berkeley: University of California Press, 1997), 155–56. "Human Universe" emerged in part via Olson's letters to his friends and editors. The initial published version appeared in *Origin* 4 (Winter 1951– 52): 217–28. Olson sent an earlier draft version to Corman "in a letter of 17 June 1951" (Olson, *Collected Prose,* 409).

15. Joseph N. Riddell, *The Turning Word: American Literary Modernism and Continental Theory,* ed. Mark Bauerlein (Philadelphia: University of Pennsylvania Press, 1996), 145.

16. William V. Spanos, "Charles Olson and Negative Capability: A Phenomenological Interpretation," *Contemporary Literature* 21, no. 1 (Winter 1980): 40–41.

17. Olson, "Projective Verse," 240; Charles Olson, "Letter to Elaine Feinstein," in *Collected Prose,* ed. Donald Allen and Benjamin Friedlander (Berkeley: University of California Press, 1997), 250.

18. Olson, "Letter to Elaine Feinstein," 250.

19. Friedrich A. Kittler, *Discourse Networks 1800/1900,* trans. Michael Metteer, with Chris Cullens (Stanford, Calif.: Stanford University Press, 1990), 25.

192   Notes to Chapter 1

Kittler claims that the discourse network of 1800 sees a change in the mother's role with regard to language. During this period the mother becomes an educator. "Pedagogical discourses disappeared into the Mother's Mouth only to reappear multiplied in the form of bureaucratic administration," and so "what Faust called a life source became institutionalized. The mother 'must be an educator' because 'the child sucks in its first ideas with the mother's milk'" (55). Unlike Kittler, Olson does not believe the voice to be entirely dominated by literacy and bureaucratic administration. For more on the commonalities and differences between Olson's and Kittler's thinking about language and media, see Abram Foley, "Friedrich Kittler, Charles Olson, and the Return of Postwar Philology," *Affirmations: Of the Modern* 2, no. 2 (2015): 81–100.

20. Here, Olson fits into a configuration of midcentury media theorists such as Harold Innis and Marshall McLuhan. McLuhan takes a particularly strong stance against dominant literary (i.e., written and printed) forms. For an argument regarding the relation between print and linear thought after Gutenberg, see Marshall McLuhan, *The Gutenberg Galaxy: The Making of Typographic Man* (Toronto: University of Toronto Press, 1962). For a history of various graphic technologies, from ancient to digital, especially in relation to the development and administration of empire, see Innis's *The Bias of Communication*, 2nd ed. (Toronto: University of Toronto Press, 2008). Innis first published *The Bias of Communication* in 1951, just a year after Olson published "Projective Verse" and at the same time that he was researching Mayan glyphs on the Yucatan Peninsula. Olson without a doubt read Innis's *The Cod Fisheries* (1940) because it touches on the history of Gloucester. See Ralph Maud, *Charles Olson's Reading: A Biography* (Carbondale: Southern Illinois University Press, 1996), 144. There is no evidence, however, that Olson read Innis's communications work that corresponds so well with his own thought and that marked a major turn in Innis's own intellectual interests.

21. Spanos, "Charles Olson," 46.

22. Thomas H. Ford, "Poetry's Media," *New Literary History* 44, no. 3 (Summer 2013): 454.

23. Brian M. Reed, "Visual Experiment and Oral Performance," in *The Sound of Poetry / The Poetry of Sound*, ed. Marjorie Perloff and Craig Dworkin (Chicago: University of Chicago Press, 2009), 279.

24. Consider, too, that the Black Mountain poets derive their moniker in part from the *Black Mountain Review* rather than from any direct association with the Black Mountain College in North Carolina in the 1950s. Although Olson and Creeley worked for the college and Creeley edited *BMR* from Black Mountain College, some of the writers associated with Black Mountain, such as Denise Levertov, maintained mostly literary ties to Black Mountain, such as through printed work in the literary journal.

Notes to Chapter 1   193

25. Olson, "Projective Verse," 245.

26. Herd, "Introduction," 3.

27. Here I approach Olson's thinking on editing, publishing, and print by way of his engagements with Cid Corman and *Origin*. His interest in these active elements of the literary field, however, crop up elsewhere in his body of work, particularly if one tracks his correspondence with editors and publishers. On seeing the proofs to the first edition of *Maximus Poems, 1–10*, for instance, Olson responded excitedly to Jonathan Williams, the editor and publisher of the Jargon Society as follows: "It was a great experience. For I was able, today, to see these poems in the clearest light—an experience which I swear one ought to remember is an experience of proofs. It leads me to believe that writer, printer, and publisher ought always to assume that proofs are very damn much a vital stage in the process of poems, just as important as final mss. In any case, another thanks, for giving me the chance to learn something: that proofs have to be faced up to from the same organic place as the writing of the stuff (here, for the first time, acquiring the clothes of type, & print)." Charles Olson to Jonathan Williams, June 24, 1953, box 434, folder 1, Jargon Society Collection, State University of New York at Buffalo. My thanks to Pete Moore for supplying me with his transcription of this letter.

28. Olson, *Letters for Origin*, 48.

29. Olson, 49.

30. It is worth noting here that Olson's turn toward the graphic coincides with his travels to the Yucatan Peninsula, where Mayan glyphs compelled him to rethink his relation to graphic inscription. For more on Olson's experimentation with graphics in his own poetry, see Nathaniel Mackey, "That Words Can Be on the Page: The Graphic Aspect of Charles Olson's Poetics," in *Discrepant Engagement: Dissonance, Cross-Culturality, and Experimental Writing* (Tuscaloosa: University of Alabama Press, 1993), 121–38.

31. For more on the context of the poem, see Butterick, *Guide*, 574.

32. The poem is signed off with a date. Olson, III.205.

33. Butterick, *Guide*, 5.

34. In one of the first book-length critical works on Olson, *Charles Olson: Call Him Ishmael* (Austin: University of Texas Press, 1979), Paul Christensen offers some balanced skepticism about the powerful place "Projective Verse" holds in criticism on Olson's work. For Christensen, too much emphasis on "Projective Verse" forecloses discussions about artfulness in Olson's poetic oeuvre. "The essay seems to take away from poetry more than it gives," he writes, "for its most explicit points condemn the conventions of artifice; offered in return are rhythm, sound, and perception—the irreducible properties, he argued, that constitute the poetic act" (70). Robert von Hallberg writes more bluntly that Olson is "influential more as a writer of manifestoes than as

194 Notes to Chapter 1

a poet" and adds that "Olson's best poetry is offered as explanation and under-standing, not as expression." See Robert von Hallberg, *Charles Olson: The Scholar's Art* (Cambridge, Mass.: Harvard University Press, 1978), 2–3.

35. One could point to challenges to the cliché of modernist solipsism in a range of work associated with the new modernist studies, which turned to material and cultural history to open modernist studies to its historical contexts. One particularly relevant example in the context of Olson and Bové's characterization of solipsistic modernism, particularly given Olson's identification of T. S. Eliot as an exemplary practitioner of closed verse, is David E. Chinitz's *T. S. Eliot and the Cultural Divide* (Chicago: University of Chicago Press, 2003).

36. Paul A. Bové, *Destructive Poetics: Heidegger and Modern American Poetry* (New York: Columbia University Press, 1980), ix.

37. A point of clarification about Gloucester's actual topography: Gloucester is not an island city. It is located on Cape Ann, which is mostly separated from the mainland by the Annisquam River. The separation of a large portion of the cape from the mainland, however, was completed as early as 1643 with the construction of the Blynman Canal, which connects Western Harbor (Gloucester's famed seafront) in the south, with the Annisquam River to the north. Topographic specificity, however, is less important here than poetic functionality. For Maximus, Gloucester is an island city, because islands provide floating worlds of sorts from which the poetic figure emerges.

38. Charles Olson to Jonathan Williams, April 11, 1953, B433F12, Jargon Society Archives, Poetry Collection, Special Collections, State University of New York of Buffalo.

39. *Oxford English Dictionary,* s.v. "figuration, *n.*," accessed September 6, 2019, https://www.oed.com/view/Entry/70074.

40. Butterick, *Guide,* 142.

41. I adopt the term "imperial romance" from Robert L. Caserio's entry on the subject in *The Cambridge History of the English Novel,* ed. Robert L. Caserio and Clement Hawes (Cambridge, UK: Cambridge University Press, 2012), 517–32.

42. Charles Olson, *Mayan Letters,* in *Selected Writings,* ed. Robert Creeley (New York: New Directions, 1966), 125.

43. *Oxford English Dictionary,* s.v. "annex(e, *n.*," accessed September 6, 2019, https://www.oed.com/view/Entry/7873.

44. For a reading of Olson's relationship with philology, see Michael Davidson, *Ghostlier Demarcations: Modern Poetry and the Material Word* (Berkeley: University of California Press, 1997), 94–115. See also Abram Foley, "Friedrich Kittler, Charles Olson, and the Return of Postwar Philology," *Affirmations: Of the Modern* 2, no. 2 (2015): 81–100.

Notes to Chapter 1   195

45. Olson, *Mayan Letters,* 129.

46. Olson's interest in a "core" of civilization echoes throughout his own work. In "The Gate and the Center," for example, Olson takes interest in ancient Sumer. He writes that "until date 1200 B.C. or thereabouts, civilization had ONE CENTER, Sumer, in all directions, that this one people held such exact and superior force that all peoples around them were sustained by it, nourished, increased, advanced, that a city was a coherence which, for the first time since the ice, gave man the chance to join knowledge to culture and, with this weapon, shape dignities of economics and value sufficient to make daily life itself dignity and sufficiency." Charles Olson, "The Gate and the Center," in *Collected Prose,* ed. Donald Allen and Benjamin Friedlander (Berkeley: University of California Press, 1997), 170. Olson's interest in Sumerian culture came by way of his correspondence with Frances Boldereff, who herself wrote a book later in her life about Joyce's interest in Hermes Trismegistus. Olson's interest in gates and centers is similarly hermetic and informed by the legacies of hermeticism, an aspect of his work in need of future study. It should be noted here, however, that Olson was also familiar with the work of L. A. Waddell, whom I discuss presently and who advanced Sumerian culture as an ancient source of Aryan cultural dominance. For more on Boldereff, Olson, and Sumer, see Robert Hampson, "'When the attentions change': Charles Olson and Frances Boldereff," in *Contemporary Olson,* ed. David Herd (Manchester, UK: Manchester University Press, 2015), 149–62.

47. Maud, *Charles Olson's Reading,* 335. Olson's other reference to Donnelly comes by way of Olson's reading of C. L. R. James. In a 1953 letter to Robert Creeley, Olson writes that "a crazy book fr a crazy man came in here, surprise, yesterday . . . sounds like a sort of Waddell & Ignatius Donnelly" (249). The book Olson refers to is James's *Mariners, Renegades and Castaways: The Story of Herman Melville and the World We Live In.*

48. Donnelly's other works include *Ragnarök: The Age of Fire and Gravel* (1883); *The Great Cryptogram: Francis Bacon's Cipher in the So-Called Shakespeare Plays* (1888); and *Caesar's Column: A Story of the Twentieth Century* (1890), which is most often compared to Edward Bellamy's more famous work of a similar nature, *Looking Backward.* For criticism on Donnelly, cryptology, and orientalist methodologies related to his work on Shakespeare, see Brian Lennon, *Passwords: Philology, Security, Authentication* (Cambridge, Mass.: Harvard University Press, 2017).

49. David Kahn, *The Codebreakers: The Comprehensive History of Secret Communication from Ancient Times to the Internet* (New York: Scribner, 1996), 878. Quoted in Lennon, 41.

50. Lennon, 41.

51. The most wide-ranging account of the relation between philology and orientalism remains Edward W. Said's *Orientalism* (New York: Vintage, 1979).

196   Notes to Chapter 1

For the role of orientalism and philology played in shaping world literature, see Aamir R. Mufti, "Orientalism and the Institution of World Literature," *Critical Inquiry* 36 (2010): 458–93. Mufti expanded this work in *Forget English! Orientalisms and World Literatures* (Cambridge, Mass.: Harvard University Press, 2016).

52. Ignatius Donnelly, *Atlantis: The Antediluvian World* (New York: Harper and Brothers, 1882), 1.

53. Donnelly, 213–36.

54. James Churchward, *The Lost Continent of Mu* (New York: Paperback Library, 1968), 5.

55. Olson, *Mayan Letters*, 129–30.

56. Olson, *Maximus Poems*, II.79.

57. Riddel, *Turning Word*, 144.

58. For more on Olson's at once amateur and "inspired" expedition in Mexico, see DuPlessis, "Olson and His *Maximus Poems.*"

59. Olson, *Mayan Letters*, 113. For a brief monograph on Charles Olson's extensive engagement with Mayan glyphs, see Dennis Tedlock, *The Olson Codex: Projective Verse and the Problem of Mayan Glyphs* (Albuquerque: University of New Mexico Press, 2017).

60. Olson, *Letters for Origin*, 50.

2. Editing and the Institution

1. James Joyce, *Ulysses*, ed. Hans Walter Gabler (New York: Vintage Books, 1986), 2.377.

2. Flann O'Brien, *The Dalkey Archive* (Normal, Ill.: Dalkey Archive Press, 1993), 7.

3. In "An Interview with John O'Brien," Dalkey Archive Press, 2000 and 2004, http://www.dalkeyarchive.com/interview-with-john-obrien/, John O'Brien states his reasons for establishing the *Review of Contemporary Fiction* in 1980, which he sees as the necessary antecedent to the press: "The writers I was interested in—Gilbert Sorrentino, Paul Metcalf, Wallace Markfield, Luisa Valenzuela—were not being written about . . . and it was difficult for me to write about them with any expectation that what I wrote would get published in journals at that time. If you wrote the 5,000th essay on Saul Bellow, you had a pretty good chance of getting it published because editors knew who he was and so publishing another essay on Bellow was safe . . . So, the critical establishment (however you want to define this, from academic journals to the *New York Times Book Review*) had a lock on what writers would be covered, as well as how they would be covered."

4. John O'Brien to Gilbert Sorrentino, October 14, 1980, M0835, box 2, folder 10, Gilbert Sorrentino Papers, Stanford University.

Notes to Chapter 2   197

5. Mark McGurl, *The Program Era: Postwar Fiction and the Rise of the Creative Writing Program* (Cambridge, Mass.: Harvard University Press, 2009).

6. Margaret Doherty, "State-Funded Fiction: Minimalism, National Memory, and the Return to Realism in the Post-Postmodern Age," *American Literary History* 27, no. 1 (Spring 2015): 89. While Doherty points out that the relationship between institutions and aesthetics is not determinative, opting for the more capacious "overdetermined," both she and McGurl emphasize a directionality leading from institutional cause to literary effect, though both trouble that directionality in sophisticated ways. Loren Glass's recent book on Grove Press and the *Evergreen Review* works in this line as well, with Glass arguing successfully for the "incorporation of the avant-garde" by reading through the lens of a very successful publishing house. I do not disagree with the approaches these scholars take. They offer maps that tell us how we arrived where we are. My position is somewhat closer to Merve Emre's in "Ironic Institutions: Counterculture Fictions and the American Express Company," *American Literature* 87, no. 1 (2015), where she conceives of a "paraliterary institution," which she defines as "an institution that uses literature to organize practices of self and sociality, but has little to do with the conventional sites and spaces of literary production" (113). Emre's position resonates with my own because she recognizes that institutions emerge from different ways of reading and interacting with literature. While Emre looks to institutions that are not traditionally associated with literary production, however, I propose that we can see such institutional derivation at work within the literary field by reading through Dalkey Archive Press's booklist.

7. McGurl, *Program Era*, 3.

8. Robert L. Caserio, "Unintelligible Specificity and the Writing of Gay Literary History," *American Literary History* 27, no. 1 (Spring 2015): 150.

9. John O'Brien, ed., *Interview with Black Writers* (New York: Liveright, 1973).

10. In "An Interview with Jeremy Davies by Michelle Pretorius," *The Bailer*, February 15, 2012, https://thebailer.com/interviews/an-interview-with-jeremy-m-davies-by-michelle-pretorius/, Jeremy M. Davies, then senior editor at Dalkey Archive Press, stated, "There would be no Dalkey Archive without Gilbert Sorrentino—our first book was a reprint of his *Splendide Hotel* [*sic*], and his advice guided a good number of the Press's early acquisitions and has great influence here to this day. (A good way to get something noticed is to say, 'Sorrentino loved this book . . .') His death in 2006 was a serious blow to the Press and American letters both."

11. Loren Glass, *Counterculture Colophon: Grove Press, the* Evergreen Review, *and the Incorporation of the Avant-Garde* (Stanford, Calif.: Stanford University Press, 2013), 1–33.

198   Notes to Chapter 2

12. Gilbert Sorrentino to John O'Brien, August 20, 1971, M507, box 1, folder 1, *Review of Contemporary Fiction* / Dalkey Archive Press: records, 1971–1974, Stanford University.

13. Sorrentino to O'Brien, July 26, 1972, M507, box 1, folder 1, *Review of Contemporary Fiction* / Dalkey Archive Press: records, 1971–1974, Stanford University.

14. Sorrentino to O'Brien, May 27, 1972, M507, box 1, folder 1, *Review of Contemporary Fiction* / Dalkey Archive Press: records, 1971–1974, Stanford University.

15. Sorrentino to O'Brien, September 27, 1974, M507, box 1, folder 1, *Review of Contemporary Fiction* / Dalkey Archive Press: records, 1971–1974, Stanford University.

16. Even critics of contemporary literature such as Kathryn Hume (whose most recent works range over dozens of books) and Caren Irr (whose work treats more than one hundred texts) can only claim to engage one aspect of contemporary literary expression. See Kathryn Hume, *Aggressive Fictions: Reading the Contemporary American Novel* (Ithaca, N.Y.: Cornell University Press, 2012); and Caren Irr, *Toward the Geopolitical Novel: U.S. Fiction in the Twenty-First Century* (New York: Columbia University Press, 2014).

17. Sorrentino to O'Brien, September 27, 1974.

18. O'Brien to Sorrentino, October 14, 1980.

19. Christine Brooke-Rose, an author whose work O'Brien has supported with both the *Review* and the press, points out in the title essay of her collection *Invisible Author* (Columbus: Ohio State University Press, 2002) that avant-garde writing and reception suffers under the strategies of male posturing, leaving many women experimentalists in the role of "invisible authors" to their more boisterous male counterparts. As Urmila Seshagiri writes in "Making It New: Persephone Books and the Modernist Project," *MFS: Modern Fiction Studies* 59, no. 2 (Summer 2013) about the London-based feminist press, Persephone Books, "Despite decades of dedicated scholarship, impassioned activism, and progressive publishing, literary culture at the turn of the twenty-first century continued to devalue the talents of women writers" (242). One interesting offshoot of Dalkey Archive is the small publishing house known as "Dorothy, a publishing project," run by Danielle Dutton and her husband, Martin Riker. Riker was second-in-charge at Dalkey Archive Press for several years before leaving the press, and Dutton worked for a brief period in design and production for Dalkey Archive. Her new press publishes women writers almost exclusively.

20. O'Brien established the press while teaching at the Illinois Benedictine College. It subsequently moved to Illinois State University for a time and then

Notes to Chapter 2

to the University of Illinois, Urbana-Champaign. In 2015, the press began a new affiliation with the University of Houston-Victoria.

21. Sorrentino to O'Brien, February 8, 1974, M507, box 1, folder 1, *Review of Contemporary Fiction* / Dalkey Archive Press: records, 1971–1974, Stanford University.

22. Gilbert Sorrentino, "Introduction," in *Cadenza* by Ralph Cusack (Elmwood Park, Ill.: Dalkey Archive Press, 1984), 5–6.

23. Sorrentino to O'Brien, August 9, 1983, M507, box 1, folder 8, *Review of Contemporary Fiction* / Dalkey Archive Press: records, 1983–1984, Stanford University.

24. Sorrentino to O'Brien, September 6, 1980, M507, box 1, folder 5, *Review of Contemporary Fiction* / Dalkey Archive Press: records, 1980, Stanford University.

25. Joyce, *Ulysses*, 9.837–42.

26. Flann O'Brien, *At Swim-Two-Birds* (Champaign, Ill.: Dalkey Archive Press, 1998), 20.

27. Anne Clissmann, *Flann O'Brien, a Critical Introduction to His Writings: The Story-Teller's Book-Web* (New York: Barnes and Noble Books, 1975), 106.

28. O'Brien, *Dalkey Archive*, 12.

29. In a letter to Sorrentino, John O'Brien wrote that he planned to name his little magazine "Black and White." His reasons were, he wrote, "1) too obvious to mention; 2) that's the way I see the world and that's the way this journal will see literature." Whether O'Brien makes reference to Sorrentino's book of poetry or to Saint Augustine's speech in his first point remains unclear. O'Brien to Sorrentino, May 10, 1980, M0835, box 2, folder 9, Gilbert Sorrentino Papers, Stanford University.

30. Gilbert Sorrentino, *Mulligan Stew* (New York: Grove Press, 1979), first unnumbered page. Due to the strange space these pages occupy in Sorrentino's novel, I number them from the first to the eleventh unnumbered page.

31. Sorrentino, first unnumbered page.

32. Sorrentino.

33. Sorrentino, second unnumbered page.

34. Sorrentino, seventh unnumbered page.

35. Sorrentino, eleventh unnumbered page.

36. Sorrentino.

37. McGurl, *Program Era*, 33.

38. Jean Allman, "Nuclear Imperialism and the Pan-African Struggle for Peace and Freedom: Ghana, 1959–1962," *Souls* 10, no. 2 (2008): 83. For the best account of the life and literary works of Julian Mayfield, see Kevin K. Gaines, *American Africans in Ghana: Black Expatriates and the Civil Rights Era* (Chapel Hill: University of North Carolina Press, 2006).

200 Notes to Chapter 2

39. Although Amiri Baraka declined to be interviewed for O'Brien's volume, he (under his name LeRoi Jones) addresses the hazards of publishing for African Americans in essays such as "The Myth of a 'Negro Literature'" (1962) and "Black Writing" (1963). In the former, he renounces most writing by African Americans as "middle class" and urges authors to write, if possible, from outside the mainstream. In the latter, Jones addresses the publishing industry and the Black writer simultaneously, warning the Black writer that "Negro Material is *hot* right now, to quote a knowledgeable white man. But even hot, there are many books by Negroes that will not be published because they, the publishers will tell you, 'duplicate our other Negro material.' Though, of course, they will publish as many duplicated junks about ofays as they can" ("Black Writing," 162). Jones again urges resistance to the mainstream of the "commercial novel in America" and the "merchant's reality" before concluding that "the Negro, as he exists in America now, and has always existed in this place (certainly after formal slavery), is a natural nonconformist" (164). Black writing's nonconformity thus resists the commercial logic of publishing "industrialists," who realize that "a book—no matter what you have to say in it—is just a commercial object, and Negro Material is not the commercial object that gets the best sales" (162). These kinds of positions on the creative and cultural industries, including publishing, anticipate the institution building that Baraka later undertook with the Black Arts Movement and after, a movement that can in part be traced in the volume in which these essays are collected. See LeRoi Jones, *Home: Social Essays* (New York: William Morrow, 1966). For a particularly thorough account in Black Arts Movement and institution building, see Jonathan Fenderson, *Building the Black Arts Movement: Hoyt Fuller and the Cultural Politics of the 1960s* (Urbana: University of Illinois Press, 2019).

40. Arna Bontemps, interview by John O'Brien, in *Interviews with Black Writers*, 6–7.

41. Ishmael Reed, interview by John O'Brien, in *Interviews with Black Writers*, 173.

42. Reed refers here to Vincent McHugh's *Caleb Catlum's America* (1936), a blend of American folklore and sci-fi told in the vernacular that has been largely forgotten, as an example of the kind of radical and innovative American fiction that gets "hidden and suppressed." Although McHugh is not African American, Reed looks to him here for that way that *Caleb Catlum's America* participates in "urban ghetto traditions." See Pierre-Damien Mvuyekure, "American Neo-HooDooism: The Novels of Ishmael Reed," in *The Cambridge Companion to the African American Novel,* ed. Maryemma Graham (Cambridge, UK: Cambridge University Press, 2004), 206. Reed includes *The Metamorphosis* by Franz Kafka, *Invisible Man* by Ralph Ellison, and *The Cabinet of Dr. Caligari* by F. W. Murnau as examples of this tradition (Mvuyekure, 206). For

Notes to Chapter 2   201

more on Reed's work as a cultural organizer through the Before Columbus Foundation, see Nicholas Donofrio, "Multiculturalism, Inc.: Regulating and Deregulating the Culture Industries with Ishmael Reed," *American Literary History* 29, no. 1 (Spring 2017): 100–128.

43. Reed, interview by O'Brien, in *Interviews with Black Writers*, 179.

44. While Dalkey Archive Press has never republished *Mumbo Jumbo*, which has not been out of print since its initial publication, it currently publishes many of Reed's other works, three of which were originally published by Dalkey Archive: *The Plays* (2009), *Juice!* (2011), and *Conjugating Hindi* (2018). Reissued works by Reed in Dalkey's list include *The Free-Lance Pallbearers* (1967), *Yellow Back Radio Broke-Down* (1969), *The Last Days of Louisiana Red* (1974)—which has the same hero as *Mumbo Jumbo*—*The Terrible Twos* (1982), *Reckless Eyeballing* (1986), and *The Terrible Threes* (1989).

45. O'Brien, *Interviews with Black Writers*, vii.

46. The tagged link for "African American" literature on Dalkey's website will bring the reader to the works of four authors: C. S. Giscombe, Rowan Ricardo Phillips, Ishmael Reed, and Jay Wright.

47. Brigitte Fielder and Jonathan Senchyne, "Introduction: Infrastructures of African American Print," in *Against a Sharp White Background: Infrastructures of African American Print*, edited by Brigitte Fielder and Jonathan Senchyne (Madison: University of Wisconsin Press, 2019), 8.

48. I am influenced here by Toni Morrison's landmark statement on race and histories of American literature in *Playing in the Dark: Whiteness and the Literary Imagination* (Cambridge, Mass.: Harvard University Press, 1992).

49. I am basing these observations on the publicly available author list for New Directions, which can be found here: https://www.ndbooks.com/author/. I made these tallies in June 2020.

50. As of June 25, 2020, New York Review Books has 140 titles listed with the tag of "American Literature." Four of these books are by Black American writers, all of whom are men: William Attaway, Harold W. Cruse, Darius James, and Darryl Pinckney.

51. Kathryn Schulz, "The Lost Giant of American Literature," *New Yorker*, January 29, 2018. According to the digital copy of the essay, it originally appeared in print with the headline of "Remainders" see https://www.new yorker.com/magazine/2018/01/29/the-lost-giant-of-american-literature.

52. Schulz.

53. Schulz. I say that William Melvin Kelley seems to have shared this opinion because Aiki Kelley is quoted as saying "We always said, we made a revolution and we lost."

54. Jones, "The Myth of a 'Negro Literature'" and "Black Writing," in *Home: Social Essays*.

202   Notes to Chapter 2

55. John O'Brien died in November 2020, well after this manuscript was completed, and so I am adding this note at proofreading. Rest in peace, John. For those interested in reading more about working for Dalkey Archive Press under John's direction, I suggest Chad Post's "Remembering John O'Brien" on *World Without Borders,* December 16, 2020, https://www.wordswithoutborders.org/dispatches/article/remembering-john-obrien-dalkey-archive-chad-post?.

56. Nathaniel Mackey, *Discrepant Engagement: Dissonance, Cross-Culturality, and Experimental Writing* (Cambridge, UK: Cambridge University Press, 1993), 18.

57. All of my records about organizing this visit were in the Gmail-hosted Dalkey Archive email, and I did not forward them to my personal account prior to leaving the position and losing access to this account. This is, then, a narrative from memory.

58. Schulz's essay points out the Kelley family's conversion to Judaism in the 1970s, and Kelley's keen interest in the Pentateuch. See Schulz, "Lost Giant."

59. This list of course has its own history. John O'Brien was keen on Robert Boles, a writer I had not heard about prior to starting my editorial fellowship at Dalkey Archive; Vincent O. Carter and Carlene Hatcher Polite were both recommended to me by Aldon Lynn Nielsen, who had introduced me to Nathaniel Mackey's work years earlier; I learned about Xam Wilson Cartier's *Be-Bop, Re-Bop* through Jabari Asim's article for *Washington Post's Book World,* "African American Literature in the Black," June 1, 1997, https://www.washingtonpost.com/wp-srv/style/longterm/books/25thann/asim.htm.

60. This information does not yet appear on Dalkey Archive's own website, but the book design on Amazon and McCarthy's own biographical information on his Harvard staff home page appear to confirm the book's release with Dalkey Archive. See "Jesse McCarthy," Harvard University, last modified October 30, 2020, https://aaas.fas.harvard.edu/people/jesse-mccarthy.

3. Editing and the Ensemble

1. Fred Moten, "Knowledge of Freedom," *CR: New Centennial Review* 4, no. 2 (Fall 2004): 281.

2. Nathaniel Mackey, "Editing *Hambone,*" in *Paracritical Hinge: Essays, Talks, Notes, Interviews* (Madison: University of Wisconsin Press, 2005), 244.

3. Nathaniel Mackey, "Introduction: And All the Birds Sing Bass," in *Discrepant Engagement: Dissonance, Cross-Culturality, and Experimental Writing* (Tuscaloosa: University of Alabama Press, 1993), 19.

4. Mackey, "Editing *Hambone,*" 244.

5. I say "almost exclusively," because some contributors to *Hambone* 1 have been difficult to identify decades later since they did not become well-known figures and perhaps did not even continue writing for publication.

Notes to Chapter 3 203

6. Susan Howe, "mute memory vagrant memory," in *Hambone* 2, ed. Nathaniel Mackey (Santa Cruz, Calif.: Hambone, 1982), 23 (the overall issue is hereafter cited in this chapter as *Hambone* 2).

7. Susan Howe, "Distance and eyes get lost (apse to read) Twig," in *Hambone* 2, 24.

8. Susan Howe, "Twenty lines of," in *Hambone* 2, 30.

9. For a reading of Howe's allusions to Spenser and the English colonization of Ireland, see Will Montgomery, "Susan Howe's Renaissance Period: Metamorphosis and Representation in *Pythagorean Silence* and *Defenestration of Prague*," *Journal of American Studies* 40, no. 3 (2006): 615–33.

10. Edward Kamau Brathwaite, "Manchile," in *Hambone* 2, 48.

11. While "prone" here most immediately connotes being susceptible to something, it is worth noting that prone also means "flat," suggesting that Brathwaite's poem seeks to confound Columbus's proposition and its eventualities.

12. At greater length Metcalf writes, "HAMBONE is a delight! Really, one of the freshest reading experiences to come in a long time. Clearly, you set out to include as wide a range as possible—I'm sure you've been told this many times—but what is remarkable is not only the range, but the quality of nearly every submission. It's a genuine all-star show—as though we all knew, somehow, we had to be on our toes. How did that happen? My personal favorites: [John] Taggart, [Susan] Howe, [Kamau] Brathwaite, and [Ishmael] Read [*sic*]. (How could anybody include Taggart and Read [*sic*] in the same magazine? Well, Nate Mackey could, that's how/who.) Cheers! [signed] Paul [Metcalf]." Paul Metcalf, "Letter to Nathaniel Mackey," November 12, 1982, Nathaniel Mackey Papers, MSS 1297, box 28, folder: *Hambone* Correspondence, 1982, Emory University.

13. John Taggart, "Very Slow," in *Hambone* 2, 6.

14. Ishmael Reed, "Ishmael Reed Replies to Amiri Baraka," in *Hambone* 2, 123. Reed's reply to Baraka was part of a different form of discrepant engagement: the agonism between two prominent African American writers. In a brief note that Amiri Baraka sent to Mackey, postmarked November 15, 1982, Baraka asks, "Is it possible (or even appropriate) to answer Ish's self-interview in yr porky pages?" Amiri Baraka to Nathaniel Mackey, November 15, 1982, Nathaniel Mackey Papers, MS 1297, box 28, folder: *Hambone* Correspondence, 1982, Emory University. Mackey replied on *Hambone* letterhead three days later: "Dear Mr. Baraka: You're welcome to reply to Ishmael's piece in HAMBONE. Whether it would be 'appropriate' (as you put it) to do so is up to you." A response was never published in *Hambone*. Nathaniel Mackey to Amiri Baraka, November 18, 1982, Box 2, folder 4, Amiri Baraka Papers, 1945–2015, Series I: Correspondence, 1945–2007, Columbia University.

204 Notes to Chapter 3

15. In a letter from 1981 that accompanied Taggart's submission for *Hambone* 2, Taggart writes, "Enclosed please find 'Very Slow,' my contribution to the new *Hambone*. If of interest, the child in the poem comes from a 1972 Viet Nam photo. Perhaps you remember it: a group of children run down an almost deserted highway toward the 'viewer'; one girl, toward the front, is holding out her arms, the clothes completely burned off her body by napalm. I'd never been able to forget her. A week ago was the ninth 'anniversary' of that bombing, ironically enough done by 'our' side." Letter from John Taggart to Nathaniel Mackey, June 15, 1981, box 71, folder 8, Nathaniel Mackey Papers, Publication Records for *Hambone*, 1981–2006, Emory University. The dates more or less confirm that Taggart is speaking of the very famous image of Phan Thị Kim Phúc taken by photographer Nick Ut, originally titled "The Terror of War" and dated June 8, 1972.

16. Mackey, "Editing *Hambone*," 246.

17. For digital access to *New World Journal*'s archive of issues, visit https://newworldjournal.org/.

18. Mackey, "Editing *Hambone*," 246.

19. Eliot Weinberger to Nathaniel Mackey, November 1, 1983, TS, Nathaniel Mackey Papers, Emory University.

20. Mackey, "Editing *Hambone*," 248.

21. This line of argumentation is indebted to the work of Timothy Yu, notably *Race and the Avant-Garde: Experimental and Asian American Poetry since 1965* (Stanford, Calif.: Stanford University Press, 2009); as well as that of Dorothy J. Wang, especially *Thinking Its Presence: Form, Race, and Subjectivity in Contemporary Asian American Poetry* (Stanford, Calif.: Stanford University Press, 2013).

22. Mellonee V. Burnim and Portia K. Maultsby, with contributions from Susan Oehler, "Intellectual History," in *African American Music: An Introduction*, ed. Mellonee V. Burnim and Portia K. Maultsby (New York: Routledge, 2006), 8.

23. Here I follow the editors of *African American Music* in using Black as an umbrella term for people of different ethnicities—African, African American, Black Caribbean—in the Americas.

24. Mackey, "Editing *Hambone*," 248.

25. Lawrence W. Levine, "African American Music as Resistance, Antebellum Period" in *African American Music: An Introduction*, ed. Mellonee V. Burnim and Portia K. Maultsby (New York: Routledge, 2006), 589.

26. Melonee V. Burnim and Portia K. Maultsby, *African American Music: An Introduction*, 2nd ed. (New York: Routledge, 2014), 25. This is a definition of "hambone" placed on the margins of the page. My understanding is that these glosses are written by the editors, even if they appear alongside chapters written by other authors.

Notes to Chapter 3 205

27. Peter H. Wood, *Black Majority: Negroes in Colonial South Carolina from 1670 through the Stono Rebellion* (New York: Alfred A. Knopf, 1975), 308.

28. *The Human Hambone,* dir. Mark Morgan (First Run / Icarus Films, 2005).

29. Nathaniel Mackey, *From a Broken Bottle Traces of Perfume Still Emanate,* vols. 1–3 (New York: New Directions, 2010), 124.

30. In addition to twenty-two book-length volumes of *Hambone,* Mackey has also coedited *Moment's Notice: Jazz in Poetry and Prose* with Art Lange and coedited with Marjorie Perloff and Carolyn Kizer the Library of America's *American Poetry* volume covering the twentieth century. The emphasis I place on the name Mackey gave his journal falls in line with Mackey's other literary work, particularly *From a Broken Bottle,* in which creative acts of naming signal the historical and theoretical interests of various band members. For a reading of "puncepts" in Mackey's work, which also considers his naming practices, see Adelaide Morris, "Angles of Incidence / Angels of Dust: Operatic Tilt in the Poetics of H.D. and Nathaniel Mackey," *Callaloo* 23, no. 2 (Spring 2000): 749–64.

31. Mackey, "Editing *Hambone,*" 246. For criticism that theorizes the avant-garde as a mechanism of incorporation to dominant discourses and ideology, see Peter Bürger, *Theory of the Avant-Garde,* trans. Michael Shaw (Minneapolis: University of Minnesota Press, 1984); see also Loren Glass, *Counterculture Colophon: Grove Press, the "Evergreen Review," and the Incorporation of the Avant-Garde* (Stanford, Calif.: Stanford University Press, 2013).

32. The most complete bibliography for Harris's work was compiled by a range of scholars associated with the Harris scholar Hena Maes-Jelinek and can be found online as *The Wilson Harris Bibliography,* hosted by the Université de Liège: http://www.cerep.ulg.ac.be/harris/whprim.html.

33. Wilson Harris to Nathaniel Mackey, April 29, 1979, box 11, folder 9, Correspondence, Nathaniel Mackey Papers, Emory University.

34. Nathaniel Mackey, "hello, and courtesy draft of essay on *Hambone,*" email message to Abram Foley, February 19, 2018.

35. Nathaniel Mackey, "The Unruly Pivot: Wilson Harris's *The Eye of the Scarecrow,*" in *Discrepant Engagement: Dissonance, Cross-Culturality, and Experimental Writing* (Cambridge, UK: Cambridge University Press, 1993), 192.

36. Mackey, "And All the Birds Sing Bass," 1.

37. Wilson Harris, "Interview," interview by Jane Wilkinson, *Kunapipi* 8, no. 2 (1986): 30.

38. Quoted in Mackey, "And All the Birds Sing Bass," 5. Some of the quotations I use follow the quotations that Mackey himself uses. Even among poets and poet–critics, Mackey is particularly shrewd in his critical reflections on his own work, particularly in the introductions to *Discrepant Engagement* and *Paracritical Hinge.* With this in mind, I try to think with Mackey while offering

206   Notes to Chapter 3

what I hope to be readings of his own critical assertions that offer further insight into Mackey's poetics.

39. *Oxford English Dictionary*, s.v., "expedite, *v.*," accessed May 3, 2019, http://www.oed.com/view/Entry/66486.

40. For an excellent introduction to Harris's own testing of an "expedition into wholeness," see his novel *Palace of the Peacock* (1960; repr., London: Faber and Faber, 1988), which narrates a surreal and mystical journey into inland Guyana. The narrative depends heavily on various images rotating through the "partial" vision of the narrator, who sees through "one dead seeing eye and one living closed eye" that correspond with the material and spiritual worlds of the novel (19).

41. Harris's *The Womb of Space: The Cross-Cultural Imagination* (1983) has also been a touchstone for Mackey with regard to cross-cultural poetics. A letter from Harris to Mackey in fact suggest that Mackey was the press's reviewer for the book when series editors John W. Blassingame and Henry Louis Gates Jr. had another reviewer fall through. See Wilson Harris to Nathaniel Mackey, March 23, 1982, box 11, folder 9, Correspondence, Nathaniel Mackey Papers, Emory University.

42. Quoted in Mackey, "And All the Birds Sing Bass," 5–6.

43. Édouard Glissant, *Caribbean Discourse: Selected Essays*, trans. J. Michael Dash (Charlottesville: University Press of Virginia, 1989), 147.

44. Howe, "Twenty lines of," 31.

45. bell hooks, "in the manner of the egyptians," in *Hambone* 2, 5.

46. Don Byrd, "from *Great Dimestore Centennial*," in *Hambone* 5, ed. Nathaniel Mackey (Santa Cruz, Calif.: Hambone, 1985), 61.

47. Kamau Brathwaite, "Dream Haiti," in *Hambone* 12, ed. Nathaniel Mackey (Santa Cruz, Calif.: Hambone, 1995), 123–185.

48. Eliot Weinberger, quoted in Mackey, "Editing *Hambone*," 247.

49. Eliot Weinberger, "Letter to Nathaniel Mackey," November 1, 1983, Nathaniel Mackey Papers, Emory University.

50. Mackey, "Editing *Hambone*," 248.

51. Nathaniel Mackey to Robert Kelly, February 27, 1980, box 78, folder 3, Kelly (Robert) Collection, Poetry Collection, State University of New York at Buffalo.

52. I am referencing the title to Mackey's introduction of *Discrepant Engagement* here, which is a line from "Black Mountain Blues." Mackey refers to Bessie Smith's version of the song.

53. Mackey, "Editing *Hambone*," 248.

54. Jacques Derrida, "Hostipitality," trans. Barry Stocker with Forbes Morlock, *Angelaki: A Journal of the Theoretical Humanities* 5, no. 3 (2000): 3.

55. The persistence of this call in Mackey's editorial poetics anticipates the theories developed in Stefano Harney and Fred Moten's *The Undercommons:*

Notes to Chapter 3   207

Fugitive Planning and Black Study (New York: Minor Compositions, 2013). Jack Halberstam outlines the most salient overlap in their introduction, "The Wild Beyond: With and For the Undercommons": "Moten and Harney want to gesture to another place, a wild place that . . . continuously produces its own unregulated wildness. The zone we enter through Moten and Harney is ongoing and exists in the present and, as Harney puts it, 'some kind of demand was already being enacted, fulfilled in the call itself.' While describing the London Riots of 2011, Harney suggests that the riots and insurrections do not separate out 'the request, the demand and the call'—rather, they enact the one in the other: 'I think the call, in the way I would understand it, the call, as in the call and response, the response is already there before the call goes out. You're already in something.' *You are already in it.* For Moten too, you are always already in the thing that you call for and that calls you. What's more, the call is always a call to dis-order and this disorder or wildness shows up in many places: in jazz, in improvisation, in noise. . . . Listening to cacophony and noise tells us that there is a wild beyond to the structures we inhabit and that inhabit us" (7). This chapter proposes that *Hambone*'s call also gestures to this wild, dis-organizing beyond. It is itself a call to disorder and to the unknown.

56. Mackey, "Editing *Hambone*," 246.

57. Sarah Blackwood, "Editing as Carework: The Gendered Labor of Public Intellectuals," *Avidly*, June 6, 2014, http://avidly.lareviewofbooks.org/2014/06/06/editing-as-carework-the-gendered-labor-of-public-intellectuals/.

58. Letter from Will Alexander to Nathaniel Mackey, postmarked 1992, box 76, folders 1 and 2, Nathaniel Mackey Papers, Publication Records for *Hambone, 1981–2006,* Emory University.

59. Letter from Will Alexander to Nathaniel Mackey, undated, box 76, folders 1 and 2, Nathaniel Mackey Papers, Publication Records for *Hambone,* 1981–2006, Emory University.

60. Letter from Will Alexander to Nathaniel Mackey, undated, box 83, folder 3, Nathaniel Mackey Papers, Publication Records for *Hambone,* 1981–2006, Emory University.

61. Typed manuscript submitted to Nathaniel Mackey by Will Alexander, undated, box 83, folder 3, Nathaniel Mackey Papers, Publication Records for *Hambone,* 1981–2006, Emory University.

62. Will Alexander, "from *Diary as Sin,*" in *Hambone* 19, ed. Nathaniel Mackey (Santa Cruz, Calif.: Hambone, 2009), 8.

63. Will Alexander, "Nathaniel Mackey: 'An Ashen Finesse,'" in "Nathaniel Mackey: A Special Issue," special issue, *Callaloo* 23, no. 2 (2000): 702.

64. Letter from Judy Platz to Nathaniel Mackey, November 26, 1982, box 21, folder 31, Nathaniel Mackey Papers, Correspondence, Emory University.

65. Nathaniel Mackey, "From *From a Broken Bottle Traces of Perfume Still Emanate,*" in *Hambone* 2, 84.

208 Notes to Chapter 3

66. Derrida, "Hostipitality," 8.

67. Mackey, "Editing *Hambone*," 245.

68. Mackey uses "innovative" to describe Black centrifugal writing in both "Destination Out" and the following essay, titled "Expanding the Repertoire," which "address[es] the question of what characterizes innovation and the question of how the term impacts or fails to impact critical approaches to African American writing." See Mackey "Destination Out," in *Paracritical Hinge: Essays, Talks, Notes, Interviews* (Madison: University of Wisconsin Press, 2005), 239. See also Mackey, "Expanding the Repertoire," also in *Paracritical Hinge*, 240.

69. Mackey, "Expanding the Repertoire," 241.

70. For the history of manifestos as an experimental political and literary form, see Janet Lyon, *Manifestoes: Provocations of the Modern* (Ithaca, N.Y.: Cornell University Press, 1999); for the relation between manifestos and avant-garde literature and politics, see Martin Puchner, *Poetry of the Revolution: Marx, Manifestos, and the Avant-Gardes* (Princeton, N.J.: Princeton University Press, 2005).

71. I am thinking of three books in particular here: Peter Bürger's landmark *Theory of the Avant-Garde*, trans. Michael Shaw (Minneapolis: University of Minnesota Press, 1984); Paul Mann's *The Theory-Death of the Avant-Garde* (Bloomington: Indiana University Press, 1991); and Loren Glass's more recent *Counterculture Colophon*. Each of these imagines either economic or discursive incorporation (or both) to be the end point of avant-gardes.

72. Mann, 4. In an odd turn of events, Mann subsequently published some of his poetry in *Hambone*. For Mann's poems, which he submitted at the recommendation of Norman Finkelstein, see *Hambone* 19 (Santa Cruz, Calif.: Hambone, 2009), 209–18. For details on Mann's submission to *Hambone*, see letter from Paul Mann to Nathaniel Mackey, June 21, 2007, box 83, folder 2, Nathaniel Mackey Papers, Publication Records for *Hambone*, 1981–2006, Emory University.

73. Some excellent criticism on race and avant-garde poetry has been published since Mackey wrote his essay. See especially the abovementioned works by Timothy Yu and Dorothy J. Wang. See also the *Boston Review*'s cluster of essays on "Race and the Poetic Avant-Garde," assembled in collaboration with Dorothy Wang and published on March 10, 2015, which can be found at http://bostonreview.net/blog/boston-review-race-and-poetic-avant-garde.

74. Mackey, "Destination Out," 239.

75. Nathaniel Mackey, *Splay Anthem* (New York: New Directions, 2006), 65.

76. Stefano Harney and Fred Moten, *The Undercommons: Fugitive Planning and Black Study* (Wivenhoe, UK: Minor Compositions, 2013), 94.

Notes to Chapter 4   209

77. For another polyvocal poetic engagement with the Middle Passage, see M. NourbeSe Philip's *Zong!* (Middleton, Conn.: Wesleyan University Press, 2008).

78. Al Young, "What Is the Blues?," in *Hambone* 2, 57.

79. Mahmoud Darweesh [*sic*], "From Beirut," in *Hambone* 3, ed. Nathaniel Mackey (Santa Cruz, Calif.: Hambone, 1983), 5.

80. bell hooks, "the body inside the soul," in *Hambone* 3, ed. Nathaniel Mackey (Santa Cruz, Calif.: Hambone, 1983), 88.

4. Editing and Eros

1. Nathaniel Mackey, "Destination Out," in *Paracritical Hinge: Essays, Talks, Notes, Interviews* (Madison: University of Wisconsin Press, 2005), 239.

2. Eileen Myles, "What about Chris?," in *I Love Dick*, by Chris Kraus (New York: Semiotext(e), 2006), 13.

3. Hebdige reportedly sought to sue Kraus, and the matter seems to have been settled out of court. Nic Zembla, "See Dick Sue," *New York Magazine*, November 17, 1997, 20.

4. Myles, "What about Chris?," 15.

5. Sylvère Lotringer, "After the Avant-Garde," in "Publishing Issue," special issue, *Pataphysics*, 2005, 18.

6. For an analysis of the early years of Semiotext(e), focusing on 1975–78, see Jason Demers, *The American Politics of French Theory: Derrida, Deleuze, Guattari, and Foucault in Translation* (Toronto: University of Toronto Press, 2018).

7. In French, nouns are gendered as either masculine or feminine. The ending "e" tends to denote a feminine noun.

8. Henry Schwarz and Anne Balsamo, "Under the Sign of *Semiotext(e)*: The Story according to Sylvère Lotringer and Chris Kraus," *Critique: Studies in Contemporary Fiction* 37, no. 3 (1996): 206.

9. Lotringer, "After the Avant-Garde," 19.

10. Eve Kosofsky Sedgwick's *Between Men: English Literature and Male Homosocial Desire* (New York: Columbia University Press, 1985) remains a foundational work for understanding the operations of male exclusivity in literary and cultural work. Rachel Blau DuPlessis's *Purple Passages: Pound, Eliot, Zukofsky, Olson, Creeley, and the Ends of Patriarchal Poetry* (Iowa City: University of Iowa Press, 2012) is a terrific reading of the role of patriarchal affiliation in literary sphere formation.

11. Of the first set of Native Agents books, which Kraus has identified as those published from 1990 to around 2002, when Hedi El Khloti joined the press and began collaborating with Kraus on the fiction list, all were written in English and most by Americans, with the exception being the Canadian writer

210   Notes to Chapter 4

and artist Eldon Garnett, who published *Reading Brooke Shields: The Garden of Failure* with Native Agents in 1995. Shulamith Firestone, who published *Airless Spaces* with Native Agents in 1998, was born in Ottawa but spent most of her life in the United States and is most widely known for her second-wave feminist work developed in New York in the 1970s.

12. Schwarz and Balsamo, "Under the Sign," 212.

13. Given this chapter's emphasis on affection's role in forms of solidarity, I must mention here Kraus's 2018 defense of Avital Ronell after Ronell had been accused of using her position to emotionally and physically harass and assault a former graduate student, Nimrod Reitman. Kraus's statement of support was made after this chapter was conceived and completed. Similar to Judith Butler's early defense, I find Kraus's early defense of Ronell mistaken and wrong. Butler has apologized for her statement; Kraus, to my knowledge, has not. For a brief overview of Reitman's lawsuit and Ronell's and her supporters' response, see Colleen Flaherty's "Harassment and Power," *Inside Higher Ed*, August 20, 2018, https://www.insidehighered.com/news/2018/08/20/some-say-particulars-ronell-harassment-case-are-moot-it-all-comes-down-power.

14. Peter Sloterdijk, *Bubbles: Spheres I*, trans. Wieland Hoban (Los Angeles: Semiotext(e), 2011), 12.

15. Chris Kraus, "The New Universal," *Sydney Review of Books*, October 17, 2014, https://sydneyreviewofbooks.com/new-universal/.

16. Chris Kraus, *I Love Dick*, rev. ed. (Los Angeles: Semiotext(e), 2006), 260.

17. David Rimanelli, "*I Love Dick*," *Bookforum*, Spring 1998, 7.

18. Zembla, "See Dick Sue," 20.

19. Joanna Walsh, "*I Love Dick* by Chris Kraus: A Cult Feminist Classic Makes Its UK Debut," *The Guardian*, November 11, 2015, https://www.theguardian.com/books/2015/nov/11/i-love-dick-chris-kraus-review.

20. Kraus, *I Love Dick*, 19.

21. Near the end of the narrative, Chris even writes a four-page reminiscence of her adolescence in New Zealand in the style of Katherine Mansfield's short story "Bliss" (246–50).

22. As we have seen, Chris places James among the handful of writers she most admires and he makes several appearances by name throughout the book (26, 50, 71, 115). Kraus also made a film adaptation of James's *The Golden Bowl* in 1984, which she titled *The Golden Bowl, or Repression*, hinting at the psychological dimension Kraus attributes to his work. Chris makes explicit reference to *The Golden Bowl* in her very first letter in *I Love Dick*. After Chris and Sylvère leave their first meeting with Dick, "Chris tells Sylvère how she believes that she and Dick have just experienced a Conceptual Fuck" (21). They discuss Chris's newfound obsession for several days before "Sylvère

Notes to Chapter 4   211

finally suggests that Chris write Dick a letter. Since she's embarrassed she asks him if he wants to write one too. Sylvère agrees. Do married couples usually collaborate on *billets doux*? If Sylvère and Chris were not so militantly opposed to psychoanalysis, they might've seen this as a turning point" (25). Sylvère then writes the first letter and self-consciously explains that "it must be the desert wind that went to our heads that night or maybe the desire to fictionalize life a little bit" (26). When Chris begins her letter, she notes, "Since Sylvère wrote the first letter, I'm thrown into this weird position. Reactive—like Charlotte Stant to Sylvère's Maggie Verver, if we were living in the Henry James novel *The Golden Bowl*—the Dumb Cunt, a factory of emotions evoked by all the men. So the only thing that I can do is tell The Dumb Cunt's Tale. But how?" (26–27). The conjunction between Chris's allusion to James and her wondering *how* to tell her own story signals the importance of James's work for Kraus. Indeed, these lines are the first in a flurry of letters that make up the book. But while *The Golden Bowl* serves as the first Jamesian intertext for Kraus, Chris's remark that her "reaction" can only be to "tell The Dumb Cunt's Tale" points subtly in the direction of James's novella of psychological haunting, *The Turn of the Screw*. Aside from the roughly echoed title—*The Turn of the Screw* / The Dumb Cunt's Tale—*I Love Dick* more clearly reflects the narrative of *The Turn of the Screw* than it does *The Golden Bowl*. *The Turn of the Screw*, that is, takes interest in how stories are told, in how something is telling or not, and in how a narrative can conceal the subject of its telling. Kraus's assertion and subsequent question that open her first letter—"the only thing that I can do is tell The Dumb Cunt's Tale. But how?"—introduce a point of commonality with James's novella: an interest in the *how* of storytelling and its relation to a gendered economy of letters.

23. Henry James, *The Turn of the Screw*, ed. Deborah Esch and Jonathan Warren (New York: W. W. Norton, 1999), 3.

24. Edmund Wilson, "Ambiguity in *The Turn of the Screw*," in *The Turn of the Screw*, by Henry James, ed. Deborah Esch and Jonathan Warren (New York: W. W. Norton, 1999), 171–72.

25. Shoshana Felman, "Turning the Screw of Interpretation," in *Literature and Psychoanalysis: The Question of Reading—Otherwise*, ed. Shoshana Felman (Baltimore: Johns Hopkins University Press, 1982), 103.

26. James, *Turn of the Screw*, 3.

27. Kraus, *I Love Dick*, 122.

28. Chris Kraus, *Aliens and Anorexia* (Los Angeles: Semiotext(e), 2013), 11.

29. Kraus, *I Love Dick*, 23.

30. Myles, "What about Chris?," 23.

31. Myles, 15; Anna Watkins Fisher, "Manic Impositions: The Parasitical Art of Chris Kraus and Sophie Calle," *Women's Studies Quarterly* 40, nos. 1–2 (Spring–Summer 2012): 224.

Notes to Chapter 4

32. Chris Kraus, "What I Couldn't Write," in *Social Practices* (South Pasadena, Calif.: Semiotext(e), 2018), 72.

33. "Semiotext(e) / Native Agents," MIT Press, last modified November 15, 2020, https://mitpress.mit.edu/books/series/semiotexte-native-agents.

34. "Semiotext(e) / Native Agents." For more on Hedi El Kholti's influential role in Semiotext(e) since roughly the turn of the century, see Aaron Lecklider, "Sexing the Semiotext(e) Whitney Biennial Box Set," *English Language Notes* 53, no. 1 (Spring–Summer 2015): 141–58.

35. Anna Poletti, "The Anthropology of the Setup: A Conversation with Chris Kraus," *Contemporary Women's Writing* 10, no. 1 (March 2016): 134.

36. Kraus, *I Love Dick*, 123.

37. Ann Rower, *If You're a Girl* (New York: Semiotext(e), 1990), 15.

38. Schwarz and Balsamo, "Under the Sign," 213.

39. Cookie Mueller, *Walking through Clear Water in a Pool Painted Black* (New York: Semiotext(e), 1990), 5.

40. Chris Kraus, *Where Art Belongs* (Los Angeles: Semiotext(e), 2011), 61.

41. Chris Kraus, *Video Green: Los Angeles Art and the Triumph of Nothingness* (New York: Semiotext(e), 2004), 196.

42. Mueller, *Walking*, 148.

43. "Moyra Davey: *My Necropolis*," Murray Guy, last modified November 1, 2020, https://murrayguy.com/exhibitions/my-necropolis/.

44. Kraus, *Where Art Belongs*, 97.

45. Kraus, *Video Green*, 83.

46. David Ratray, *How I Became One of the Invisible* (New York: Semiotext(e), 1992), 7.

47. "Alden Van Buskirk," Poetry Foundation, last modified October 20, 2018, https://www.poetryfoundation.org/poets/alden-van-buskirk.

48. Rattray, *How I Became*, 28.

49. Alden Van Buskirk, *Lami*, ed. David Rattray (San Francisco: Auerhahn Society, 1965), 9.

50. Kraus, "New Universal."

51. "Author and Critic Chris Kraus' Papers Arrive at NYU's Fales Library and Special Collections," NYU News Release, January 15, 2016, https://www.nyu.edu/about/news-publications/news/.

52. Chris Kraus, "This Is Chance," in *The Chance Event, wherein . . .* , by Becket Flannery (Bogotá: Athénée Press, 2020), 31.

53. Flannery's *The Chance Event, wherein . . .* had not yet been published when I learned of its existence in April 2020. I am immensely grateful to Flannery and Jennifer Burris Staton, editor and publisher of Athénée Press, who provided me with a digital copy of the book prior to its publication. This coda would not have been possible without their generosity.

Notes to Coda

54. Flannery, 4.

55. Diana Taylor is not mentioned in Flannery's book, but her landmark study *The Archive and the Repertoire: Performing Cultural Memory in the Americas* (Durham, N.C.: Duke University Press, 2003) anticipates the direction Flannery takes in his thinking on affect, archives, and the locations of cultural memory.

56. Flannery, *Chance Event*, 8.

57. Kraus, "This Is Chance," 24.

58. Kraus, 31. Flannery notes in one of his essays that this sacred land was, in 1996, still under threat from the possible Yucca Mountain nuclear waste repository—proposed in 1987 and finally scrapped by the Obama administration in 2011 after decades of local, regional, and international resistance. See Flannery, *Chance Event*, 16.

59. Quoted in Flannery, 16.

60. Flannery's exploration of the structural biases of chance in fact begins with an excerpt of an interview between him and Kraus where he brings up a scene from Kraus's *Aliens and Anorexia* in which a young woman on a solo hitchhiking trip is raped, a story that itself echoes another from Mueller's collection. Kraus notes, "The sort of chance of the unprotected young woman is rather predetermined." Flannery, *Chance Event*, 41.

61. Eileen Myles, "Endorsement," MIT Press, last modified July 28, 2020, https://mitpress.mit.edu/books/airless-spaces.

62. Flannery, *Chance Event*, 44.

63. Kraus, *I Love Dick*, 23.

Coda

1. Peter Gizzi, "On the Conjunction of Editing and Composition," in *Paper Dreams: Writers and Editors on the American Literary Magazine*, ed. Travis Kurowski (Madison, N.J.: Atticus Books, 2013), 231.

2. For reports on the intensified and ongoing contraction of the academic job market after the 2008 recession, see "Reports on the MLA Job Information List," Modern Language Association, accessed July 19, 2019, https://www.mla.org/Resources/Career/Job-List/Reports-on-the-MLA-Job-Information-List.

3. Janice Lee, "About," accessed July 8, 2020, http://janicel.com/about/.

4. For specific numbers on the rise of the U.S. creative writing program, see Mark McGurl, *The Program Era: Postwar Fiction and the Rise of Creative Writing* (Cambridge, Mass.: Harvard University Press, 2009), 24–25.

5. *Merriam-Webster*, s.v. "entropy," accessed July 10, 2019, https://www.merriam-webster.com/dictionary/entropy.

6. For the relationship between Olson and the discourse of the sciences, especially physics, see Peter Middleton, "Discoverable Unknowns: Olson's Lifelong Preoccupation with the Sciences," in *Contemporary Olson*, ed. David Herd (Manchester, UK: University of Manchester Press, 2015), 38–51.

Notes to Coda

7. Charles Olson, *Letters for Origin, 1950–1956*, ed. Albert Glover (New York: Paragon House), 50.

8. See Robert von Hallberg, *Charles Olson: The Scholar's Art* (Cambridge, Mass.: Harvard University Press), 1–3.

9. For more on Olson's careerist and institution-building work, see Libbie Rifkin, *Career Moves: Olson, Creeley, Zukofsky, Berrigan, and the American Avant-Garde* (Madison: University of Wisconsin Press, 2000).

10. I should note here that McGurl's study of the program era addresses fiction more or less exclusively, and that poetry's place in it is less clear. This gap should be addressed by Kimberly Quiogue Andrews's forthcoming book on *The Academic Avant-Garde* in American poetry. Many thanks to Kim for sharing some of her work in manuscript form.

11. "About," *Entropy*, accessed July 7, 2020, https://entropymag.org/about/.

12. I say "in theory" here because Wikipedia suffers from a remarkable gender gap, where only a small minority of editors are women. For an analysis of this gap in terms of the infrastructures upon which Wikipedia operates, see Heather Ford and Judy Wajcman, "'Anyone Can Edit,' Not Everyone Does: Wikipedia's Infrastructure and the Gender Gap," *Social Studies of Science* 47, no. 4 (2017): 511–27. Ford and Wajcman also cite relevant research on Wikipedia editing and economic precarity and access.

13. It is worth noting, for instance, that while Wikipedia content is created by free editorial labor, this labor produces significant earnings for search engines such as Google. Who makes Wikipedia inquiries via the Wikipedia search function, after all?

14. "About," *Entropy*.

15. According to Lee's books page (https://janicel.com/project/imagine-a-death/, accessed May 11, 2021), *Imagine a Death* will be released in September 2021 by a fascinating arts initiative known as the Operating System—a terrific subject for some future study. For more on the Operating System, see http://www.theoperatingsystem.org/, last modified November 10, 2020.

16. "About," *Entropy*.

17. Kate Thompson, "Write When Language Fails with Janice Lee of Entropy," *Lit Mag Love*, November 27, 2017, https://www.litmaglove.com/janicelee/.

18. Janice Lee and Jared Woodland, "Apocalypse Withheld: On Slowness and the Long Take in Bela Tarr's *Sátántangó*," *Entropy*, May 15, 2014, https://entropymag.org/apocalypse-withheld-on-slowness-the-long-take-in-bela-tarrs-satantango/.

19. Lutz Koepnick, *The Long Take: Art Cinema and the Wondrous* (Minneapolis: University of Minnesota Press, 2017), 102.

20. For an especially illuminating analysis of Tarr's films in relation to Lee's

Notes to Coda 215

Damnation, see Jon Wagner, "Introduction," in *Damnation,* by Janice Lee (Los Angeles: Penny-Ante Editions, 2013), 11–15.

21. The descriptive methods developed by Sophie Seita in her book on *Provisional Avant-Gardes: Little Magazine Communities from Dada to Digital* (Stanford, Calif.: Stanford University Press, 2019), methods derived and adapted from book history and textual studies, might provide different kinds of insights into *Entropy.* The space required for that kind of descriptive methodology, however, lies outside the scope of this brief coda.

22. "Boltzman Entropy Award for Emerging Voices in Nonfiction," *Entropy,* July 22, 2015, https://entropymag.org/boltzmann-entropy-award-for-emerging-voices-in-nonfiction/. Although this award never got off the ground, *Entropy's* announcement for it illuminates the editors' interests.

23. "Masthead," *Entropy,* last modified November 25, 2020, https://entropymag.org/masthead/.

24. Roxane Gay, "Too Many of Us, Too Much Noise," in *Paper Dreams: Writers and Editors on the American Literary Magazine,* ed. Travis Kurowski (Madison, N.J.: Atticus Books), 276.

25. Jacques Rancière, *Béla Tarr, the Time After,* trans. Erik Beranek (Minneapolis: University of Minnesota Press, Univocal Publishing, 2013), 68–69.

26. Thompson, "Write When Language Fails."

27. Thompson.

28. Thompson.

29. Rancière, *Béla Tarr,* 63–64.

30. Although it does not address editing or her own work in publishing specifically, Lee has written a painful and passionate essay of her own experience trying to have her most recent book published, and the harmful structures of power and authentication that much of the publishing industry still upholds. See Janice Lee, "Books Are Not Products, They Are Bridges: Challenging Linear Ideas of Success in Literary Publishing," *Vol. 1 Brooklyn,* December 4, 2019, http://vol1brooklyn.com/2019/12/04/books-are-not-products-they-are-bridges-challenging-linear-ideas-of-success-in-literary-publishing/.

31. I am thinking for this last point not only of *Entropy's* support of a wide variety of writers and editors in general but also of the platform's more explicit support for those who have suffered abuse—including sexual violence—as a result of academic hierarchies and power structures, such as was the case with Seo-Young Chu, who published her widely circulated account of rape at Stanford on *Entropy* on November 3, 2017; see "A Refuge for Jae-In Doe: Fugues in the Key of English Major," https://entropymag.org/a-refuge-for-jae-in-doe-fugues-in-the-key-of-english-major/. Since then, *Entropy* has initiated a series called WOVEN, published under the editorship of Sylvia Chan, which is a "dedicated safe space for essays by persons who engage with #MeToo, sexual assault and

216 Notes to Coda

harassment, and #DomesticViolence, as well as their intersections with mental illness, substance addiction, and legal failures and remedies. We believe you. If selected for the series, we want to provide the editorial and human support such that our conversation continues long after the stories and names have changed." This is the editorial description of woven that accompanies every piece in the series. In June 2020, Chan wrote a moving statement to honor two years of woven and the people who came forward with their stories; see "Two Years in Woven," *Entropy*, June 24, 2020, https://entropymag.org/two-years-in-woven/.

Index

academia, 25, 28, 58, 64, 66–69, 73, 82, 122, 128, 163–65, 173
Ader, Bas Jan, 150
Adorno, Theodor, 3, 19–22
Albiach, Anne-Marie, 114
Alexander, Will, 115–16
Alighieri, Dante, 37
Allman, Jean, 199n38
American Scholar, 69
Andrews, Kimberly Quiogue, 214n10
Antin, Eleanor, 141–43, 145
Asim, Jabari, 202n59
Assembling, 2–5
Atlantis, 56
Attridge, Derek, 23
Aub, Max, 114
Auerbach, Erich, 9–10
Augustine, Saint, 77–78, 199n29
avant-garde, 71, 94, 104, 110–11, 121, 198n19, 205n31, 208n70, 208n71, 208n73

Baraka, Amiri, 11–13, 86, 89, 91, 97, 186n41, 200n39, 203n14. *See also* Jones, LeRoi

Barnhisel, Greg, 183n21
Barth, John, 14–16
Barthes, Roland, 183n23
Baudrillard, Jean, 130, 158, 160
Bauz, Luis, 158
Beardsley, Monroe, 21
Becker, Julie, 145, 154
Bellow, Saul, 9
Benjamin, Walter, 153
Bérard, Victor, 55, 58
Berthold, Robert, 111
bibliography, 53–54
Blackburn, Paul, 12
Black Mountain College, 25, 191n11, 192n24
Black Mountain Review, 69, 191n11, 192n24
Blackwood, Sarah, 115, 186n41
Blanchot, Maurice, 6
Boldereff, Frances, 11, 43, 195n46
Boles, Robert, 92, 202n59
Bontemps, Arna, 66, 84–85
book history, 22–23, 87, 183n21
Bové, Paul, 47–48, 194n35
Bowers, Andrea, 150

218 Index

Brathwaite, Kamau, 96–97, 110
Brier, Evan, 182–83n20
Brooke-Rose, Christine, 198n19
Brooks, Cleanth, 10, 184–85n31
Brophy, Brigid, 68, 72
Brouillette, Sarah, 181n2, 182–83n20
Buell, Lawrence, 184n23, 184n27
Bürger, Peter, 205n31, 208n71
Burroughs, William S., 132
Butterick, George F., 189n1, 191n11
Byrd, Don, 110

Cage, John, 21
Callaloo, 111
Carroll, Jordan S., 183n21
Carter, Vincent O., 92, 202n59
Cartier, Xam Wilson, 92, 202n59
Caserio, Robert L., 65, 194n41
centrifugal poetics, 19, 21, 104–8, 120–25
Chan, Sylvia, 215–16n31
Chatwin, Bruce, 128
Chinitz, David E., 194n35
Christensen, Paul, 193–94n34
Chu, Seo-Young, 215n31
Churchward, James, 55–58
Clay, Steve, 183n21
Clissmann, Anne, 199n27
Cold War Modernists (Barnhisel), 183n21
colonialism, 96–97
Conjunctions, 111
"contemporary literature," 66–73
Corman, Cid, 25, 40–45, 62, 165–66, 191n11, 193n27
Cortázar, Julio, 114
Creeley, Robert, 25, 34, 41, 53, 191n11
crypto-philology, 56–60, 184–85n31, 195n48
Cusack, Ralph, 74

Dalkey Archive Press, 7, 25, 63–92
Darnton, Robert, 184n24
Darwish, Mahmoud, 100, 114, 124–25
Davey, Moyra, 153–54
Davidson, Michael, 194n44
Davies, Jeremy, 197n10
Delany, Samuel R., 17
Deleuze, Gilles, 130. *See also* Guattari, Félix
DeLillo, Don, 9
Demby, William, 87, 91
Demers, Jason, 209n6
Derrida, Jacques, 22, 114–15, 118, 130
di Prima, Diane, 12–14, 186n41
discrepant engagement, 95, 97–98, 106
Doctorow, E. L., 17
Does Writing Have a Future? (Flusser), 181n5
Doherty, Margaret, 64–65, 197n6
Donnelly, Ignatius, 55–57, 195n47, 195n48
Dorn, Ed, 13
Dorothy, a publishing project, 18, 198n19
Douglas, Marcia, 88
Drucker, Johanna, 183n21
DuPlessis, Rachel Blau, 186n41, 189n4, 190n6, 196n58, 209n10
Dutton, Danielle, 18, 198n19

Eagleton, Terry, 22
Eburne, Jonathan P., 182n18
editing: as art, 1; as carework, 115–20, 152, 164, 174 (*see also* Blackwood, Sarah); as collective practice, 14, 26, 41, 44, 93, 109, 123–24, 165–68; as component of projective poetics, 29–62; as disordering method, 2–5; as gatekeeping, 2–3,

167, 172; and hospitality, 112–20; as process of assembling, 2–5, 13, 17, 41, 94; as rerouting of desire, 127–61; utopian drive of, 5, 30–31, 49, 166–68, 176; as work, 6–7 (*see also* labor)

"Editing Hambone" (Mackey), 93–94

Eliot, T. S., 11, 185n36, 194n35

Ellison, Ralph, 9, 26, 66, 84, 200n42

Emre, Merve, 197n6

ensemble, 26–27, 99–100, 115

enslaved people, 93, 102, 109

enslavement, 101–2, 108

Entropy, 27–28, 163–76

Eshleman, Clayton, 111

Felman, Shoshana, 138–39

Fenderson, Jonathan, 200n39

Fenollosa, Ernest, 36

Ferrini, Vincent, 29–34, 50, 52, 62, 189–90n5, 191n11

Fiction Collective, 16–17

Firestone, Shulamith, 160–61, 209–10n11

Fitzpatrick, Kathleen, 184n23

Flannery, Becket, 158–61

Flaubert, Gustave, 136

Floating Bear, The, 12, 186n41

Flusser, Vilém, 181n5

Ford, Thomas H., 39, 188n4

Foucault, Michel, 3, 9, 34

4 Winds, 29–34, 49–50, 52, 189n5

Fulton, Len, 13–14

Funkhouser, Christopher, 184n23

Gaddis, William, 17

Gaines, Ernest J., 26, 86

Gaines, Kevin K., 199n38

Garnett, Eldon, 209–10n11

Gay, Roxane, 5, 172

Giles Goat-Boy (Barth), 14–16

Ginna, Peter, 181n4, 184n25

Ginsberg, Allen, 191n11

Gizzi, Peter, 1, 6, 163

Glass, Loren, 71, 181n2, 184n28, 188n64, 197n6, 205n31, 208n71

Glidden, Christina, 154

Glissant, Édouard, 104, 108–9

Grant, Gavin J., 18

"Great American Novel, the," 9, 184n27

Green, Henry, 68

Groenland, Tim, 183n21, 189n68

Grove Press, 71, 79–80

Guattari, Félix, 130. *See also* Deleuze, Gilles

Haggard, H. Rider, 55–56

Halberstam, Jack, 206–7n55

Hambone, 6, 7, 26–27, 93–125, 127

hambone (musical practice), 94, 100–104

Hambone (vernacular figure), 93, 100–104, 108–9, 161

Hampson, Robert, 195n46

Harney, Stefano, 123, 206–7n55

Harper, Michael S., 66, 94, 95

Harris, Wilson, 104–7, 206n40, 206n41

Hawkins, Joan, 134

Hebdige, Dick, 127, 209n3

Heidegger, Martin, 47, 59

Henderson, Bill, 2

Hepworth, Doug, 159

Herd, David, 32, 41

Herodotus, 58

Heti, Sheila, 134

HIV/AIDS crisis, 151–52

Hölderlin, Friedrich, 188n58

hooks, bell, 94, 110, 125

Hornick, Lita, 12, 186n41
hospitality, 114–20
Howe, Fanny, 154
Howe, Susan, 96–97, 110
Hughes, Langston, 88
Hume, Kathryn, 198n16
Hungerford, Amy, 183n21
Hyams, Edward, 53

Innis, Harold, 192n20
Interviews with Black Writers
(O'Brien), 66, 82–88
Irr, Caren, 198n16
island as poetic trope, 45–52

James, C. L. R., 195n47
James, Darius, 88
James, Henry, 27, 136–39,
210–11n22
Jamison, Leslie, 134
Jargon Society, the, 49, 193n27
Jones, Hettie, 12, 186n41
Jones, LeRoi, 11–13, 89, 186n41,
200n39. *See also* Baraka, Amiri
Joyce, James, 63, 66, 74–75

Kahn, David, 56
Kelley, Aiki, 89, 91, 111
Kelley, Jess, 90
Kelley, William Melvin, 88–92
Kelly, Robert, 7, 112–13
Kerouac, Jack, 12, 132
Kessler, Stephen, 124
Kholti, Hedi El, 145
Kittler, Friedrich, 191–92n19
Koepnick, Lutz, 169
Korn, Henry James, 2
Kostelanetz, Richard, 2–5
Kraus, Chris, 7, 27, 127–61
Krystufek, Elke, 150
Kulchur, 12, 71, 186n41

labor: academic, 164, 172–73, 175–76;
intellectual, 7, 26, 28, 100, 119–
20, 122, 165–67, 175
Lee, Janice, 7, 27–28, 163–76, 215n30
Lennon, Brian, 56, 187n53, 195n48
Lerner, Ben, 134
Levertov, Denise, 192n24
Levine, Lawrence W., 101–2
Link, Kelly, 18
literary celebrity, 9, 64, 184n28
literary field, 2, 8, 16, 19, 64, 68,
100, 181n3, 197n6
literary history, 71, 73–79
literary journals, 28, 40–41, 93–98,
110–16, 166–67, 191n11. *See also*
little magazine
little magazine, 33, 43, 62, 69
logocentrism, 35–36, 38–40
Lotringer, Sylvère, 128, 130–31
Lyon, Janet, 208n70

Mackey, Nathaniel, 6, 7, 19, 26–27,
90, 93–125, 193n30, 202n59,
203n14
Maes-Jelinek, Hena, 205n32
Mailer, Norman, 9, 124n28
Major, Clarence, 26
Make Now Books, 18
Manly, John Matthews, 185n31
Mann, Paul, 121, 208n72
Markfield, Wallace, 196n3
Maud, Ralph, 56
Mayan glyphs, 25, 30, 60, 62,
192n20, 193n30
Mayfield, Julian, 84, 199n38
McCaffery, Larry, 17
McCarthy, Jesse, 92
McDonald, Peter D., 22–23
McGrath, Laura B., 183n21
McGurl, Mark, 14–15, 64–65, 81–82,
214n10

Index

221

McHale, Brian, 14–15
McHugh, Vincent, 200n42
McKay, Claude, 85
McLuhan, Marshall, 192n20
Melville, Herman, 31, 132
Merchants of Culture (Thompson), 181n3
metaphysics, 30–31, 33, 47–49, 54–56, 59, 62
Metcalf, Paul, 97, 196n3, 203n12
Meyers, Calvin, 160
mimeograph, 13
modernism, 25
Morris, Adelaide, 205n30
Morrison, Toni, 17
Mosley, Nicholas, 68, 73
Moten, Fred, 93, 123, 206–7n55
Mu (lost continent), 55, 57–58, 149, 152, 160
Mueller, Cookie, 132, 147–50, 160
Mulligan Stew (Sorrentino), 78–82
Murnau, F. W., 200n42
Mvuyekure, Pierre-Damien, 200n42
Myles, Eileen, 128, 134, 161

NEA (National Endowment of the Arts), 65
New Criticism, the, 10–12, 21, 22, 25, 47, 185n31
New Directions, 87–88
New York Review Books, 88, 201n50
New York Times Book Review, 16
Nichols, Miriam, 190n6
Nichols, Stephen G., 9–10
Nielsen, Aldon Lynn, 202n50
Nishikawa, Kinohi, 183n21
Noon, 18

O'Brien, Flann, 63, 66, 74–79, 81
O'Brien, John, 26, 64, 66–72, 196n3, 202n55

Olson, Charles, 7, 10, 13, 19, 24–25, 29–62, 122, 161, 165–66
orientalism, 56–62
Origin, 40–45, 62, 69, 165–66, 191n11, 191n14, 193n27

Papaleo, Joseph, 90
Perrin, Tom, 184n26
Petry, Ann, 26, 87
Phoenix Book Shop (Greenwich Village), 13
Pizarnik, Alejandra, 114
Platz, Judy, 117–18
Polite, Carlene Hatcher, 92, 202n59
poststructuralism, 128–30
precarity, 164–76
Price, Leah, 8, 22, 23
print, 30–32, 35–45
Program Era, The (McGurl), 14–16, 65, 81–82
proofs, 193n27
Provisional Avant-Gardes (Seita), 183n21
publishing, 2, 5, 7–9, 14–18, 24–26, 30–34, 41, 43–45, 62
Publish-It-Yourself Handbook: Literary Tradition and How-To, The, 2
Puchner, Martin, 208n70
Pynchon, Thomas, 9, 17, 166–67

Ra, Sun, 97
Racial Imaginary Institute, 89
Rancière, Jacques, 172–73, 175
Rankine, Claudia, 89
Rattray, David, 132, 143–45, 154–57
Reed, Ishmael, 17, 26, 66, 84–86, 94, 97, 200n42, 201n44, 203n14
Reitman, Nimrod, 210n13
Review of Contemporary Fiction, 64, 66, 71–73

Index

Riddel, Joseph, 36, 59
Riker, Martin, 18, 198n19
Rimanelli, David, 133
Rivera, Reynaldo, 158
Ronell, Avital, 210n13
Ross, Fran, 87–88
Rosset, Barney, 79
Roth, Philip, 9
Rothenberg, Jerome, 183n21
Rower, Ann, 132, 146–47

Said, Edward W., 195n51
Scarpati, Vittorio, 152
Scher, Julia, 158
Scholem, Gershom, 153
Schulz, Kathryn, 88, 92
Sedgwick, Eve Kosofsky, 209n10
Seita, Sophie, 183n21, 189n68,
   215n20
Semiotext(e) (journal), 128–30
Semiotext(e) (publisher), 127–28;
   Native Agents series, 130–32,
   145–58
Seshagiri, Urmila, 198n19
Shepp, Archie, 94
Sinykin, Dan N., 181n3, 182n20,
   183n21
slavery, 87, 100, 103, 123, 200n39
Sloterdijk, Peter, 27, 131–32
Small Beer Press, 18
Smith, John, 52
So, Richard Jean, 183n21
Sorrentino, Gilbert, 66–71, 73,
   78–82, 86, 186n41, 196n3,
   197n10
Spahr, Juliana, 183n21
Spanos, William V., 36, 38, 45
Speculum (journal), 9
Spenser, Edmund, 96
Spivak, Gayatri Chakravorty, 22
Stono Rebellion, 102

Sukenick, Ronald: "Author as Editor
   and Publisher," 16–17
Sumer, civilization of, 195n46
Swift, Jonathan, 16

Taggart, John, 97, 204n14
Tarr, Béla, 28, 168–71
Tedlock, Dennis, 196n59
Thoburn, Nicholas, 3
Thompson, John B., 181n3
Thompson, Rachel, 173
Tieryas Liu, Peter, 163, 166
Tillman, Lynn, 184n27
Toomer, Jean, 84–85
Totem Press, 12, 186n41
Trocchi, Alexander, 132
Turner, Catherine, 183n21
Turn of the Screw, The (James),
   136–39
Twain, Mark, 132
Twersky, Lori, 150–51

Ulysses (Joyce), 63, 74–75

Valenzuela, Luisa, 196n3
Van Buskirk, Alden, 154
Vareschi, Mark, 184n24
Veggian, Henry, 184n31
von Hallberg, Robert, 166,
   193–94n34

Waddell, L. A., 55, 58, 195n46
Walsh, Joanna, 134
Wang, Dorothy J., 204n21
Washington, Margaret, 102
Weil, Simone, 134
Weinberger, Eliot, 110–12
Wellek, René, 10, 185n31, 185n36
Whitehead, Alfred North, 31, 59,
   190n8
Wideman, John Edgar, 26, 91

Index

Wieners, John, 13
Wilderson, Frank B., III, 123
Williams, Diane, 18
Williams, Jonathan, 49–51, 193n27
Wilson, Edmund, 138–39
Wilson, Robert A., 13
Wimsatt, William, 21

Woodland, Jared, 169, 175
Woolf, Douglas, 73
writing systems, 36–37, 57, 60

Young, Al, 94, 124
Yu, Timothy, 204n21
Yūgen, 12–13, 186n41

ABRAM FOLEY is lecturer in English at the University of Exeter, where he is codirector of a newly launched master's degree program in publishing.

Lightning Source UK Ltd.
Milton Keynes UK
UKHW020246110522
402785UK00003B/188